Understanding Teache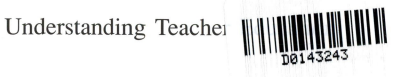

Understanding Teacher Education
Case Studies in the Professional Development of Beginning Teachers

James Calderhead and Susan B. Shorrock

The Falmer Press
(A member of the Taylor & Francis Group)
London • Washington, D.C.

UK   The Falmer Press, 1 Gunpowder Square, London, EC4A 3DE
USA   The Falmer Press, Taylor & Francis Inc., 1900 Frost Road, Suite 101, Bristol, PA 19007

First published in 1997

A catalogue record for this book is available from the British Library

Library of Congress Cataloging-in-Publication Data are available on request

ISBN 0 7507 0398 9 cased
ISBN 0 7507 0399 7 paper

Jacket design by Caroline Archer

Typeset in 10/12pt Times by
Graphicraft Typesetters Ltd., Hong Kong.

Printed in Great Britain by Biddles Ltd, Guildford and King's Lynn on paper which has a specified pH value on final paper manufacture of not less than 7.5 and is therefore 'acid free'.

Every effort has been made to contact copyright holders for their permission to reprint material in this book. The publishers would be grateful to hear from any copyright holder who is not here acknowledged and will undertake to rectify any errors or omissions in future editions of this book.

Contents

Acknowledgments

The research reported within this book would not have been possible without the cooperation of many students and teachers. In particular, twenty student teachers gave generously of their time and patiently tolerated our many attempts to document in detail their experiences of learning to teach. Throughout this process, the authors greatly admired the students' integrity and professional dedication and are extremely grateful for the time and sincere effort that they devoted to this research. The authors also gratefully acknowledge the sponsorship of the Economic and Social Research Council, who provided the financial support for this project.

Chapter 1

Teaching and Teacher Education

Defining Teaching and Teacher Education

'What makes a good teacher?' is a question that has intrigued and challenged philosophers, researchers, policy-makers and teachers for many centuries. It is also a question that has generated diverse answers, varying in their nature and degree of specificity in different countries and across different periods in history. Educational thinkers and writers have variously emphasized different aspects of the teaching role — the teacher as expert in their subject; the teacher as facilitator of learning; the teacher as a motivator and source of inspiration; the teacher as upholder of moral standards. Recent educational policy documents in the UK, and in many other countries, have tended to become more prescriptive in the views of teaching which they support — often construing teachers as the deliverers of a prescribed curriculum, necessitating the acquisition of particular skills and competences. At the same time, media reports would suggest that public expectations of schools and teachers have become more extensive: schools are not only institutions in which children acquire knowledge and skills, they are also places where children learn to socialize and cooperate with others, learn about the world of work and prepare for responsible citizenship.

Views about the role of the teacher are culturally embedded. Substantial variations in how school teachers think about their roles and responsibilities have been found across France, Spain and the UK, for example. Spanish teachers, working within a democratic management system, in which headteachers are elected from amongst teachers within the school, have been found to be more likely to think of teaching as a collaborative activity and to have a stronger sense of responsibility to the local community (Laffitte, 1993). French school teachers, on the other hand, tend to think of their role as relating much more to expertise in their subject specialisms and do not regard their responsibilities as encompassing the pastoral care that their English counterparts value more highly (Broadfoot, Osborn, Gilly and Brûcher, 1994; Planel, 1995).

How we conceptualize the work of teachers inevitably influences how we think about their professional preparation, and ultimately shapes suggestions for the further improvement of teacher education. Zeichner (1983) and Feiman-Nemser (1990) provide interesting classifications of ideologies, or conceptual orientations, in teacher education which they suggest have characterized reform movements within the United States over the past century. These orientations refer to a body of values and beliefs about teaching and teacher education that at different points in history have been particularly influential in shaping the nature of initial teacher education courses. The *academic orientation*, for example, emphasizes teachers' subject expertise and sees the quality of the teacher's own education as his/her professional strength; in this view, a sound liberal arts education is seen as the crucial ingredient of teacher preparation. The *practical orientation*, on the other hand, emphasizes the artistry and classroom technique of the teacher, viewing the teacher as a craftsperson; it therefore attaches importance to classroom experience and apprenticeship models of learning to teach. The *technical orientation* derives from a behaviourist model of teaching and learning, emphasizes the knowledge and behavioural skills that teachers require and has been associated with microteaching and competency-based approaches to teacher education. The *personal orientation* emphasizes the importance of interpersonal relationships in the classroom, often derives support from humanistic psychology, and views learning to teach as a process of 'becoming' or personal development; in this view, teacher education takes the form of offering a safe environment which encourages experimentation and discovery of personal strengths. The *critical inquiry orientation* views schooling as a process of social reform and emphasizes the role of schools in promoting democratic values and reducing social inequities; an important aspect of teacher education is therefore seen as enabling prospective teachers to become aware of the social context of schools and of the social consequences of their own actions as teachers; within this orientation, teacher education functions to help teachers become critical, reflective change-agents.

These ideologies or value positions are clearly identifiable across national boundaries. In many countries one can distinguish similar, competing ideologies or orientations in how teaching and teacher education are viewed. Arguably all of these orientations offer a perspective on teachers' professional preparation and all simultaneously have implications for the design of teacher education courses, although frequently they appear to vie with each other for precedence in the prevailing language with which teacher education is publicly discussed, rather than being thought of as complementary or mutually relevant and informative. Inevitably, learning to teach involves the acquisition of certain knowledge and skills, but teaching is also a matter of individuality and personal expression; it is also often subject focused, but teachers' actions are embedded within a particular institutional context to which they need to adapt and which may well require them to analyse critically its nature and structure and its contribution to the overall goals of education. Teacher education, in effect, is too complex to be characterized by any one of these orientations alone, and inevitably encapsulates aspects of them all.

Reform in Teacher Education

Over the past decade or two, an increasing level of attention has been paid to teacher education, accompanied by more profound questioning of its nature and purpose. In the UK, this has partly been stimulated by professional concerns — an awareness amongst some teacher educators that the quality and relevance of initial training could be improved, and a willingness to experiment with new approaches (e.g., Benton, 1990; Ashton, 1983). A second factor has been the increasingly high public profile of education itself: the demands upon schools and teachers have grown and this has raised questions about how teachers are best trained for their work. Finally, teacher education has also become embroiled in economic and political arguments. Education throughout the Western world is one of the major consumers of public funds, often only ranking behind defence, health and social services. In times of recession and cuts in public expenditure, teacher education, amongst other areas of educational expenditure, has not escaped scrutiny and the drive for value for money. Concerns with quality and efficiency have become commonplace, and combined with a policy of introducing competitiveness and markets into all areas of public service, have in the UK led to some radical reforms in teacher education, imposed from central government.

In 1990, the Department for Education introduced alternative means of training school teachers. Two new schemes were proposed. One was termed the *licensed teacher scheme*, which enables trainees over the age of 26 and with at least two years of higher education experience to be trained on the job. The licensed teacher would work in a school and be paid a salary for a two-year period. The training was to be tailored to their specific needs and would be provided by their employer. At the end of the two-year period, the employer would make a decision as to whether to recommend the trainee for qualified teacher status. The second scheme was the *articled teacher scheme* which was to be delivered in partnership between schools, local education authorities and higher education institutions. The local education authorities, however, were to take the leading role in terms of organization, financial control and monitoring of the scheme. Trainees were to spend two years in training — 80 per cent of this time being on attachment to schools where their training would be overseen by a mentor.

HMI evaluations of school-based training pointed to the highly variable nature of the provision and to the need for teachers to be much better trained to take on their new mentoring roles (HMI, 1991). Despite these reservations, however, the Department for Education pressed ahead with its reforms, introducing legislation in 1992 governing the nature of initial teacher training courses. This specified that one-year postgraduate secondary teacher training courses must involve two-thirds of the time spent in school, and the course must be delivered in partnership between schools and higher education institutions, with teachers playing a major administrative and teaching role (see DfE, 1992). Similar reforms were also introduced to primary teacher training (see DfE, 1993), although less time was required in school in recognition of the breadth of the primary curriculum for which student teachers have to be prepared. In addition, schools are now also being encouraged to provide their own initial training courses either by themselves or in partnership with higher education institutions. The establishment of a separate funding council for teacher education with a specific mission to encourage school involvement reflects the determined attempt of central government to wrest control of teacher education from higher education institutions and introduce what is perceived to be a more practical, apprentice-like form of training, which can be supplied by a wide range of providers in competition. More recently, central government has proposed reforms aimed at influencing the content of teacher training by enforcing a standardized national preservice teacher training curriculum (DfEE, 1996).

The UK is not alone in the rapid move towards school-based teacher education. The US, Australia and the Netherlands have experienced similar trends, though not always for the same reasons. In several areas of the US, Professional Development Schools have emerged which have a strong focus on professional development activities, including the initial training of teachers, and specialist staff in schools are taking on roles previously undertaken by teacher educators in higher education (see Stallings and Kowalski, 1990). In the Netherlands, concerns with quality, effectiveness and value for money in public services are similarly fuelling interest in a form of school-based training that resembles an apprenticeship as opposed to traditional university-based courses which are perceived to be overly academic (Wubbels, 1992).

In other countries, however, there is a trend in the opposite direction. In France, for example, primary teacher education was until recently undertaken by the equivalent of colleges of education, and secondary teacher education was virtually non-existent, relying heavily upon the subject studies within university degrees as the major qualification for teaching. In an attempt to improve both the status of primary teaching and the quality of training, new university level institutes were created to offer four-year degree courses covering the subject matter of the primary curriculum, the pedagogy associated with the various subject areas and matters concerning child development and children's learning. Similarly in Italy, where secondary teacher training has not traditionally been compulsory, there is an awareness of the need for teachers to be better prepared in the teaching and learning of their subject, and postgraduate courses in teacher training are becoming much more widespread (see Buchberger, 1992; Eurydice, 1995). Teacher training in Scandinavia, on the other hand, has in recent times involved education to Masters level, with the integrated study of subject matter, pedagogy and educational studies; this form of training still retains strong levels of public and professional confidence.

The rapid move towards school-based teacher education in several countries has probably as much to do with political, economic and ideological factors as it has with any genuine concern for, and understanding of, quality in teacher education. The argument that teaching is best learned in the classroom has little theoretical or empirical justification, although in the UK it has had some strong advocates in the right-wing Centre for Policy Studies. The main justifications they have offered for this move seem to lie in two arguments. First, the claim is made that teacher education courses have evolved with a bias towards unproductive theorizing and a leaning towards left-wing ideology, at the expense of an essential focus on subject matter, and the techniques of imparting knowledge and managing children in classrooms. Lawlor (1990), for instance, criticizes ITT courses for their obsessive concern with multiculturalism and special needs which she views as products of 1960s left-wing thinking rather than as matters relating to practical teaching. Second, O'Hear (1988), a philosopher at Bradford University, argues that teaching is a practical activity and can only be learned in practice. Drawing on Gilbert Ryle's (1949) distinction of 'knowing how' and 'knowing that', he argues that learning to teach, like learning to ride a bicycle, is largely a matter of 'knowing how' and can only be learned from one's own trial and error practice and under the supervision of an experienced practitioner.

Such a view, however, presents an oversimplification of the processes of learning to teach. Even if learning to teach could be regarded as purely a matter of acquiring a practical skill, even moderately complex human skills are not learned simply through trial and error experience and coaching. Learning to ski, for example, by strapping on boots and skis and taking to the snow can be a potentially dangerous exercise. Furthermore, where practical skills are learned through trial and error, rarely are high levels of accomplishment achieved by practice alone. For example, in learning to ski, the skier can develop useful theoretical knowledge — about how the ski works, about how the skier's distribution of weight on the ski affects its actions, about how movements of the body are used to control the direction of the skis, and about the appropriateness of particular techniques in different terrain. Good ski instructors similarly require much more knowledge than simply the 'know-how' of how to ski themselves. They need to develop a language for communicating with the novice about the physical sensations and movements that skiing involves; they also need an understanding of the processes of learning to ski — what kinds of difficulties novices encounter, what are useful learning activities, how might they be sequenced, what advice, analogies, concepts, explanations are useful to learners to help them judge their own performance and improve upon it. Learning to ski well is certainly much more than trial and error learning under the watchful eye of an expert. Similar arguments could be made for almost any area of moderate or complex human skill. When considering much more complex skills, such as teaching, which require reasoning (about how to deal with new specific situations), the development of complex relationships (that enable teachers to maintain children's interest and communicate with them) and moral judgments (about what is appropriate action for teachers and schools to take), 'knowing that' and 'knowing how' are clearly simplistic divisions, leaving out of the account, for instance, the 'knowing why' and 'knowing when'.

Understanding Teacher Education

Given the diverse and contradictory ways in which teacher education is being shaped, a fuller understanding of what teachers do and the processes by which teachers learn to teach is evidently needed. Although teacher education may at present be being driven by an alternative agenda, any genuine improvements in the quality of teacher education require a clearer understanding of the processes involved and how they are most appropriately facilitated. Claims currently abound concerning potential ways of improving teacher education, involving, for instance, an increase in the level of subject study for intending teachers, or an increase in the practical component. Such claims, however, are premised on very simple models of the nature of teaching and how teachers learn to teach. They leave out of the account the complexity of the tasks that teachers undertake, and the different kinds of learning that these most likely involve. Learning how to plan a lesson, how to relate to 7-year-olds in a classroom, how to present oneself as a teacher in the classroom, how to work collaboratively with other teachers, how to analyse and improve one's own practice and to consider the long-term goals of education require quite different approaches to learning.

The purpose of this book is to report an ESRC-funded project that studied twenty student teachers over a two-year period, with the intention of exploring the processes of learning to teach. Ten of the students were on a two-year articled teacher training course, the other ten were on a conventional one-year postgraduate certificate in education course which was largely institution-based with intermittent periods spent in schools. All of the students were training to become primary teachers.

The project aimed to improve our understanding of the processes of learning to teach, principally by attempting to answer such questions as:

- What kind of background and experience do the student teachers come to teacher training with, and how does this influence their experience of training and induction?
- What kind of knowledge and understanding do they acquire in the process of learning to teach? How do they acquire it? And how does it inform their classroom practice?
- What are the major factors that interact and facilitate the processes of learning to teach? How, for instance, do institutional, supervisory, personal and activity factors interrelate with one another?
- How can we understand the processes of professional development in initial teacher education, and what might its implications be for the design, organization and assessment of preservice training?

Chapter 2 reviews some of the key literature that has reported previous research in this area and which provides some of the theoretical frameworks for the analysis of the data collected in this study. Chapter 3 describes the methodology of the research project, pointing out how the data was collected and analysed and how the case studies described in Chapters 4 to 7 were constructed. The main findings of the study are reported in Chapters 8 and 9. Chapters 4 to 7 describe four case studies, two from each of the training programmes, overviewing the development of the student teachers over the two-year period. Chapter 8 looks across all of the cases and comments on some general themes concerning the students' learning and experiences. The final chapter discusses some of the practical questions facing teacher education today and considers how research might help to understand teacher education processes and how it might help to direct teacher education in the future.

In the literature on teachers' professional development, there are sometimes clear distinctions drawn between 'teacher education' and 'teacher training'. More recently, the distinctions have become blurred and the two terms seem to be used almost interchangeably, both referring to the overall professional preparation of teachers. That is the understanding on which the terms have been used throughout the book, though further consideration of possible distinctions between them is made in Chapter 9.

Chapter 2

Learning to Teach

During initial training and their first few years in the classroom, many teachers, perhaps even the majority, experience difficulties in learning to teach. Managing children, developing appropriate relationships in the classroom, getting to grips with the subject matter, planning activities which involve children and help them learn, monitoring children's understanding, becoming part of the social and institutional structure of the school, are all common sources of difficulty and anxiety (Veenman, 1984; Knowles and Cole, 1994). It is therefore somewhat surprising that within the profession itself, initial training and support for induction into the profession often appear to have been awarded scant attention or prestige.

Yet the task of preparing teachers for the profession is a complex and challenging one. In designing teacher training courses, difficult decisions have to be faced about the structure and content of the courses, about when experience in school is best introduced and how students are most appropriately prepared for it, about the roles of the personnel involved, and about how student teachers are suitably assisted in coming to terms with the substantial demands of the school and the classroom. Similarly, teacher educators are faced with many individual decisions with particular student teachers in specific contexts: How do you best support a student in difficulty? How do you help them learn? What do they need to know and do? How do you help them select from, and learn from, the wide range of experiences that they are exposed to in schools?

These decisions, however, seem more often to be based on the intuition or craft wisdom of the teacher educator, built up over several years, or upon prevailing ideologies within education or the constraints of official guidelines than upon any clearly articulated and tested understanding of how student teachers learn to teach or how professional development might alternatively be designed and delivered. But what knowledge might usefully be drawn upon in designing, implementing and evaluating courses of initial teacher education? In searching for such knowledge one might conclude that there are few theoretical models to draw upon in thinking about the nature, context and purpose of the teacher educator's work. Teacher educators even appear to lack a common language for talking about their work. There have been several imperatives to innovate in teacher education, though the resulting changes have themselves rarely been systematically evaluated, and as a result there is little in the way of a body of evidence about what works, why and when. Attempts to improve teacher education, particularly recently, have often been motivated by political or ideological concerns, rather than by a thorough understanding of the nature of teachers' work and the processes of becoming a teacher.

Inevitably, however, when action is taken to improve teacher education — such as moving larger proportions of time to school experience, changing the structure of the course, recruiting different expertise amongst teacher educators, emphasizing subject matter content rather than pedagogy — assumptions are implicitly or explicitly made about teaching and how teachers learn to teach. In the pursuit of systematic improvement in the quality of teacher education, it becomes important that this action is based on a secure, well-founded understanding of teachers' professional development. A conceptual framework is required which enables us to appreciate the experiences of student teachers and how these relate to their developing practice, and which helps us to identify the factors that are influential in the student teacher's professional growth. It is in the creation of such an understanding that research has an important role to play. The more we come to know about student teachers' experiences, how their practice in the classroom develops and the factors that impinge upon this development, the more able we are to construct models or theories of professional growth that will be able to shape the construction of future courses, inform the training and induction of teachers and serve as guides for action for teacher educators, dealing with the complex task of helping student teachers to learn the practice of teaching.

Research on Teacher Education

Up until relatively recently, research on teacher education has not been a major focus within the field of educational research. Only over the last two decades has research in the field developed to the extent that it can now support several specialist international journals of high standing and warrant many national and international conferences convened to discuss and disseminate research findings and their implications for practice.

Some of the early research in teacher education was concerned with student teacher evaluations of their own professional education. Questions such as whether student teachers value their initial training, and which parts are perceived by them to be most useful predominated the agenda. Interestingly, several of these studies, carried out over a period of time, have pointed to a similar trend (see Lanier and Little's 1986 review). Student teachers appear to be dissatisfied with the bridge between theory and practice. Their perception of what happens in their college or university-based part of the course seems difficult to reconcile with their practical experiences in the classroom. Often the students value more highly the practical aspects of their course, and they tend to identify more readily with their supervising teachers than with their university tutors, particularly towards the end of their professional training when they are close to taking up appointments in schools themselves. Such general trends have been reported in numerous studies in different countries and with respect to courses of training involving quite different structures and different personnel. It is therefore interesting to consider why there is such a level of dissatisfaction with initial teacher education. Why does it appear to be so little valued? Why do practising teachers themselves often not rate their professional training highly? Why are these findings apparently so consistent over time, place and curricular and institutional context?

Several possible answers could be offered for these findings. First of all, teaching perhaps has a culture which attaches importance to personal and practical experience. Teaching is action-oriented, and action in the classroom is more readily associated with teachers' work than reading, reflection or private study. Even in staffroom discussions of teaching competence, the number of years of experience as a teacher are often equated with professional effectiveness, or are at least considered more significant than academic or professional qualifications. This has been suggested to be a peculiarity of teaching and in contrast to other professions. Lanier and Little (1986), for example, point out how comparable studies of medicine and law indicate that practitioners within these fields typically value their initial training and place a great deal of emphasis on the knowledge that is acquired from the university context. A second possible explanation lies in the complexity of the teaching task and the knowledge and skill that teachers develop. Perhaps there is just so much knowledge that experienced teachers ideally need to acquire that attempts to make this knowledge accessible to student teachers in a short period of initial training, and at a time when it is meaningful to them and can be readily assimilated and related to practice, inevitably results in problems of mis-timing, overload, and perceived irrelevance. In becoming a teacher, there is too much to learn in too short a time. Other explanations lie in the different types of learning in which student teachers engage, and the difficulties of constructing courses that enable this learning to be developed in a coherent and well-coordinated manner (see Calderhead, 1991). It has also been suggested that the frequently reported finding that student teachers value practical experiences far above college-based training is an artefact of the situation they are in. McNally, Cope, Inglis and Stronach (1994) suggest that classroom practice stands out as being the most significant element of professional training to student teachers because of its vividness and its emotional associations: students develop strong emotional attachments to the teachers and children they work with, and the events they experience in schools themselves stand out as vivid memories which transcend the more mundane aspects of their college-based professional training. Experience in school is therefore more readily and enthusiastically mentioned in any retrospective evaluation of their course. Grossman (1992), in a series of detailed case studies of secondary school student teachers, found that much of their planning and teaching did derive from university-based parts of the course, and student teachers acknowledged the helpfulness of these courses in relation to specific lessons or aspects of their teaching, which is in contrast to the more generalized perception that they typically have of field experience itself being the valuable part of the course. The college or university contribution may simply be less readily noticed and therefore less likely to be acknowledged by students.

These tentative answers, however, pose many further questions. Clearly, the teacher training experience is a complex one, and explorations of this complexity lead to a questioning of both the content and process of the students' learning. What learning is involved in becoming a teacher? Is there a distinctive professional learning process? Is learning to teach different from learning subject matter or learning performance skills and, if so, in which respects?

Research on Early Professional Development

Research in teacher education cannot at present offer one comprehensive theory of professional development. Very many variables clearly influence the growth of teachers' practice and it is difficult to order and categorize these in a way that provides one meaningful and coherent account of teacher development that might guide the organization and management of teacher education. Nevertheless, inquiries into the professional growth of teachers have tended to cluster around five particular models that emphasize specific aspects of learning to teach, and that construe the learning process in characteristic ways. Each highlights certain aspects of the process of learning to teach and also raises particular questions about how student teachers are most appropriately prepared for their work as teachers.

The *enculturation*, or *socialization into the professional culture, model* emphasizes the socializing processes in professional development. Teaching is portrayed as a demanding task that occurs in a powerful material and ideological context. The organization and physical resources of schools and, perhaps more significantly, the beliefs that are not only held and valued within the institution but have become embedded within its many taken-for-granted practices, inevitably exert a powerful influence upon the new teacher, sometimes referred to as the 'wash out effect' (Zeichner and Tabachnick, 1981) since they may dominate and over-rule the practices learned in college. In this perspective, learning to teach is viewed largely in terms of induction into the institutional values and practices, the ways of thinking and acting that predominate within the school. Lacey (1977) describes the strategies adopted by new teachers in school to negotiate their way amongst these pressures, changing to fit in with some of the school values and practices, managing to influence others, and going along with some, though not essentially believing in them, for strategic reasons in order, for example, to gain acceptance within the school.

Zeichner, Tabachnick and Densmore (1987) propose that the socialization process is in fact more complex because schools generally contain multiple ideologies in the form of groups of teachers who mutually support particular subject ideologies or particular notions of teaching and learning. The task of the new teacher becomes one of weaving their way amongst these often identifying with one like-minded individual or group of teachers from whom they can seek support. In one longitudinal study of two student teachers, Rust (1994) charted the growth of students' quite child-centred views of teaching and learning during their initial training programme, followed by a reversal to more control-oriented beliefs about teaching when faced with the practicalities of teaching in their first year of employment. Rust suggests that the pressures of teaching in school led the students to emphasize fitting into the school, particularly into its control-oriented ethos and practices, and they were ill-prepared to develop their own teaching style or to deal with the negotiations that are necessary to develop one's confidence and status in an institutional setting. In their review of teacher socialization, Zeichner and Gore (1990) suggest that the literature contains several models of teacher socialization, which place differing emphases on the influence of the institutional context and the individual teacher's potential to change existing values and practices. Socialization perspectives on professional development, however, have succeeded in highlighting the complex interactions that occur between an individual's own values, beliefs and practices and those of the school, and also the importance of the individual's capacity to negotiate and manoeuvre within a powerful ideological context. These perspectives draw attention to the importance of 'political skills' amongst student teachers, and raise questions about how students might be better prepared to develop and defend their own practice within an institutional context.

The *technical*, or *knowledge and skills, model* is perhaps the most often cited perspective on learning to teach which emphasizes the knowledge and skills teachers acquire that contribute to classroom practice. In the 1960s and 1970s, this was popularly defined in terms of classroom behaviours. Several attempts were made to develop microteaching or skill development programmes, focusing, for example, on questioning skills or the management skills involved in transitions from one activity to another. These programmes relied particularly upon the large amount of 'process-product' research emerging at that time, which attempted to link teaching behaviours to children's learning outcomes. More recently, teaching skill has been conceptualized cognitively as well as behaviourally, in terms of ways of understanding practice and the actions to which such understandings lead. Several studies comparing experienced and novice teachers have demonstrated how the experienced teacher has a much more sophisticated understanding of their practice. The experienced teacher appears to have access to a wide range of knowledge that can be readily accessed when dealing with classroom situations and which can help in interpreting and responding to them. The novice teacher, on the other hand, makes simpler, common-sense interpretations of classroom events, and is less able to anticipate possibilities and act accordingly. Berliner (1987), for example, demonstrates how student teachers and experienced teachers judged to be 'expert' differ in the interpretations they make when observing videotapes of classroom interaction. The student teachers' descriptions of the videotaped excerpts tended to focus on the physical attributes of the children and the layout of the classroom, whereas the experienced teachers were more able to infer the situation and context, to hypothesize about children's difficulties and speculate on what might happen next. The experienced teachers had a wealth of context-specific knowledge on which they could draw in order to interpret and explain the situations.

The knowledge that teachers call upon in planning their work, teaching in the classroom and later evaluating their work is highly varied, including knowledge of children, teaching strategies, the curriculum, school rules, the availability of materials, etc. Teachers' knowledge also takes different forms, some of it is clearly propositional and is relatively easily articulated; other aspects of their knowledge are embedded within action and are more easily demonstrated than put into words. One aspect of teachers' knowledge that has received particular attention in recent years has been that concerning subject matter. In the UK, several surveys of teachers' practice based on HMI observations have suggested that teachers who are insecure in their subject knowledge tend to adopt a slavish adherence to textbooks, reliance on narrow questions, an inability to extend children's answers and an overprescriptive method where the teacher remains within a safe routine (HMI, 1987). Such observations have directed attention to the importance of the extent and quality of teachers' subject knowledge. Largely stimulated by the work of Shulman (Shulman, 1986; Wilson, Shulman and Richert, 1987), several studies, both in the US and the UK, have investigated changes in student teachers' understanding of the subject they teach. These have suggested that a large amount of time is spent in the first few years of teaching relearning the subject matter for the purposes of teaching it. Shulman suggests that in order to teach a subject one needs both a breadth and depth of knowledge, a rich factual knowledge base with many interconnections which represents a much more thorough understanding than that which is achieved purely as a learner. In addition, teachers develop knowledge which enables them to facilitate understanding in others. Shulman refers to this as *pedagogical content knowledge* — knowledge of examples, anecdotes, experiments, and difficulties that are commonly experienced, knowledge which helps teachers to communicate the subject matter.

Since children's own backgrounds vary considerably and they approach a subject with particular understandings of their own, teachers, it is argued, need a wide repertoire of pedagogical content knowledge to cater for children's individual differences. The analogy that 'works' for one child, for example, may be completely meaningless to another. One example of pedagogical content knowledge that Shulman and his colleagues present is of a novice teacher faced with the task of teaching Julius Caesar to a class of 14-year-olds. Believing that the children will not be enthusiastic about the play, he uses his knowledge both of the play as a drama about moral conflict and of the children and their interests to construct a task where he asks the children to imagine they are second in command on the Starship Enterprise and that Captain Kirk, their best friend, is becoming big-headed and is beginning to take decisions that risk the lives of his crew — what would they do? This situation is used to lead into a discussion on loyalty and morality. The teacher uses his knowledge of the subject, and of the children and their interests, to introduce the play in a way that captures their attention, engages them in considering the theme of the play, and enables them to empathize with the characters, setting the scene for more in-depth study. In the process, the teacher also adds to his own pedagogical content knowledge. Developing this knowledge not only requires an understanding of the subject, but an understanding of children, their abilities and interests and how they tend to respond to different situations, an appreciation of different teaching strategies and how various types of classroom activity might be managed. Developing pedagogical content knowledge, in fact, seems to require the orchestration of a wide variety of knowledge about teaching.

Studies suggest that there is an enormous diversity of knowledge that the more experienced teacher possesses — not only about subject matter, but about children, teaching and the classroom context — that enables teachers to make sense of classrooms and to monitor and shape their classroom routines and behaviours. Shulman (1987) argues that it is important to attempt to make this knowledge base explicit, not only for the purposes of facilitating teacher education, but from the point of view of maintaining the professional status of teaching. It is through 'codifying the wisdom of practice' and making the knowledge base of teaching explicit that teaching can stake its claim to being a profession alongside others which are similarly built upon a body of substantial and specialized knowledge.

Teaching, as well as being a practical and intellectual activity, is also a *moral endeavour*, and this has formed the basis of an alternative way of conceptualizing learning to teach. Teaching involves caring for young people, considering the interests of children, preparing them to be part of a future society, and influencing the way in which they relate to each other and live. The ethic of caring has been claimed to be a central facet of teaching (Noddings, 1986; Valli, 1990), often valued by teachers, parents and children, but frequently unacknowledged in discussions of professional development. In addition, important moral issues concerning equality within our society are implicit in the way in which schools and teaching are organized and the ways in which academic rewards, in the form of qualifications, are distributed, and this can raise several moral dilemmas for teachers in their practice.

Lyons (1990), drawing upon a series of interviews with secondary school teachers, demonstrates how moral dilemmas abound within their professional lives. One teacher, for example, who saw himself as a showman, was quite extrovert in lessons and was well liked by students had become used to his particular teaching persona, which gave him satisfaction in his work and was successful in terms of generating pleasant classroom relationships. At the same time, however, he had to face concerns about whether he was doing what would best promote the children's learning — does he give up the role that he finds satisfying and which endears the children to him in order to serve the best interests of the children? Lyons argues that because teaching involves a sense of mission and because teachers often have strong commitments to certain values and ideas, as well as having certain conceptions of their professional and personal self, and of the subject and how it should be taught and learned, dilemmas inevitably become a frequent characteristic of teachers' thinking. Should a teacher, for example, let a disruptive child skate through the year without learning much in order to maintain reasonable order and a pleasant life? Should the teacher with a commitment to a constructivist view of teaching and learning resort to more didactic methods because these are what are accepted within the school? Lyons argues that teachers cannot avoid moral dilemmas, and that these often require extensive deliberation in order to be managed or resolved.

Olson (1992) suggests that in many countries recent concerns with educational standards and instrumental attempts to manipulate the processes of teaching and learning towards certain areas of scholastic attainment have resulted in the moral dimension of teaching becoming obscured. He argues that implicit in all teaching acts are certain value judgments and that in education today these may well be at odds with the basic values to which teachers, and teaching as a profession, might wish to adhere. Part of a teacher's professional development, he suggests, is to enquire into what those values are, to regain control of those values and to seek to promote a closer level of agreement between values and practices. Becoming a teacher is viewed as a process of professional self-actualization in which coming to terms with values and conflict are a significant part.

Within the formal curriculum of teacher education, moral dilemmas probably receive scant attention, yet clearly these dilemmas can present new and emotionally and intellectually challenging situations to the new teacher. These are aspects of teaching that often remain unexplored and undiscussed. Left to wrestle with them on their own, student teachers may find such dilemmas to be a source of considerable stress (Knowles and Cole, 1994) that may even lead them to consider leaving the course and abandoning their teaching career.

Several studies have recently emphasized *the close relationship between the personal and the professional in teachers' work*, and the need to consider personal development in any model of teachers' professional development. Several different aspects of the personal dimension have been emphasized in the literature. First of all, it has been found that teachers approach teaching with various ideas and images of what teachers' work is like based on their own individual past experiences, including previous work experience, experiences as a parent or childhood experiences of school (Johnston, 1992; Calderhead and Robson, 1990). This is often a metaphoric way of thinking about teaching (Russell, Munby, Spafford and Johnston, 1988) in which past experiences are used as models for reasoning about the nature of teaching and what teachers do. In case studies of experienced teachers, Elbaz (1983) and Clandinin (1986) have used the term 'personal practical knowledge' to refer to the working knowledge that teachers have that is imbued with teachers' own lived experience.

Second, teachers' personalities themselves are an important aspect of their work as teachers (Clark, 1988). Teachers are to some extent performers in the classroom, required to establish working relationships with their pupils, to command their attention and respect, and to ensure the smooth running of their classes. Such tasks intrinsically involve teachers' personalities, and part of teachers' professional development requires teachers to engage in self-learning, becoming aware of their own personal qualities and how other people respond to them, so that they can take greater control in their interactions with others.

Bullough, Knowles and Crow (1991) suggest that learning to be a teacher requires the development of a professional self-concept. This is achieved, they argue, through a reassessment of oneself and the context in which one works, particularly the individuals with whom one interacts. In their studies of student teachers, they suggest that metaphors are frequently used to conceptualize aspects of the self, to give coherence and meaning to life and to capture a teacher's core self-perception. Students were found to enter teaching with metaphors of themselves as teachers (such as teacher as nurturer, or teacher as subject expert) but, when explored, these were often found to be unrealistic or fantasy-like. When these changed and became more stable professional metaphors, they sometimes also influenced how students felt about themselves. They report the case of one teacher, for instance, who became much more positive, enthusiastic and confident in her personal life once uncertainties about her professional identity were resolved.

Reflection has recently become a popular term in the context of teachers' professional development. Many teacher education courses, both preservice and inservice, claim to be based upon a reflective practitioner model (Furlong, Whitty, Barrett, Barton and Miles, 1994). The enthusiasm for reflective practice may be partly accounted for in terms of the current attractiveness of many of the principles that have come to be associated with it: helping teachers to analyse, discuss, evaluate and change their own practice; heightening teachers' awareness of the contexts in which they work; enabling teachers to appreciate the moral and ethical issues implicit in their practice; to empower teachers to take greater control over their own professional growth and to influence future directions in education. At a time of uncertain educational change and when, in some countries, there are strong pressures to view teachers as technicians and implementers of a curriculum devised by others, the rhetoric of teachers as reflective practitioners — educators with a purpose, able to take control over their own futures — has an obvious appeal. What reflective practice actually looks like, however, is less clear. Several notions of reflection have been used to support quite a diversity of practices.

Schön (1983, 1987) has been one of the most influential writers in this field. Although he has written about professional practice in general, including such fields as social work and psychotherapy, his own studies have mainly focused on architecture and town planning. He argues that one of the major problems with professional education in general is that it focuses on standard scientific theories and how to apply them to straightforward cases. In reality, however, real problems, he suggests, can often not be solved in this way. Skilful professional practice depends less on factual knowledge and rigid decision-making models than on the capacity to reflect, interactively framing the problem as well as working out possible solutions. He identifies two forms of reflection which have been readily applied to a teaching context (see Grimmett and Erickson, 1988). One, which he terms *reflection-in-action*, refers to the processes of monitoring and adapting one's behaviour in context. Because teaching is complex and unpredictable, teachers cannot rely entirely on routine ways of coping with situations. Teaching therefore involves a process of acting, reflecting on the effects of one's actions and constantly adapting one's behaviour to the situation and purposes at hand. A second type of reflection, termed *reflection-on-action*, places emphasis on after-the-event evaluation. Teachers, after a lesson or after the day is over, may reflect back on particular events, analysing where difficulties arose, considering how they might be surmounted and deciding on the future directions their teaching might take.

Schön argues that reflection-in-action constitutes the artistry that lies within professional action, and that the skills involved can only be acquired in the practice setting. Schön therefore places particular emphasis on practical experience under supervision and highlights the importance of the mentor in inducting the novice into ways of thinking and acting.

Several researchers (e.g., Carr and Kemmis, 1986; Court, 1988) have also pointed towards a more deliberative form of reflection in which teachers engage —

reflection that is more searching, philosophical and critical. These are occasions when teachers think more about the purposes of education, their own personal and professional goals and the value of their own practice.

The nature of the reflection that teachers engage in, however, may well differ from that of architects and town planners. Clarke (1995), in a series of case studies of student science teachers over a thirteen-week field experience, aimed to track what student teachers reflect about and what facilitates or impedes their reflection. He argues that the term 'reflective incident' was inappropriate in characterizing the substance of their reflection. While reflective themes were born of incidents, they were extended and interwoven across multiple personal and classroom contexts rather than being episodic. In addition, Clarke suggests that the relationship between student and mentor was less smooth and more problematic than Schön depicts. The mentor's suggestions didn't always work, support could turn to criticism, relationships between student and mentor could obstruct potentially profitable learning. The nature of reflection and the means of supporting it were found to be more complex than suggested in Schön's original classification.

Recent writings on reflective teaching have considered what the cognitive, affective and behavioural components of reflection might be: what are the skills, knowledge bases, attitudes and predispositions that make reflection possible, and how might these be facilitated amongst teachers at different stages in their career? Do student teachers need to be taught how to reflect and is this different from the support needed by more experienced teachers in their reflection? Do student teachers need to have a basic mastery of teaching before reflection on practice is actually possible? Researchers and teacher educators have also focused on the content of reflection: is all content an equally appropriate subject for reflection, and how does one prioritize the subject matter for reflection? (see Calderhead and Gates, 1993).

Certainly, enthusiasm for reflective teaching has led to much experimentation in teacher education (see Clift, Houston and Pugach, 1990; Valli, 1992) and the development of a wide range of techniques and approaches to encourage and foster reflection in both preservice and inservice courses. These have included techniques such as journal writing, action research, and the use of research evidence and empirically derived theory to provide alternative conceptual frameworks for the analysis of practice, as well as the development of certain principles of training and defined roles of the trainers that relate to the overall 'reflective' philosophy and organization of a course.

The implementation of reflective teacher education has not been without its difficulties, however. Creating a course that helps student teachers to become more analytical about their practice and to take charge of their own professional development is a task with a number of inherent dilemmas. How do teacher educators reconcile their traditional role as a gatekeeper to the profession with that of mentor and facilitator of reflection? The goals of reflective teaching are extremely ambitious — what is reasonable to achieve in preservice education and what can only be achieved in the much longer term? How does a teacher education institution foster reflection when in schools much greater importance is attached to immediate, spontaneous action than to reflection and evaluation? Does reflective teaching require a particular supportive, collaborative ethos in school in order for the efforts of teacher educators to be effective? The development of reflective practice in preservice and inservice courses has not proved easy and there are many questions posed by current research and development efforts.

Synthesizing Research on Learning to Teach

From research on learning to teach, we can conclude that teaching, and the processes of learning to teach, are highly complex and place heavy demands, of a cognitive, affective and performance nature, upon the student teacher. Each of the models discussed above identifies an important set of variables relating to professional development, but each gives only a partial picture of the total process. Each focuses on a particular aspect of teachers' work, though clearly all of these represent dimensions of teachers' practice and are closely interrelated. Learning to teach involves the development of technical skills, as well as an appreciation of moral issues involved in education, an ability to negotiate and develop one's practice within the culture of the school, the development of personal qualities and an ability to reflect and evaluate both in and on one's actions. Each of these areas may make quite different demands upon the learner and entail different forms of professional growth. Furthermore, the learning required of them may be different from the learning in which they have previously been engaged in higher education: learning to become a teacher contrasts sharply in its demands from learning mathematics or learning history, for example. Learning to be a teacher requires multiple forms of learning. Learning to teach the concept of ratio is different from learning to present oneself as a teacher in the classroom, or learning to relate to reluctant learners, or learning how to plan the curriculum, or how to work with one's colleagues or how to cope with one's own anxieties (see Calderhead, 1991). Not only does learning to teach involve different forms of learning, but since student teachers start out with many different abilities, types of expertise and background experience, their routes in the process of learning are inevitably quite varied. Just as children come to the classroom with different background experiences that influence their learning, student teachers approach initial training with different pasts on which to draw, different aspirations and expectations, and different repertoires of relevant skills, abilities and knowledge.

Research to date has identified a diverse range of factors that could potentially influence the professional development of beginning teachers — factors within the school, within the training programme and within the individual. Research has also to some extent mapped out the key players in the process of professional development. From the student teacher's perspective, the most influential actors to shape their developing practice are the college tutor and the mentor or supervising teacher. The influence of the college tutor is perceived by the student teacher to be less, and to decrease over time, whereas the opposite is generally perceived to be the case for the supervising teacher (Guyton and McIntyre, 1990). The actual impact of the university tutor on the student teacher's practice, however, may be more substantial than is immediately recognized by the student (Grossman, 1992). Another two groups of key players are also suggested in some studies. One is the peer group. Student teachers may be reluctant to share some of their concerns and ideas with those who are perceived to be authority figures, and discussions within the peer group of student teachers may serve an important supportive function (Hawkey, 1995). The other is the children themselves, who provide a constant source of feedback to the student teacher about their abilities as a person and a teacher (Knowles and Cole, 1994).

In conclusion, it can be argued that research has a vital role to play in teacher education. Although initial training courses may be involved in a continuous process of fine-tuning and ongoing development, substantial improvements in the field are dependent on a fuller understanding of what learning to teach involves. Exploring the various aspects of professional development that research has highlighted, seeking a fuller understanding of the processes of learning to teach and identifying the factors that facilitate or impede that learning are tasks that can further our appreciation of teacher education and provide a reasoned and supported basis for its future development.

Chapter 3

Researching Learning to Teach

As the studies reviewed in Chapter 2 reveal, the processes of learning to teach have been investigated in numerous ways. Researchers have pursued their work from a variety of theoretical and disciplinary perspectives, have adopted different foci and have used diverse research methods and procedures to collect and analyse data. Attempts to understand the experience of novice teachers' learning to teach have taken researchers along different conceptual routes. The result, not surprisingly, is a partial, patchy and poorly organized knowledge base, and little effort so far appears to have been directed towards synthesizing this knowledge or developing more comprehensive theoretical frameworks for understanding the professional growth that occurs in the early stages of a teacher's career.

The design of any empirical research study establishes how data is to be collected and analysed, and is affected by the questions posed and also by the theoretical framework within which the study is constructed. This study started out with an awareness of the multiple perspectives adopted in attempts to understand teachers' development. It also began with a belief that creating a more comprehensive theoretical framework was desirable and might also be achievable through an exploration of the overall experience of student teachers during their preservice courses and early teaching careers. It is through the experience of the students that the many significant factors identified in the research literature impinge upon the teachers' developing practice, and therefore a fuller understanding of the students' experience might serve to synthesize and develop existing interpretive frameworks.

Several general questions helped initially to frame the research design reported on in this book:

- how do student teachers think about teaching, learning, subject matter, themselves and the process of becoming a teacher before the start of their teacher training course?
- how do these conceptions change and develop in the process of becoming a teacher?
- what features appear to facilitate or impede this development?
- how does a study of these changes help us understand the processes of professional development, and result in a more comprehensive theoretical appreciation of the processes involved?

These questions served as broad guides in the initial stages of the research. They focused on areas of the students' experience that existing research literature and the authors' own experiences in teacher education suggested were significant. However, they also implied various assumptions about learning to teach. They assumed, for instance, that students start out in teacher education with certain knowledge that undergoes change or development and which is significant in shaping the new teacher's practice. Whilst this might suggest a cognitive psychological perspective, these questions were chosen for their centrality to the process of learning to teach, and therefore as an obvious starting point, rather than with the intention of making them an exclusive focus, tied to one particular theoretical perspective. The study was undertaken with an awareness of differing perspectives on learning to teach and a readiness to include alternative questions and data collection procedures should these appear at any time to be pertinent to understanding the students' experiences and the processes of professional growth.

In order to track the changes that occurred in the thinking of student teachers, it was decided that a relatively small number of students would be studied quite intensively over at least the period of the training and, where possible, longer. A case-study approach which built up detailed descriptions of the students' experience was selected as an appropriate methodology. A sample of twenty student primary teachers was eventually chosen from two different training courses at the same institution — a college of higher education in the south-west of England. The involvement of student teachers from two separate courses, one a conventional year-long PGCE course, and the other a two-year articled teacher course, enabled a wider range of course design and supervision factors to be included in the study, since each course had its own particular philosophy of preparing teachers and quite different course design features which one might expect to have some influence in shaping the students' early experiences. The length of the study enabled the PGCE students to be followed through into the first year of their appointments in school, where appointments were obtained, and the articled teachers to be followed through the full two years of their school-based course.

The Students

The students were recruited to the study on the basis of two criteria. First of all, the broad aims of the study and the time demands it was likely to make were explained to both student groups, and volunteers were invited. Secondly, students on the PGCE course were only selected if they were normally resident within easy travelling distance of the college and were seeking first appointments in the same area. The inclusion of the latter criterion was to ensure that the follow-up of the students in their first year of full-time teaching could be feasibly conducted.

All of the students were graduates, with first degrees in subjects ranging across arts (10), languages (1), sciences (2), humanities (5), home economics (1) and psychology (1). Other characteristics of the sample are summarized in Table 3.1. In terms of age, gender, academic background and previous work experience, they were comparable to the usual graduate intake for primary teacher education in this

Table 3.1:   *Characteristics of the student teachers*

	Total N	N female	N with > 3 years' work experience	N over 26	Age Range
Articled Teachers	10	10	8	7	22–43
PGCE Students	10	7	5	5	23–48

college. The PGCE course in 1991–92, the first year of the study, had a total intake of eighty-three and the articled teacher training course, an experimental school-based scheme, had an intake of twelve.

The Preservice Training Courses

The PGCE course was a year-long course in primary education, preparing class teachers for the 4–11 age range. The course began with an induction week in which the students were introduced to the college facilities, their tutors and to the structure of the course. A major event in the induction week was a field trip to the local docks which formed the basis of some initial project work. The purpose of this was to enable the students to get to know one another, but also to use it as a basis for exploring the teaching and learning that was involved in field-based projects. The main part of the course was structured around three terms of approximately twelve weeks each. The structure of the terms followed a similar pattern. Each began with a period of college-based work, followed in terms one and two with a period in which the students would be attached to a school for one day per week, followed in turn by a block school experience. The block school experience (BSE) became longer as the terms progressed. The demands upon the students also increased in subsequent BSEs: according to the course handbook, the first BSE was intended 'to allow students to extend their professional skills and responsibilities'; the second 'to be confident with a much wider range of curriculum areas, to teach at least 60 per cent of the class timetable and to be able not only to plan work, but begin to make simple assessments of children's progress'; by the third BSE it was expected that students would be able 'to undertake at least 80 per cent of the class timetable and to show, as soon as they are able, the qualities which any headteacher would expect to discover in a newly qualified and competent primary school teacher'. The college-based courses focused largely on the teaching of the primary school curriculum, with the emphasis being on maths, English and science. The first term also contained a course on multicultural issues and a brief course on microcomputers in education, and the second term included a course on special needs. Throughout the year, a further course on Professional Perspectives dealt with general issues such as theories of teaching and learning, organization and planning, evaluation and assessment, and the National Curriculum. (See Table 3.2 for details.)

The overall structure of the course was greatly influenced by the criteria laid

Table 3.2:   The structure of the PGCE course

	College-based Courses	Day Attachment	Block School Experience
Term 1	• Curriculum Courses (English, Maths, Science, Creative and Expressive Arts) • Professional Perspectives • Multicultural Issues • Micros in Education	one day per week in weeks 6–9	3 weeks in weeks 9–12
Term 2	• Curriculum Courses (English, Maths, Science and Technology, Social Studies, Creative and Expressive arts) • Professional Perspectives • Special Needs	one day per week in week 4–8	4 weeks in weeks 8–12
Term 3	• Curriculum Courses (English, Maths, Science, Social and Integrated Studies, Physical Education) • Professional Perspectives		7^1/$_2$ weeks beginning in week 3

down by the Council for the Accreditation of Teacher Education in circular 24/89, which specified minimum contact time for study in the field of subject application and also minimum periods of practice in schools.

Assessment for the course consisted of seven written assignments and an assessment of teaching practice. Four of the seven written assignments were in curriculum areas (English, maths, science, expressive arts), two related to the professional perspectives course, and a special study was an open-choice school-based study. Assessment of teaching practice was made jointly between college tutor and school staff. The views of the class teacher and the senior teacher in the school responsible for managing the school placement (usually the headteacher) would be formally sought by the college. Assessment of practice was made against a set of specified competences in the areas of planning and preparation, presentation and organization, class management, evaluation and personal/professional qualities. The overall judgment was one of pass or fail.

Each student on the course was allocated a personal tutor whose role was to provide academic, personal and professional guidance. On school practice, students would be visited approximately once a week by a college tutor, but tutors were assigned to particular schools rather than students, and therefore a different tutor might be visiting on each school placement, and this would most likely be someone other than the student's personal tutor.

Table 3.3: The structure of the articled teacher training course

Term	Content	Timing	Location
Before the start of the course	School-based Induction	2 weeks	Base School
Mid-September	College-based Induction	3 days	
Term 1	Main Programme (4 days in School, 1 day in College)	12 weeks	Base School
Term 2	Main Programme (4 days in School, 1 day in College)	12 weeks	4 weeks teaching focusing on different primary age phase
Term 3	Main Programme (4 days in School, 1 day in College)	12 weeks	4 weeks teaching in a different primary school; Pre-school visits
Term 4	Main Programme (4 days in School, 1 day in College)	12 weeks	Visits to secondary schools
Term 5	Full School Experience	School Term	Base School
Term 6	School-based project; Teaching	Half a term on each	Visits to other schools, Curriculum Centres, etc.

The Articled Teacher Scheme was one of sixteen pilot schemes developed throughout England. It was jointly managed by the local education authority and the college. The course lasted two years, aimed to prepare the student teachers for teaching the 4–11 age range and involved 80 per cent of course time being spent in schools. It began with a two-week period of observation in schools, followed by a three-day introduction to the course and college facilities; both of these were completed before the beginning of the college term. Throughout most of the course, the students spent one day per week in college and the other four days in school. In the fifth term, the students were based entirely in school, and the sixth term was divided between teaching, carrying out a school-based project relating to their own curriculum specialism, and various further professional development activities. For most of the course, the students were assigned to work in one class with an allotted mentor, who had received a small amount of training to undertake this role. However, the course also involved four weeks being spent with another age range within the same school, and an additional four weeks were spent in a second primary school (see Table 3.3). There were also occasional visits to nursery schools and secondary schools.

While in schools, students were expected to carry out a series of structured tasks which might involve observation, assessment of children or the teaching of particular lessons. In addition, the student was expected to work alongside the class teacher, and also to undertake a progressively increasing amount of teaching on their own. The course design allocated one half-day per week for school-based mentoring. The intention was that this would occur away from the classroom, and would enable the mentor to talk through the student's progress with him/her and to discuss the student teacher's own practice and emerging understandings of teaching.

Time in college followed a similar pattern to that of the PGCE course, with 70 per cent of the time being allocated to the primary school curriculum, focusing mostly on English, mathematics and science; 15 per cent on professional issues; and 15 per cent on aspects of teaching and learning.

The course was assessed through coursework assignments and an assessment of the practice of teaching. In each of the first four terms, two assignments were to be completed each term, one always related to the variety of tasks carried out each week in school, the second related to an aspect of the core curriculum (terms 1–3) or assessment (term 4), requiring the study of a topic in depth. The final term involved the completion of a school-based project, relating to the student teacher's own curriculum specialism as reflected by the area of their previous degree studies.

On the articled teacher training course, each student teacher was expected to maintain a profile which served as a formal written record of formative evaluations over the two years of training. Comments were written termly by the student teacher, the mentor and the college tutor, and action plans were agreed for future development. At the end of each term, the students were given feedback regarding their progress, and in term 2 a formal assessment was made in the practice of teaching. The final decision on whether students had passed the practice of teaching element of the course was based on assessments of their performance in term 5, by which time it was expected that the student would be assuming full responsibility for 75 per cent of the class timetable. The assessments were jointly made by the schools (usually the mentor in conjunction with the headteachers) and the college tutor.

The Research

The design of the study was very much influenced by Miles and Huberman's (1984) conception of qualitative research as an interactive and iterative process in which data is collected in response to some initial questions; this data is then reduced and interpreted, and in so doing further, often more specific questions, or questions concerning verification, are generated which in turn guide subsequent data collection and analysis. Consequently, after each phase of the data collection a preliminary analysis was conducted which helped to direct further stages of the enquiry.

The principal means of data collection was the semi-structured interview. In effect, these took the form of conversations about practice in which there was a particular focus, a series of issues or questions to address, but in which there was a great deal of scope for the students to talk about these matters in whatever way they chose or to guide the conversation to aspects of their development which they considered to be relevant or more important. The focus of the conversations shifted across the two-year period, changing, for example, from motivations for entering teacher education and ideas about teaching and learning in the very early stages of the project to more specific college and classroom experiences as students began to undertake these. Some of the interviews were preceded by a period of classroom observation: the field notes from which provided the main agenda for discussion and often provided particular examples of teaching or learning that stimulated a wider discussion. Significant features of these interviews included providing the students with the opportunity to take the lead in directing the conversations so that their experiences were authentically recounted, and also allotting specific time in which the conversations could take place, allowing students the opportunity to talk at length should they so choose. To ensure that the students felt at ease and were able to concentrate on the issues at hand, interviews were often conducted where it was convenient for students and where the interview was likely to be undisturbed. This varied on different occasions, including the college, the school and the students' own homes.

Interview data was also supplemented by a questionnaire and rating scale at the end of the first year. The content of this was derived from the first year interviews, and served the purpose of checking the students' earlier claims and attempting to assess the strength of some of their views. One of the data collection rounds also involved collecting students' and mentors' interpretations of video extracts of contrasting styles of teaching as a means of exploring and comparing the cues used to interpret classroom processes.

During the first year, each of the students was contacted three times per term in order to collect data concerning their practice and experience. In the second year, students were contacted three times in the first term and twice in each of the other two terms. The reduced number of visits in the last two terms enabled the research officer to spend whole days working with the students in the classroom and to develop a fuller appreciation of their practice: students were interviewed before the start of the day about their planning and at the end of the day about the day's activities and significant events within it. The objective behind coupling observation with the interview was to be able to probe more effectively into students' understandings of their own practice. In addition, the mentors of the articled teachers were interviewed in the summer term of the first year on their approaches to supervision and their understanding of student teachers' professional development. All interviews were tape recorded and transcribed soon afterwards, and ongoing analysis was used to inform further data collection. The nature and focus of each point of data collection is listed in Table 3.4.

An important feature of the research design was its attempt to be responsive to the ongoing data collection, analysis and interpretation. Whilst time constraints often acted against this process, in that the next phase of data collection would be looming before the earlier data was fully evaluated, this approach to the research served five quite distinct though often interrelated functions in the research process.

Table 3.4: The focus of data collection sessions

	Data Collection Stage	Method	Focus
Term 1	1	Semi-structured interview.	Personal background; motivation to teach; ideas about teaching and learning and learning to teach.
	2	Semi-structured interview.	Initial reactions to the course; the contribution of their own degree studies; students' observations in school; children's learning.
	3	Semi-structured interview.	Own learning; 'high spots' and 'low spots' on the course; educational views; children's learning; anticipated future development.
Term 2	4	Video analysis (students watched 3 video extracts of teaching and were individually interviewed on their interpretation of these). *This exercise was also undertaken by the articled teacher mentors.	Student's interpretation of teaching styles and classroom processes; student's own expectations for similar lessons/contexts.
	5	Semi-structured interview.	Experience in school(s); students' own learning; their own reflective journal writing.
	6	Observation of lessons, preceded and followed by semi-structured interview.	Pre-session: planning, expectations. Post-session: planning, organization, learning outcomes, roles, future planning.
Term 3	7	Semi-structured interview.	Role of mentors; experience with mentors.
	8	Observation of lesson, preceded and followed by semi-structured interview.	Pre-session: planning, source of ideas/strategies. Post-session: students' evaluations of own teaching.
	9	Rating scales and follow-up interview (a list of 73 statements about teaching abstracted from previous interviews were presented to students who were asked to represent their agreement/disagreement on a 1–5 scale). In follow-up interview, students selected key points to discuss and elaborate.	Range of aspects of teaching and learning in schools, and learning to teach.

Table 3.4: Cont'd

Data Collection Stage	Method	Focus
10	Semi-structured interview with *mentors, supervising teachers and college tutors.*	Supervision; professional growth; role of mentors; work with students.
Term 4 11	Semi-structured interview.	Expectations for year ahead; personal aims, concerns; context of student's teaching; (for PGCEs) planning for the first day of teaching.
12	Observation of lesson preceded and followed by semi-structured interview.	Pre-session: planning. Post-session: student's evaluation of lesson, particularly children's learning.
13	Semi-structured interview.	Students' own accounts of professional growth to date.
Term 5 14	Whole-day observation followed by semi-structured interview.	Student's planning; justifications for practice; interpretations and evaluations of own practice and children's learning.
15	Whole-day observation followed by semi-structured interview.	Student's planning; justifications for practice; interpretations and evaluations of own practice and children's learning.
Term 6 16	Whole-day observation followed by semi-structured interview.	Student's planning; justifications for practice; interpretations and evaluations of own practice and children's learning.
17	Semi-structured interview (in advance of the interview students were sent a selection of transcripts from previous interviews to form a basis for discussion of their development).	Student's own professional development over the 2-year period.

Verification

The analysis of interview transcripts often raised ambiguities or apparent inconsistencies. Specific questioning in further interviews could then be used to check alternative interpretations. For example, in one interview a student talked about her ideas for organizing maths sessions. These involved a complex set of group-work activities. It was unclear at the time whether these represented her intended practice or actual practice or were simply ideas that she had picked up from college lectures without thinking them through; later interviews and observations clarified these points. In another instance, a student who had expressed a strong desire to establish warm, sympathetic relationships with children appeared readily to adopt a more formal authoritarian approach in one of her teaching practices. This apparent inconsistency was later presented to the student who explained that she had felt under pressure to conform to her supervising teacher's expectations in order to achieve a successful teaching practice, but that she was actually very opposed to the kind of authoritarian relationship that her supervising teacher had established with the children.

Elaboration

The ongoing analysis sometimes identified comments which gave incomplete accounts or comments that warranted further exploration. Often these were general remarks made by students where particular examples would have been helpful and illustrative, or were remarks that, in the context of other data about the student, seemed unusual, interesting or significant and raised further questions. For example, during an early interview one mature student seemed to attach considerable importance to children working in groups. His classroom practice also revealed a strong commitment to group work. It was only in later interviews, however, that it was discovered that his previous training and experience as a manager of a group of laboratory technicians was providing him with ways of thinking about his role as a teacher in terms of maintaining a team spirit and managing collaboration.

Conceptual Analysis

Collectively, the analysis of interview data would often suggest the importance of particular concepts or lines of enquiry which consequently guided the research study. For example, towards the end of the second term, students frequently commented about 'finding themselves as a teacher', or stressing 'the personal element in teaching'. Such comments, together with earlier emphases on the importance of personality and different styles of teaching led to subsequent discussions being more focused on the personal interests and satisfaction that the students saw themselves obtaining from teaching, how they viewed the relationship between their own personal attributes and teaching, and on what they perceived as an identity transition in becoming a teacher.

Developing Lines of Enquiry

The analysis of student teachers' responses to certain lines of questioning sometimes raised issues about the most appropriate means of gaining access to their thoughts and beliefs. Early in the study, for instance, students were asked questions about how they viewed the maths, science and language curricula in the primary school and what they thought were the purposes of teaching these subjects. Generally, students had great difficulty answering these questions or they would occasionally give what appeared to be textbook-like definitions of the purposes of science education, such as 'science is important because it helps to develop children's enquiry skills'. Such answers may have been attributable to the fact that the students had thought little about the nature of the primary school curriculum and had not yet clarified their ideas about the possible purposes and justifications for different subject areas. Yet, at the same time, it seemed unlikely that the students had started out in the course without any ideas of what primary science, maths or language work might be like.

This consideration led to experimentation with alternative ways of trying to access the understandings that the student teachers might have. Throughout the entire study, in fact, it was found that student teachers had great difficulty answering general questions about subject matter or the curriculum. However, probing aspects such as the planning, the organization, or the rationale for a specific observed science session, connected much more readily with the ideas and assumptions that the students had accumulated about the subject and its associated teaching and learning methodology. One student, for example, was asked to outline his planning for the day which included a science activity designed to introduce the topic of minibeasts. After the student had discussed his ideas, he was then asked to explain what he felt was the best way to promote learning in science. Rooted in a concrete example, the student was readily able to verbalize his own ideas about the importance of practical activities in children's learning and the need for 'hands-on' activities.

Identifying Areas of Change

Ongoing analysis also helped to identify areas where one might expect change to occur and which might usefully be monitored over the course of the study. A few of the students, for example, gave surprisingly detailed accounts at the very beginning of the first year of how they saw themselves learning to teach. This provided a reference point in later interviews whereby they could comment on and compare how their ideas had changed. One student, for example, expressed her ideas about learning to teach as 'involving three distinct elements — the personal, the professional and the academic'. This view persisted throughout the course and was occasionally used as a framework to describe her experiences, but was also raised by the interviewer at the end of each year as a means of probing how her ideas about learning to teach might have developed.

Another student expressed the view quite firmly at the beginning of the course that as long as the teacher achieved the 'right atmosphere' and developed the 'right relationships', children would readily cooperate with the teacher and would be keen to 'go on in their own way' with the ideas that the teacher had sown. These ideas persisted for a long way into the course and were probably a major contributor to the fact that he experienced serious classroom management difficulties. His expectations that children would be cooperative and reasonable were often not met, but it took many challenges to these beliefs before the student eventually began to adjust his thinking about how to organize classroom activities and manage children.

The ongoing interactive process of data collection, analysis and interpretation enabled quite detailed accounts to be built up of the students over the research period. In the first year of the study, data was collected on all twenty student teachers. In the second year, only four of the PGCE students obtained full-time teaching posts from September, although another two took up posts in January: all these students were included in the second year of the study. Of the remaining four student teachers, one moved to take up a teaching post in the north of England, the others obtained employment outside teaching, due to a combination of financial pressures and the non-availability of teaching posts in the region.

The Analysis

The data collection over the two-year period yielded a substantial volume of transcript material. Although some ongoing analysis had occurred during the data collection in order to guide the research process, the final analysis still required all of the transcript material to be reviewed again. The aim of this review was to produce a case history over the two-year period for each student teacher. This process involved each student's transcripts being read to identify significant events or processes that appeared to explain the professional development of the student. Two factors were borne in mind in identifying 'significance' — first of all, existing theoretical models which have identified certain factors (such as past educational experiences or personal images of teaching) as important influences on teachers' practice, and; second, the significance that students themselves seemed to place on certain events or processes (e.g., through repeated mentions, or through their own emphasis). These events and processes were then used to construct a case account of each student teacher, clustering them under some general headings (such as educational background, early images of teaching, professional relationships, understanding the core curriculum) to provide a common structure that would enable later comparisons across the cases to be made more easily, but also with some idiosyncratic headings where these seemed appropriate for the particular case.

The construction of case histories was a very time consuming process, involving between ten and twenty drafts and redrafts. Often a case history draft would itself raise questions about the student concerned and would necessitate a return to the transcripts to try to provide a fuller account. Occasionally, an interpretation that appeared with one student might also trigger an enquiry with another and would require a further analysis of the data to check this out. In the final stages of drafting the case studies, attention was also given to the fact that these would be read by people unacquainted with the students or their college or school contexts, and there was a need to provide the necessary contextual detail to make the accounts meaningful to an unfamiliar audience.

A second stage of the analysis was to look across these case histories and to identify general trends about the processes of learning to teach. Whereas the objective in the first stage was to describe the individual development over the two-year period, the second stage involved explicit comparisons amongst the students in an attempt to abstract major developmental characteristics, together with the main factors that either facilitated or impeded the students' professional growth.

Examples of four contrasting case histories are provided in Chapters 4–7, and the overview of the case histories is provided in Chapter 8.

Validity

A major issue in any research project concerns the validity or trustworthiness of the data and its interpretation. This is as true of quantitative research, where various assumptions might be made in the design, use and interpretation of results of research instruments, such as questionnaires or interview schedules, as it is of qualitative research where there are large volumes of transcript material capable of having multiple interpretations.

The nature of validity takes different forms in different projects. In a quantitative questionnaire study, for example, there may be no ambiguity in the coding and tallying of responses, but there may be significant questions of validity concerning whether all respondents understood the questions in a similar way, or whether their responses were thoughtfully considered or represent more immediate or even flippant reactions. Similarly, in quantitative studies of classroom interaction, the number and type of interactions amongst teachers and pupils may be reliably recorded, but there are issues of validity to consider when attempting to identify patterns of interaction or to interpret their purpose and significance.

In this study there were two aspects of validity that were thought to deserve particular attention. The first concerned the accuracy of the students' own reports. By far the main source of data in the project was the self-reports of the students themselves. They were asked about their conceptions, experiences and beliefs, and about significant events that occurred in their training. An important issue to consider is the extent to which individuals can accurately monitor and comment upon such matters, and whether the research situation might itself construct a social situation in which the students feel obliged to justify or over-rationalize their thoughts and behaviour, or perhaps become defensive and withhold or distort the data that the study was seeking to reveal. By asking students questions about their experience of learning to teach, would they, for instance, feel compelled to invent answers when they were unable to provide genuine ones, would they construct after-the-event justifications rather than provide accounts of their experience at the time, would they wish to present an image of themselves which was more idealized than the reality?

Several steps were taken to minimize the effects of those factors which were considered likely to invalidate the data:

1 Students were assured of confidentiality — the interview data would stay within the research team and would only be reported anonymously.

2 The researchers also devoted considerable time to developing the trust and confidence of the student teachers to ensure honest cooperation.

3 The broad objectives of the research were explained to the students. It was also explained that some questions would be asked that might be difficult to answer and that if students were not able to answer the questions, an acknowledgment of this was preferred rather than any contrived answer or justification.

4 At the end of the first year, a rating scale was constructed from many of the common statements that students had made over the year. Data obtained from completion of this scale provided a means of checking the strength of the claims students had made previously.

5 One of the researchers was in touch regularly with the student teachers' classrooms, mentors and college tutors, and was in a position to observe and discuss particular events that occurred and to check on events that students reported as significant. The familiarity that the researcher had with the context probably helped to keep interviews focused on the experienced reality of the situations, and made justifications or deceptions (even unwitting self-deceptions) less likely.

It was expected that such strategies would help to allay any fears that the students had about self-disclosure, would provide a safe and comfortable social environment in which they could talk about their experience, and would create a relationship in which the students shared the same commitment as the researchers to develop an honest insight into their emerging practice.

A second possible source of invalidity lies in the interpretation of the data. Faced with the task of reducing a large amount of transcript material, it is possible to form several different interpretations. How then can the researcher guard against being influenced by his/her own prejudices, or being unduly influenced by particularly memorable or noticeable events that attract attention but may be uncharacteristic or relatively insignificant overall? Three main strategies were adopted in this project to ensure the trustworthiness of the interpretations being made. First of all, the interactive and iterative nature of the data collection and analysis enabled a constant verification, elaboration and checking out of interpretations. Tentative interpretations could therefore be tested against further data that was collected specifically to assess the interpretations themselves. For example, interviews with one student early in the project seemed to suggest that 'neatness' and 'being in control' were important aspects of the teacher she sought to become. Further probing through open-ended questioning that allowed confirming or disconfirming evidence to emerge, led her in a subsequent interview to offer the following self-analysis: 'I suppose it's your baggage, the way I've been channelled in going to a Girl's High School perhaps, a very academic school . . . I suppose I've become an attention to detail type of person.' Secondly, in assembling the case histories, the transcripts were read independently by both researchers who identified significant events and processes, which were then discussed before inclusion. A high level of agreement was usually found in the selection of significant features. Where differences occurred, these resulted in a re-reading of the transcripts for further evidence concerning the identified feature; this usually led to the corroboration of one or other interpretation, and occasionally led to a new interpretation that incorporated both previous ones. A third aspect of ensuring validity was the students' own verification. The case history of each student was presented to them at the end of the two-year period. The students were asked to read and comment on the case histories, paying particular attention to the accuracy of the interpretations that had been made of their experiences over the two years. The students, in fact, tended to make few comments, and very rarely disagreed with the case history accounts.

None of these validity checks are on their own particularly strong. Students asked to verify the interpretations of the transcript data, for example, may feel somewhat pressured to conform, or may have difficulty remembering the actual events that are being referred to. Collectively, however, the steps taken to ensure valid data collection and analysis have attempted to guard against the major areas of bias that might influence a project of this kind.

Ethical Considerations

Any project that delves deeply into the thoughts and experiences of individuals raises a number of ethical issues concerning the appropriateness of the research methods, the interpretation of data, and the confidentiality of findings. In the process of such research, the researcher is deciding what is significant in the perspectives of others. The researcher's interpretation may be at odds with the ways in which the students would normally wish to characterize themselves. For example, discussions about their motivations for teaching and their experiences of learning to teach may reveal personal and private matters that would normally not be discussed, particularly with a stranger. The student teachers, like all human beings, had anxieties about their children and their spouses, experienced financial worries, and sometimes had deep emotional concerns that affected how they thought about their work as students and teachers or that influenced what they were willing and prepared to talk about. The extent to which such matters were pursued or explored required sensitive negotiation and trust: the researchers trusting the student teachers to report faithfully upon their experiences, and the student teachers trusting the researchers to maintain confidences and at the same time not to misrepresent or misuse the data they acquired.

A further ethical issue concerns the impact of the research on the student teachers themselves. Inevitably, frequent probing interviews about one's experience over a two-year period are likely to heighten awareness of one's own actions and also clarify thinking about one's role and personal and professional goals. All of the students reported being affected by the research in these ways, though they perceived them as beneficial outcomes which aided their development as teachers.

In order to pursue this line of research, open trusting relationships had to be developed between the researchers and the students. To this end, the students were informed at the beginning of the purposes of the research, and they were given unrestricted access to the transcripts of their own interviews and to the interpretations that the researchers made of these. In reporting the research, all the names of the students, teachers and children have been changed in an attempt to preserve their anonymity.

Chapter 4

Case Study One — Adam

Introduction

Adam is a PGCE student, specializing in the later primary years. The first of his three teaching practices, however, takes place in a village infants' school, consisting of 200 pupils. Adam works in a class of Year 2 (6–7 year olds) children where the children are grouped by ability for all classroom-based activities. For the second practice, Adam joins a large urban junior school, in which he works with a class of Year 4 (8–9 year olds) children. The school's catchment area is predominantly middle class. Although the children are seated in groups, the teacher mainly teaches the class as a whole. The final teaching practice offers Adam yet another contrast, being in a modern, well-resourced, village primary school specifically built to support an integrated curriculum, with classrooms consisting of several activity bays, and the whole school being open plan.

Entry to Teacher Education

Adam, a 25-year-old history graduate, claims his interest in teaching has always been at the 'back of his mind ... gnawing away from early experience'. Memories of his own education are very positive. He recalls being well liked by peers and staff, and being strongly supported by his parents who were keen for him to do well in school. His mother, an infant teacher, appears to have instilled in him a deep respect for the profession, and he frequently comments on the hard work and dedication that underpins effective teaching.

Adam attended the local infant, junior and secondary schools, all of which had a largely middle-class catchment area and well-established parental support. It seems that both Adam's upbringing and educational experiences have provided a strong sense of warmth and security, as well as 'moral behaviour', and many of his memories centre upon these features. For example, his second year infant teacher is described as 'a very, very caring teacher ... I felt very lucky to be in her class ... and that's stayed with me'. He also refers to two particular teachers from his years in the sixth form, whom he also holds in high esteem. Their relationships with pupils, and the examples of behaviour which they set within the school, are viewed as very important aspects of teaching and learning. Insights gained from his mother's commitment to the profession seem to have enabled Adam to empathize with the thinking of these, and other, teachers:

... seeing the way they acted and interacted with the class ... They were obviously very intelligent people but they were very interesting as well and they could draw things out of pupils rather than stuffing things in. I think just by seeing them and thinking they were good figureheads to follow. They were leading by example. And they were also setting standards not just in the classroom but from their ideas and thoughts and beliefs. You could see what their ideals were and what they thought was the correct way to behave in society, as well as in the classroom. That can teach you more than just necessarily the facts.

Other memories serve to demonstrate his strong sense of justice. He recalls, for example a 'physically awkward' teacher who was the butt of pupils' jokes. Thoughts of this still appear to incense Adam because, in his view, the pupils failed to appreciate the teacher's hard work and dedication. Another particularly strong memory involved a teacher in junior school who demonstrated disappointment and irritation when Adam and another boy did not work as expected. The incident appears to have shaken Adam at the time, though he totally accepts the teacher's reaction:

One of the strongest [memories] was having a project ripped up and put in a bin in my fourth year because I was talking. We'd all been given different projects that we could choose and my friend and I — and it was a Friday afternoon — did a project on newspapers. We were literally just picking up a paper, cutting it up and plonking it in a scrapbook. Anyway the teacher caught me talking, saw the project and went berserk, rightly so I realize now. But it did affect me because he went to town on me. I didn't cry, I just felt ashamed because I'd messed him about. He had trusted us to do a good job and I didn't. I thoroughly deserved his rebuke.

Adam attributes his decision to enter teaching to the influence of the two teachers he had admired during his sixth-form education, as well as his experiences as a youth worker during his degree studies. He reports being sure that he wanted to teach prior to going to university, but he decided to study history first because he enjoys the subject so much, inspired by the teacher whom other children had ridiculed.

Following his degree, Adam sought short-term employment to relieve financial pressures, and for nine months worked in a chartered accountant's office, the clerical nature of which he found tedious. In his spare time, he again undertook weekly voluntary work in the Boys' Brigade, defining one of his roles there as 'a teacher'. He reports deriving enormous personal satisfaction from the young people's achievements, something he associates only with teaching:

I was making galleons with them out of cardboard and they came out really well. From what you'd shown them they went away and produced something brilliant. I had a real sense of satisfaction. I think that's another reason I'm going into teaching. Job satisfaction is important. It's great to see a child come into your class at a certain level and go out at a higher one. You see results. In my previous job it was just praise from the manager, but that's not satisfaction for me. So for my own needs it's the sort of job I need to do . . .

From the accountant's office, Adam moved into insurance work. He reports that to his surprise he enjoyed the social life and interpersonal contact so much that he delayed his application to the PGCE course for a further few years.

Looking back on his experiences since school, Adam feels that his recent employment has served to improve certain skills, such as numeracy, and being able to communicate confidently with adults, and he also expects his youth work to be valuable in preparing him for teaching. He seems to have a clear view of the kind of teacher he would like to become, and is able to pinpoint specific skills he feels are very important, such as 'being able to talk to children appropriately'.

Prior to the course, Adam claims to have no illusions about teaching and how demanding it will be. He expresses a strong commitment to becoming a teacher, and for him the essence of this is being with children. He anticipates that in any class there will be a range of ability, and recognizes that to date he has had little experience of children's learning difficulties, having worked only with able, mostly middle-class children. At this stage, he associates learning difficulties with poorer social backgrounds, and deficits on the part of the child.

> One thing I've got to do is special needs learning. I was with this girl who was backward, trying to teach her to read and maths . . . I know you shouldn't bracket kids together, but they are a certain bunch, but I haven't had any experience with children with special needs.

Images of Teaching

Adam's early images of teaching can be seen to shape much of his thinking over the next two years and he describes these in terms of two aspects — the personal and the professional. Within his personal aspect of teaching are two significant themes, the moral and caring. In considering his own qualities as a teacher, Adam emphasizes his sense of commitment: 'I have a lot to offer the children, 100 per cent input'. His caring personality and interest in children's learning are also viewed as important in helping him as a teacher to exert a powerful social influence. Developing the individual, building their self-esteem and sense of worth and encouraging 'moral behaviour' are seen as central to his role as a teacher:

> . . . the idea of developing that child to be an individual and an individual who can stand on their own two feet . . . and won't feel intimidated by going up [to secondary school] and by children from other schools who may be brighter than them. Make sure they realize that every child in the

class has something to offer. They may not be the best mathematician or footballer, but there isn't a child there who hasn't got something they can offer the rest of the class. So building up their esteem, their knowledge that everyone is worth something and that they are worth something to you as a teacher and to their individual classmates. Also making sure that they have a good sense of how they should act in society outside the school. I don't mean mucking about, but they must have an idea of what is moralistic and what isn't. Some children aren't necessarily naughty, they just don't know what is right and wrong. They're not being naughty because they want to be naughty. So you have to teach them the correct way to behave.

The second aspect of Adam's images relates to 'professional qualities'. For example, self-organization is seen as a very important asset which Adam is convinced that effective teachers, such as his mother, possess, and that he, by nature, does not. Adam anticipates that self-organization will be the most demanding part of teaching for him. He is determined, however, to develop this ability, accepting that this may mean that he will have to change his usual ways of working.

Adam also identifies organization within the classroom as the key to promoting effective learning, particularly in providing for the needs of a wide range of ability, and in ensuring that a suitable learning environment is established. However, Adam is fully aware that, prior to the course, he is unclear of what organizational strategies might be needed to foster children's learning:

Basically I think the teacher is going to have to be able to organize the class so that . . . some activities are going on which don't need constant supervision and where the children can just get on with it. And they might not be of a completely learning nature. I don't know. I'm not hot on knowing what activity a child can actually learn from or whether an activity is just going to be reinforcing his knowledge or developing a skill rather than acquiring knowledge.

The idea of combining firm management and good organization with a strong sense of community and mutual respect within the classroom continually emerges in Adam's ideas about teaching. He sums up his own desired teaching persona as:

Someone who instructs from the base of their knowledge, but also sets examples and standards of correct ways to perform tasks and behave. Instruction not just from what you know but from how you act.

Year One — Learning to Teach

Adam feels that in comparison with studying for his degree where the aim was to gain knowledge 'simply to pass an exam . . . You train and train, peak at the exam point and then you go intellectually flabby and it's gone', the PGCE course is about 'assimilating knowledge for use in the future . . . So . . . you have to think of its relevance and how you're going to use it'. He finds it difficult 'to get into the swing of things' in the first few weeks in college, and the course 'hard to acclimatize to' because much of the content is 'quite intellectual rather than practical':

> The first three weeks I didn't like going in but [now] I've actually gone on attachment days and found the relevance of what we were being told. So there were practical things to hang [the theory] on and since I've done my attachment days I've found it a lot easier . . . I've enjoyed it but found it difficult to pinpoint where it was going for the first few weeks.

Although Adam 'couldn't quite see' where the course was aiming, he 'wasn't getting particularly worried about it but just trusted it was going as it should', demonstrating the level of trust he puts in those in positions of authority.

Topics such as 'multiculturalism' and 'child abuse' are described by Adam as the 'nitty-gritty' of teaching, but he finds them difficult to relate directly to the classroom. At this stage, he wants to be given knowledge and recipes for action which he can turn to immediate use. As the term progresses towards the first teaching practice, Adam becomes much happier, reporting that the lectures are more practical and that, 'I'll go off to my BSE (block school experience) armed with activities, games and things to use which college has suggested'. He ponders whether he could produce such ideas himself because he imagines that being able to do so is part of the intrinsic satisfaction of teaching:

> . . . it doesn't matter where the ideas come from, whether they're from your head or someone else's resource, doesn't matter as long as you know where to pitch it and you can introduce it in an interesting way so that children really get interested. I don't think it matters where they come from but I think you get immense satisfaction if you do think of your own ideas and see it through.

One of Adam's greatest concerns at this time is getting the 'pitch' right. The message he has gained from college is that this is crucial. He suspects that a game on money, involving a piggy bank, which he had planned for Year 2 pupils and carried out on the attachment days as part of a maths assignment 'was pitched slightly too low for some of them' as the children had no difficulty in playing the game. However, he reasons that this is better than pitching it too high because 'you just get these blank expressions'. It is from experience that he expects to get 'the right level', and learning to teach at this stage is seen as 'the old story of learning by your mistakes'.

One particular idea from college is the use of picture books with later primary children, and Adam is surprised by the wealth of activities that can be generated from them. He reports that the books excite great interest amongst the children, and serve to stimulate 'good discussion'. Coupled with his own memories of stories at school, the experience serves to convince Adam how effective they can be, and he goes on to use stories as a starting point for topics in the future.

One picture book activity, however, is seen by Adam as a 'bit of a disaster' because the discussion does not develop as he expected. The college course emphasized the importance of open-ended questioning but Adam struggles to understand why his attempts at this do not appear to be working. Here he describes how he and another student taught the session:

> We did 'The Whale Song' . . . I had the whale music in the background and read it to them, but it was just a bit of a flop really. I didn't get what I wanted from them. What they were talking about regarding the book was quite interesting, but it wasn't what I wanted. It's difficult because you've got to give open questions and if you don't get what you want, that's that. You can't give closed questions just so that you get responses you want . . . They certainly got that the whales sang . . . There was a look of amazement on their faces that whales actually made that noise. That was good and you could hear them talking about it the next day. That was great because it showed they'd taken notice of the book and it made an impression, but we were asking character questions about the grandfather and things . . . But it didn't move as much as we expected it to . . . I think the problem was that we actually loved the book and we were trying to tell the children they'd enjoy it.

Prior to the placement, Adam had been worried that he would encounter children with behaviour problems, but afterwards reports his relief that he had coped with all the difficulties he had encountered. In fact he appears very satisfied with his classroom performance, and reports being pleased with the teaching persona he achieves — relating to the children 'on a friendly basis, but still able to step back . . . if necessary, if they were misbehaving . . .'. A skill he claims to have developed further is that of using 'more precise language with the children' and being able to 'pitch it at a level they could relate to'.

Adam feels that the thing he enjoyed most about his teaching practice 'wasn't so much the instruction, as a kind of pastoral thing'. Specific events he pinpoints as significant serve to further boost his self-image, such as 'reaching' Michael, a 'real little toughie' by getting him to 'open up' about the 'problems at home', and who, 'towards the end . . . was almost like a shadow following me around'.

In talking about learning to teach, Adam emphasizes the importance of planning. Attending an INSET day in which the school plans for the whole year, Adam appreciates the relevance of long-term planning and the structure that this provides. Planning, however, is of less importance at the moment than classroom organization and management:

> One thing I've realized is that discipline is just so important. You can plan whatever you like but if the children aren't going to listen or whatever, you might just as well throw it out the window. There's a fairly fine line

because you don't want to be authoritarian. You want the noise to be creative and it's getting the fine balance. You have to keep one ear for the child you're talking to and one ear out there to see what's going on.

Through being able to observe his class teacher, Adam feels that he has gained much insight into these aspects, particularly as in this practice he only manages groups, and not the whole class. His observations are evaluated against the image of the teacher Adam is striving to become, and his ideas of what education is for. Already his early idealism has become tinged with the reality of what he feels can be achieved in practice:

> I felt the top group were left to get on on their own a bit and that could be to their detriment. I don't know. It's difficult because with SATs and things like that you want all your children to try and get through. And hopefully the top group are going to get through, so in a way it seemed to me that they're left to express themselves and the others are pushed so that as many as possible are pushed through the SATs. That's probably not what is happening, but that's the impression I got. A lot of time spent on the lesser able pupils. It's just a dilemma I can never see going away. That's not just SATs. You've got to get to a standard. Once some have reached that standard then it's going to be human nature to try and drag the others up too. But it just seems a shame that you can't drag those up and push the others on further. But with thirty-one children that's going to be really difficult.

When Adam joined the course, he had expressed considerable opposition to grouping children according to ability. However, Adam now ponders the efficacy of various forms of grouping as he anticipates the greater responsibility of the next practice, and, further ahead, how he would like to organize his own class. He comments on the wide range of ability within the class, which he admits has taken him by surprise, particularly the 'high fliers', whilst there are some children who 'couldn't put two words together'. In the class he works in, the children are ability grouped, and Adam is surprised how well this seems to work with younger children, 'even though we've got a group called the red group who are obviously less able and a black group who are able . . . But you don't see any animosity or feeling of being put down by the brighter ones at all at that age'. Adam claims that he has not fully made up his mind on this yet. Though he acknowledges that ability grouping 'works' in the classroom he is in, he still asserts that he is morally opposed to the idea of labelling children. Trying to 'devote attention to each child' and 'spreading' himself across the 'whole class situation' are the greatest concerns Adam has at the end of the first term.

After a few weeks of the college input, Adam has come to the view that 'all children learn differently, so that's one of the hard bits of the job'. He also reckons that how the teacher organizes the class will affect when and how children learn.

However, he is all too aware that his ideas are very hazy, expecting that he will gain more understanding of children's learning from talking to other teachers and that generally he just needs 'more practice'.

After the first practice, Adam is struck by a particular insight which he makes use of in his future teaching:

> I think a lot of the learning goes on in an unrecorded fashion, just talking you can hear them picking up ideas from each other. One thing I have noticed is that a lot of the children would teach each other. They'd get the idea and say 'You don't do it like this, you do it like this' and they'd show them. So then both children are operating on different levels. One child is communicating with the other and the other is listening and reacting.

During the first term, Adam uses a reflective journal as advocated by the college. He writes in diary form because it shows 'progression, rather than just statements here and there'. He reports that the act of writing is a valuable emotional outlet during the first few weeks when he feels that he is 'learning so much . . . [because] in the early stages things are thrust on you and you're desperate to write them down'. The content records his feelings, information he has acquired, and events, such as incidences of bullying, from which he feels that he has learned. When reading back over the journal, Adam cites discovering greater insights, such as understanding Michael:

> One of the main things was about this child Michael, who was quite aggressive and a toughie. He was a nice child and there was one time he was misbehaving and I said he shouldn't do it and he said Mr F. [Adam] was going to hit him. I thought at the time, 'Crikey this child has seen situations when frustration naturally leads to aggression' . . . [Then] I wondered if *I'd* been putting over an aggressive feeling. I had to reflect on that . . . especially in the case of Michael. He was always clinging and was desperate to be close, [so] if he'd thought I was aggressive, he wouldn't have done that. Later Michael [told] me that his brother hit him quite a bit and it dawned on me slightly then [that this was why he said I might hit him]. The two brothers shared a room and the elder one was 12 and just hit him . . . I did then understand him better . . . it seemed to clarify the situation in my mind.

By the middle of the spring term, however, Adam reports that he no longer uses this aid to reflection. He claims to have developed an understanding of key issues or 'facts' and that he must now engage in 'distilling them into opinions . . . it's like a gradual dawning and you get certain opinions . . . it just develops'.

Adam, however, claims that writing assignments is still very useful because the 'odd events and thoughts here and there' contained within his memory or the journal can then be 'tied together in a package'. For example, Adam argues that the assignment on professional perspectives helped him to make further sense of Michael's behaviour in relation to ideas about how to deal with misbehaviour and bullying. A strong sense of morality and justice is also evident in Adam's written assignment:

> Tattum and Herbert [authors of books on deviance and disruption] argue that you should not bully the bully as this will add credibility to his behaviour . . . I feel that it is important to talk to both the bully and the victim and ask the bully to justify his actions. If any justification is offered, the teacher should crush it until the bully realizes that there *is* no justification for violent or abusive behaviour. After this I would ask the bully whether they felt that they should apologize to the victim for their behaviour as this can have the affect of raising the victim's self-esteem by putting them in a position where they can accept or refuse the apology . . .
>
> This occurred with Michael when I witnessed him hit another child. After asking him the reason for his actions and no explanation was forthcoming, I told him how upset I was with such behaviour, and asked him whether he should apologize to the child concerned. He went over to the child, obviously ashamed of himself and apologized. The child accepted his apology and I didn't see Michael strike another child again. If, however, he had hit the child again he would not have had a second chance to apologize in case he felt that apologizing was a way of escaping punishment.

For the next practice, Adam is able to identify those areas of the curriculum in which he feels more confident, and those in which he feels unsure. For example, Adam is keen to do physical education (PE) because he has really enjoyed the course, and is now offering PE as a subsidiary subject. He feels that the course has provided him with a much wider perspective of physical education, and that he can now distinguish different 'qualities of movement'. He also now reports being able to see himself teaching dance, which before had 'conjured up horrendous night-mares of students in leotards jumping about'. On the other hand, Adam is aware that his own work in art is quite limited and that he lacks the necessary skills. As a result, the art he decides to do 'will involve something like brass rubbing'. Adam hopes that his skills in art will improve through 'being in a school where there is a strong art feel to it' or through talking to an arts specialist, as well as 'just being in the classroom and chatting to the teachers'.

Working within a second school allows Adam to make comparisons of various aspects of teaching which serve to sharpen his ideas about what he wants to achieve in his own teaching and the kind of school he can see himself working in:

> The whole ethos of the schools are different . . . C. [the second school] has very young staff, three teachers who've just finished their probationary

year and they all went in together from this college. And some other teachers who've been in teaching for four years. So the average age is about 28. Last time they were a lot older. There's a very friendly jovial atmosphere in the staffroom and it's really good. Last time you weren't allowed in the staffroom because of restriction on space. But you couldn't feel a part of the set-up. I feel I'll fit in a lot better here.

Adam seems thoroughly excited by the prospect of working with his new class teacher, June. He reports that he finds her a lot easier to get on with and anticipates that he will be given helpful comments about his teaching: 'There was no feedback at all really last time. Basically on my last practice I didn't know how I was doing. This time she's made it quite clear that she doesn't hold her comments back, which is great. I don't mind criticism . . . and hopefully she'll give me an objective evaluation as someone who knows the children and that sort of thing'.

The teacher Adam is working with is an experienced student supervisor. From her discussions with Adam, and previous knowledge of the philosophies of the college staff, June realizes that, coupled with Adam's last school experience, he is oriented towards group work. Although she warns Adam that the children are used to whole class teaching whilst sitting in groups, she encourages him to organize the class as he wants. Prior to taking on responsibility for the whole class, Adam seems to have well thought out ideas about how he might do this. He synthesizes his early conceptions about teaching, his experiences to date, what he has learned from college and what he feels is expected by the teacher and the school. For example, whilst, on the one hand, Adam is keen to try out group work because of the quality of discussion and practical work this approach can produce, on the other, he feels that he should maintain the organization the children are used to because he can see that the teacher has 'such good control' when teaching the whole class, and through modelling her approach he feels 'really in control from early on'.

Added to this are the constraints that resources may bring to bear, and so Adam decides that he will use group work for science only:

[This is] the way I see it going. A progression on different subjects to do with wheels. And get to a point where they realize where wheels came from, what they're used for, the forces acting on them . . . At G. [the first school] it was all group work. The children were just grouped for the whole day on ability. [Here] she basically does whole class teaching for most of the time, which is hugely different . . . if I was going to do an integrated day I'd have to explain to them how it operated. For science activities, for instance, I would do an integrated [approach]. Possibly over two mornings . . . The activities I'm devising involve an object which you can only have one of and so it's resources really.

Adam is aware that he is going to be assessed, and therefore also makes pragmatic decisions about how he will project himself as well as organize and manage the class:

> Whichever teacher you're under, I think you try and take on some of their traits because at the end of the day, rightly or wrongly, you feel that the children understand that approach and the teacher is going to be sympathetic to your approach because it's so in keeping with them. I don't necessarily say that's a good enough justification for doing it.

Adam admits that if the class teacher hadn't encouraged him to organize the class as he pleased he would have had to rework his science activities. As it is, he feels confident that the children will 'enjoy group work,' and his only concern at this point is that the children may become anxious or excited. This, Adam sees, must be resolved by 'an explanation beforehand of why they're doing it'.

When Adam is observed in the classroom, he has already undertaken two science sessions. In the first session he reports that there were 'children dashing around' after him with their 'hands up', which was something he had not expected: 'At one point I had about twelve children after me and it was a disaster!' As a result Adam now insists that the children stay at his table and wait for him if they have a query. At the same time Adam feels that the children are now more responsive to his voice in terms of being quiet and listening.

Below he describes how he intends to run this third session, for which he appears to have formed a clear framework for teaching a science lesson. The extract clearly indicates the complexity of decisions he is capable of making about the curriculum, organization and time management, resourcing, and pupil movement. His framework appears to have been formed through the sessions in college which have provided him with a basic structure of a science lesson, along with science resource books from the library, his own reflections and the feedback he has received from another teacher:

> It's a science activity following on from work that they've done in the first week involving friction and moving objects, things like that. They're going to be grouped on tables where they normally sit, so the groups are going to be between four and six, which I think is a nice number. It's OK on resources and they can all contribute to the experiment, rather than having too many sitting back and watching. That's how it went last time.
>
> That's a total number of twenty-eight children. There'll be three different experiments going on, but they'll be duplicated so two groups will do one sort of experiment but they'll obviously have their own resources. So six groups doing three experiments. And hopefully if they work hard enough we should be able to get them to do two experiments. The first session I did with them we only did one. I was a bit lax with them and Chris was in observing me and he said perhaps I should try to push them a bit more the next time, so the next time I did and they can get two done. There's a set format as to how I get them to write up the experiments. They observe first and record. First of all they'll be sitting down and duplicating the record sheet of how far something has travelled. One of the

group can read the card to them and then we'll do the experiment and they'll write it up in a manner which is 'equipment', 'what we did' and 'what we found'. They know that already, but I'll put it on the board anyway . . . they do a diagram as well. I must admit it came on the spur of the moment because in the first session it occurred to me that I hadn't explained how to write up the experiment so I jotted it on the board. It has actually stuck with them because even when they're doing other work they come up and ask about it. So they have got it into their heads that that's how it should be done. Hopefully it should go better because they've now [had] experience of science and they know what to do and know about noise levels. There will be chatting and talking and hopefully not too many children will be coming up saying that one or the other isn't contributing to the group because I have told them to discuss it. There is one group in there who just don't get on and they won't discuss and they'll be complaining but I hope that's been sorted out since the last session. If it's not, you sometimes have to watch that group closely to see if it has sunk in.

The ideas that Adam uses within the session are drawn from a number of sources, including his own idea for lubricating surfaces with washing-up liquid, some Science Horizons workcards for testing forces, and the school science adviser's suggestion for testing forces by sending model cars and lorries down a ramp. Adam reports that he has tested out each experiment; although he is slightly worried that something might go wrong with the lubrication activity, he is reassured that the work has been planned as thoroughly as he is able to. To aid the organization, Adam designed work cards which he thought were self-explanatory, but he anticipates that he will be looking to see if the children 'shoot their hands up' if there are any problems. He also expects to keep an eye on the car experiment because the 'boys might find them a temptation'.

As to what Adam anticipates the children learning, he explains this in terms of accurate recording and appropriate use of the equipment, discussions in the group to develop predictions and explanations and the children being able to justify their actions. The children's report writing is also regarded as an important outcome of the session.

Field notes taken during the lesson describe the session as noisy and lively, however the children appear to understand the format of the lesson and Adam's expectations for them. When the children enter the room after playtime, there is a sense that he has been accepted as the teacher, and that he is comfortable in this role — individual children go up to speak to him, Adam smiles and puts his hand on their shoulders, a gesture which seems to be used to indicate friendliness and is then used to steer the children away from him, signalling that he wants to start the lesson. When Adam introduces the lesson, he commands their attention well, and appears to have a clear picture in his mind as he tells the children what they are going to do. He reinforces expectations for behaviour and how he wants the children to work, and generally projects a business-like approach. He is still obviously quite nervous though and his voice sounds a little tense.

As the groups are working, Adam projects a good sense of awareness of the children's activity. Although the groups are quite noisy with some children going off to look at other groups or playing with the model cars, Adam seems to have the groups under sufficient control that he is able to step in and control off-task behaviour, and at times, manages to stay with individual groups to discuss problems, such as when the washing-up liquid causes the model cars to stick rather than acting as a lubricant. Throughout the session, Adam is constantly active and, although not flustered, he works extremely hard to ensure that the activity runs according to plan.

The general impression is that this is how Adam regards effective teaching — children learning through experience. Adam confirms this after the lesson when he says that the children were learning 'by experience, seeing things happen' and that group work allowed the children to 'learn from each other'. It also appears that Adam is genuinely very committed, wants to 'give his best to the children', and expects to have to put a great deal of energy into being successful.

Commenting on the lesson, Adam feels that 'it wasn't too bad', although the 'timing was a bit out' and the children didn't all complete two experiments. He is able to discuss what had occurred with clarity and detail. He recognizes that the work cards had caused problems for some children because there was 'more for them to read than last time when it was very punchy'. As he had expected, some of the children started to play with the model cars and he had to deal with some minor misbehaviours, but Adam judged that the lesson was successful in that the children appeared to learn what he expected. The problem with the lubricant is viewed philosophically and Adam resolves to tell the children that he had honestly expected a different result and to guide them towards understanding what happened. This remark reflects the role that Adam believes he ought to adopt during the session and he expresses the view that children must 'discover for themselves' and that he must not 'give them the answers'. However, his experiences seem to tell him that this is not altogether wise. Below he describes how he saw himself during the session:

> I think really just picking up on problems they might have on the worksheets and things like that. I felt that I'd given them things to learn by. To start with I felt I was just going round ironing out any little problems they might have had and then I was definitely actually teaching them. At times I felt I stepped in a bit too much, whereby I was putting words into their mouths. They said the marbles made no difference at all [to the outcome of one of the experiments] and I couldn't believe that for a second, so I then did it with them and showed them. And they noticed it did make a difference. So I had to step in a bit there. You have to keep an eye on it and if they get the wrong end of the stick, whilst you don't want to dampen exploring and discovery, you have to give suggestions and suggest having another go to see if it's exactly right. Rather than saying 'It's codswallop'. There's no point in that. If that's what they discovered, that's what they discovered. I'm just showing them that perhaps what they discovered wasn't quite 100 per cent.

In the afternoon session, Adam intended to bring the whole class together so 'we can see what we, as a whole class, came up with and hopefully by then hands will pop up from different groups and they'll remember it and they should be able to answer it. We'll discuss it and that will be it'. This, Adam anticipates, will not only serve as an efficient indicator to him as to what the children have learned, but it seems that he expects the act of 'bringing it together as a whole class' to help the children to see the connections between the various experiments in relation to the topic in order to form more 'integrated knowledge'. This would also seem to be an important act for Adam to undertake as it allows him to adopt a clear leadership role which seems integral to his images of teaching.

This second practice is generally very successful, and the school indicate that they would like Adam to apply for a teaching post which will be advertised the following term.

For the third practice, Adam is placed within a school which he reports is again 'very different' from the previous schools. The Year 5 children he works with are organized in mixed ability groups, and the school uses an integrated approach to the curriculum. Adam describes the teacher as 'very quietly spoken' and, because the 'philosophy of the school is to diffuse rather than have a confrontation' he gains the impression early on that 'the children could get away with things'. Adam senses that the teachers 'back down', which he is uncomfortable with as he feels 'order is so important'.

However, as before, Adam feels strongly that he is obliged to conform to his supervising teacher's practice and initially he adopts what he perceives to be the teacher's approach to management, even though he reports this is not his preference, and that unlike his last practice, he does not feel 'in control'. Although the children in the class are generally perceived to be pleasant and cooperative, two new class members have recently joined, and they present serious behaviour problems for Adam and encourage some of the other children to be disruptive. In this situation, Adam wants to act to assert his authority, but is afraid to do so in case the class teacher is offended. He suspects that whilst he can relate well to his teacher, tension could arise in the relationship because of their different personalities, and that he has 'to tread a very careful path'. Certainly on the visit made to the school, the impression was gained that the teacher seemed very anxious to show that she was an experienced and competent teacher who had much to offer the student. Perhaps the fact that the teacher had not actually worked with a student before meant that she did not recognize the discomfort that Andrew was feeling until he reached a very low point.

For the next few weeks, he not only experiences behaviour problems in the classroom, but is also exhausted by the preparation and teaching. When he fails to assert himself in certain situations, he experiences a lack of control, and to an extent a loss of respect from the children. In these situations he seems to view himself as 'weak' and, as he had previously described the teacher, 'pleading with the children'.

At the same time, Adam struggles with the organization of the integrated day, which stands in sharp contrast to the whole class teaching of the previous practice.

Below he describes, at the end of the year, how he views an integrated day, and how this has affected the way he planned. He also voices his misgivings about the approach:

> If you're doing integrated, you've got to think about timing more because if you have groups who are finishing and they can't get on, you have to really work out to as close as possible time-wise so that each group will finish at about the same time . . . It's easier once you get to know the children and you know what sorts of things they're capable of in terms of doing things in a certain time, especially art things. I can usually gauge that, say, an hour to do a nice sketch. Obviously it depends how structured it is. If it's really structured you can tell how long it will take by doing it yourself to a certain extent. Whether it's open or closed. If it's open then questions come to the surface that can be time consuming. If it's closed then they just do it and finish it.
>
> I think children do benefit from that style of learning. But I found personally that it was ever so hard to manage. That, I hope, is due to lack of experience. But apart from juggling so that they're all on task, to actually float around and pick up on their language and the understanding they're demonstrating from what they're doing, I just found it very difficult. I just didn't have the time or physical presence to do that. All I was left with was the work they produced and some of it had been a collusion and sometimes they'd copied. I think it's difficult, apart from moving them, because you can't actually say what that child has learnt . . . One group might be doing history, one doing English, one doing science. Then you tick when a particular child has finished that particular work. On the last day you're getting all their stuff together and you find that one child has one piece of work he's done in six weeks. I just don't think I was capable of running it because they can just become invisible and you wouldn't see them. It's awful to say, but I'm sure there were a couple of girls working really hard and I didn't even talk to them because in this busy environment there are noisier children demanding your time. I think the quieter children in a busy integrated day can just disappear and drown.

At one point in the third practice, Adam reports that his feelings are at such a low ebb that he is considering leaving the course. Fortunately the half-term break provides a welcome respite. Knowing that one of the difficult children is leaving, Adam eventually resolves to make a fresh start for the second part of the practice. Coupled with greater experience in managing an integrated day, he is determined to enact a teaching persona he feels happier with when he assumes full responsibility for the class. Shortly afterwards, he completely loses his temper with the class, and reports that, to his amazement, the class teacher approves of this, and that it is only then that she reassures him that her 'calm' approach is founded upon the respect and confidence that she has established over time, and that it would be difficult for any student teacher to achieve this.

This experience stays with Adam, and he often refers to the incident. At the time, Adam seems rather resentful towards the teacher for allowing him to suffer for so long. In time, however, he takes a more positive view and retells the incident more in terms of a rite of passage in which he won the teacher's support, and where he could have avoided the situation if he had had the confidence to act as he saw fit:

> The funny thing was, she was waiting for me to erupt at the class and I was deliberately not doing it because I thought it would upset her. When it finally got to the point where I exploded and she came in afterwards and I thought she'd really have it out with me she said, 'Thank goodness for that. I wondered how long it would take for that to happen' and I was shocked. That's when she said to me, 'I realize you wanted to get them under your control and you felt intimidated because I've got them there so I don't need to shout and bellow, but you haven't.' So there I was walking on glass for a few weeks and finally I thought if I had to have a big bust up with her then I'd have to because it couldn't go on or I'd be out. As it happened that's what she was waiting for, which was great.

As a result of this, and other experiences, Adam comes to identify modelling as a significant problem in learning to teach. Whilst he would now advocate advising students to 'be themselves', he acknowledges that this is complicated by the student's need to have a 'starting point', and to gain the sympathy and approval of the teacher:

> It's like L plates really. You feel you're going through the motions. A lot of it is performing, not for the children but the teacher you're under. I would like to think that if I had students they wouldn't feel they had to adopt my style because I don't think you can properly . . . I tried to adopt that 'first softly softly' approach and it almost led to my downfall. I'd definitely advise anyone going into TP [teaching practice] to be themselves. Obviously listen to advice, but don't adopt a manner and style that you can't get on with.

During Year 1, discussions with Adam constantly reveal a very positive orientation towards the various professionals he has worked with. In the first practice, he praises the 'empathy' of the teacher towards the children, and on the second he values the 'constant appraisal' provided by the teacher. Even on the final practice, when he experiences so many problems, Adam feels that he has been given lots of useful 'contextual information' about the class, and values having been trusted to experiment and learn by his mistakes.

Adam reports that all his college tutors have been helpful and that their contribution to his professional development has increased as he has taken on more responsibility. In particular, he appreciates the support of a male tutor on his third practice who greatly helped when he felt low, and who provided practical advice on how he might improve his management of the class. For example:

> Rather than just having a lesson for 40 minutes, [the tutor suggested] punctuating it by putting them all together to discuss certain points and giving them a rest from the constant buzz . . . and after break, the lesson was continuing and I immediately put into practice what he'd just told me and I could see a difference straightaway. They don't just give you advice for the sake of it, but you can use it and it works straightaway. It's practical.

At the end of the year, Adam is quite satisfied with his teaching although he recognizes that he 'still has much to learn'. He reports being 'daunted' by the idea of 'structuring days in terms of routines' and by '. . . tailor[ing] people's work a lot more specifically than I have done . . . I think it's going to take a lot of time and effort because you have to tailor work so that the children can fulfil their own potential'. He anticipates that he will learn these mainly from his own experience.

Adam had previously anticipated that he would have to change within himself in order to become a teacher, and he feels that this has happened. These personal changes are spoken about with great pride:

> I feel that I look at myself a lot more and what I do, and feel more responsible. I just feel a lot happier in myself because it's what I've always wanted to do. It's changed my lifestyle because for the first time I'm doing something I actually want to do, rather than just earning money. I feel a lot more content, which I think has come out in other areas of my life, socially and what have you. I feel I can look at things from a child's point of view. A lot of people would say I did that before, but last week I spent about two hours looking at spiders in the garden because I had to do it with minibeasts. If you'd told me a year ago that I'd be doing that, I'd have thought I'd got a screw loose!

Year Two — Being a Newly Qualified Teacher

Adam is delighted to secure the full-time post, teaching Year 4 in the school in which he undertook his second teaching practice. He describes the school as being formal, with a high level of support and professionalism amongst the mainly young staff, and with high parental expectations of academic achievement. Additionally, he respects the headteacher who he feels manages the school effectively, providing strong leadership as well as a forum for debate amongst colleagues. Adam reports feeling very comfortable with the school's philosophies.

As the first term approaches, Adam claims that he wants to focus on two particular aspects of his work which he has previously identified as the keys to successful teaching: first, behaviour management and relationships with the children, and second, planning and organization.

Adam expects the first term to be 'a survival experience' because even though he had taught at the school for four weeks, he is sure that there is much for him to learn and much that he is unaware of:

For instance, it's quite a formal set-up. I think I prefer that to the other school, which was more integrated and that didn't really coincide with my style of teaching. But things like teaching handwriting and formal comprehension! Things I have never done before on TP, because a lot of it [before] was to do with topic work, and the nitty-gritty comprehension and stuff are going to be new to me.

Within the early weeks he reports that teaching has taken over his life and that he is struggling to keep up with its incessant demands:

When I'm at home in the evening doing something else, I find myself back in the classroom. Every night I have a nightmare about the class. The only time I switch off is when I play football. I'm sure I'll switch off in time, but at the moment it's just constant . . . I think I must say to myself 'Right, it's 5.00 pm. If it's not done I'm going home' and forget about it. At the moment if it's not done I stay on to do it.

He expects things to get easier as his confidence grows, and he reports that this is happening day by day, with his classroom actions 'coming more naturally', and being able 'to think on my feet' more. However, having acquired the habit on teaching practice of regularly evaluating his own performance, he feels that he has not had the time in the first term of his new appointment to step back and think about his teaching, and that time for evaluation would be useful to him:

At the moment I'm just giving work out, marking it, working out whether they've understood it and then talking to them, but not really looking at my own delivery. There are times when I've given a horrendous introduction and they've gone off and done it all wrong.

Professional Relationships and Support Networks

Adam's views about the support he receives within the school are largely unchanged throughout the year. He genuinely feels well supported by all the staff, and appears to be very fond of many of them, and they of him. Judging by several visits to the school, the staffroom atmosphere seems as Adam describes it: 'a strong sense of teamwork' and 'everyone gets on really well'.

Adam is clearly proud to be part of such a team, and he attributes the ethos within the school to the headteacher's leadership, describing him in glowing terms:

He's just got that calm, jovial but deep down serious commitment. That's his attitude. That comes across. He has absolute confidence in his staff and they have confidence in him. When you've got a situation like that, everyone's self-esteem in this school is high. You read about teachers' morale, but here I don't see teachers moaning about anything because he doesn't moan. We don't moan at each other or about situations really . . . at staff meetings . . . we take it very seriously . . . It's really good because everyone can just give their views and everyone talks or disagrees. That's the only place it ever happens. Paul says, 'This is the time for disagreement if there is any. Off you go', and we have a discussion and at the end of it no-one has taken it personally.

Within the school Adam sees himself as the 'young male on the staff, likes a good laugh in the staffroom, sometimes a bit cheeky'. He perceives that: 'The way I operate here is very similar to the way I worked at [insurance office] in terms of getting on with people. Similar thing. I can't work without a bit of a joke and some fun, either in the staffroom or the kiln room [a retreat for the staff who smoke] or wherever.' It is clearly important to Adam that these dimensions of his personality find expression. Equally he reports with considerable pride that, by the end of the year, staff begin to ask his advice about teaching history, and that he is to join a subject coordination team with the local secondary school. He is looking forward to participation in this as he believes it will help him to become better established in the area.

Although he has an official mentor whose help and advice he appreciates on a day-to-day basis, Adam generally turns to June, the parallel class teacher with whom he had worked on teaching practice, and Sian, a young teacher, for support. Similarly he reports that other members of staff are aware of the difficulties facing a newly qualified teacher and also give him encouragement.

> I often talk to June because she's next door and she was my teacher on TP and I can't help seeing her as a kind of mentor. She's as much a mentor as the deputy. I'm always going in there and she's been great. She'll come in and say 'I wouldn't have done that with your display' and I ask her what I should do and she'll tell me. Nothing to knock your self-esteem, but if it doesn't work she'll say so. She says it because she wants me to succeed and have a good start. There are two or three other teachers who make a point of just wandering in and saying 'That's brilliant' and then they'll wander back out again. They don't have to do that. It's because it's my first year and you're one of them. If everyone feels high in their self-esteem then it goes throughout the school. If people go around feeling they're useless all the time then it's not a happy school . . . I don't think there's one person I wouldn't approach with a problem. Sometimes it depends who is in the staffroom and I say 'This happened today. What would you have done?' They're really open like that. I don't feel they're going to say, 'Guess what Andrew said to me the other day?' There's none of that.

The deputy head, who is near to retirement, is Adam's official mentor, and is regarded by him as 'very experienced'. Whilst she and Adam do not have scheduled meetings, he reports that her door is always open and that she's never too busy to see him: 'Even if she's doing something important she'll drop it for a chat. You always see results as well. If she says she's going to do something, she does it immediately.' This is greatly appreciated by Adam, especially mid-way through the first term when he reaches a 'flash point' with a particular child in his class.

Adam recognizes that he is very frustrated by Chris, a pupil awaiting a statement for special needs, who experiences serious behavioural and learning difficulties, a point which is supported by observations in the classroom. On a number of visits, it is noted that Chris exhibits poor levels of concentration, seems to find it difficult to stay in his seat and is often wandering around. At the same time, he frequently disturbs other children, although he is never observed to be aggressive in any way. When Adam does try to work with him on an individual basis, they both seem to talk easily but not about his work! Whenever possible, Chris is removed from the class by the learning support teacher, and there is the general impression that the school has not taken a longer term view of his educational needs as it is anticipated that Chris will be given a place within a special school. Other staff and the child's parents appear to be extremely sympathetic towards Adam, and encourage him to accept that he should just try to do whatever he can for the time being. Adam, however, feels that he cannot cope with the demands of being a newly qualified teacher and having a pupil with such learning difficulties, and appears to distance himself from the responsibility of meeting Chris's needs, yet he seems to feel guilty about this at the same time. It also seems that he is rather resentful of being put in such a position but he does not openly criticize the school staff, as he generally feels so positive and very loyal towards them. For example, during one interview, Adam appears somewhat indignant, using the third person to describe the position he is in '. . . you've got an NQT who is trying to get to know the job and they've got thirty children and him [Chris]'. He later transfers to the first person:

> . . . the first few weeks I was getting really frustrated and then I just gave him work to keep him ticking over really . . . if I didn't make that decision then I would get so frustrated it would be untrue. Better just to admit defeat. I can't say I've given up on him, but I'm certainly not going to sit down and devise a whole term's work just for him.

When the flash point with Chris occurs, Adam finds both June and the school staff highly supportive:

> I marched into her room and said 'I can't have that kid in my class any longer' and she said 'Oh dear' and put the kettle on . . . and she says 'We can't have that' and she got on the phone straightaway [to arrange a meeting with the parents] . . . she was very supportive and she's 100 per cent behind me and what I do. She often just puts her head round the corner to see what he's up to, offers herself if he gets too much so that I can send him to her . . . the whole of the staff have said that if it gets too much I can send for them. But I haven't had to do that yet. Things can't be that bad. I think the critical point has passed.

Adam also credits the headteacher with maintaining a clear understanding of the problems that face newly qualified teachers, and how they might be supported. He has termly meetings with Adam, and looks at, and comments upon, his plans and record books on a very regular basis: 'I honestly believe that Paul sees his role with a NQT as setting them up for a good career. He knows I'm not going to be here forever but he'll put [so] much into that first and second year because that really does form how you go for the rest of your career.'

Behaviour Management and Relationships with Children

Adam has always emphasized the importance of establishing the 'right relation-ship' with the class. This view was even reflected in his response to three videoed extracts of classroom practice, viewed early in the course, where he identified very positively with a male teacher whom he saw as 'teaching whole class with the children seated in mixed ability groups' while 'walking freely around the room amongst the children' who, in turn, were 'well behaved but relaxed enough to respond freely enough to open [ended] questions'.

His experiences in classrooms during the first year also seem to confirm his early view that the teacher should try to create an 'ethos in the classroom, which pro-motes success' while being 'firmly in control'. Achieving control in other teachers' classrooms has, at times, proved difficult, and Adam is aware that there have been occasions when he has felt so stressed that he has actually lost his temper, even on his second teaching practice which was very successful. On one such occasion, he reports being very angry — 'almost uncontrollable' — when some boys are off-task, even though Adam is sure that they understand what to do. This is remin-iscent of the incident Adam recalls from his own past when he was severely reprim-anded for playing around with the newspaper cuttings. Just as he had reported that he felt he had let the teacher down, so Adam seems to feel that when the children mess about, this is a personal slight against him.

When the new academic year begins, Adam reports being advised by the other staff to 'hit 'em hard!' and 'don't laugh until Christmas!' This he is determined to do, reasoning that it is also important to 'go in and be confident because if I appeared nervous or disorganized in any way then it would immediately transmit itself to the children'. At this point, he perceives that his role is to 'ensure that they learn and that the class doesn't degenerate into a riot'. Whilst Adam is sure that they will like him in time, he convinces himself that he is not necessarily there to be liked, because it is better to 'drill the children [into] the basics and get them the way you want them . . . Then you can have a happy class for the rest of the year. If that initial half term goes a bit haywire, then I think you'd have problems. You're going to have to stand there and face it for a whole year'. Early in the year, he reports that his strategy to remain aloof is actually forced upon him by the pace of work, and he senses that he is not really developing a relationship with the children. As the term progresses, he becomes increasingly dissatisfied, realizing that he wants to become more relaxed, to share a sense of humour with his class, and so enjoy his teaching more. At the end of the first term he recalls the point when he makes a conscious decision to change the relationship:

> For the first three weeks I was on my back and didn't know where I was. I wouldn't say I didn't like the children in the class but I just thought it was my job to teach them . . . I wasn't particularly close to [them] and I went in really hard and was quite miserable with them to get them to knuckle down and do as they were told really. Now the turning point when I started to enjoy it was when I went home one weekend and I'd been hard on them again, or rather firm, and I sat down and thought, 'I don't think I've laughed once in front of those children in three weeks. I haven't smiled or cracked a joke.' So I thought they were ready for me to ease up a bit. If you spend the time being a total grouch then it's time wasted because you don't enjoy it. I started to ease off and make a few jokes here and there. If things arose I made light of it and I've enjoyed it a lot more since then.

Adam reports that as he becomes more confident and gets to know the children better, he tries out games and 'little tricks' to control them, such as putting his hands in the air, which the children have to copy when they become too noisy, although as he realizes this can quickly lose its effect: 'Now a lot of them put their hands up but they're still talking so I'll have to try something different.' He also tries counting to ten if he asks them to sit down and they don't respond straight-away. By employing other strategies, Adam feels that he improves his control over the children because it 'means that when I do get cross they do stop and think, "Gosh, he must really be upset now because he's getting cross"'.

By the end of the first term, Adam claims that in fact he feels annoyed on far fewer occasions because he better understands the children:

> I think I've become more wary about incidents that arise between children in the playground and classroom, flash points in terms of action. When someone says 'He kicked me', whereas before I would have said 'Did you?' now I try to get to the bottom of it and nine times out of ten both parties are guilty, and I tend to sit back a bit more rather than fly off saying 'This child has been kicked. I must sort it out'. If a child can't walk then I'd get really cross, but if it's a kick — don't get me wrong, I don't let it go — but I try to sort it out without getting too heated.

Whilst Adam seems to feel less threatened by children's misbehaviour in the class-room, the account of his reaction at the time when one child is reprimanded by the headteacher in assembly in the summer term suggests that he continues to feel personally responsible if they misbehave within the wider school community:

> Some days . . . they just upset me and they know they've put me in a foul mood. In assembly someone was told off in my class so I came in and just

looked at them and there was silence. I didn't say anything, but just kept on frowning. It wasn't a particularly nice day, virtual silence all day, but it was a way of reinforcing being in control.

Observations of Adam in the latter part of the first term indicate that he is increasingly able to refine his voice control in order to effect anger or disapproval. When doing this, Adam reports that he feels more detached and likens himself to an actor:

When I get upset or angry or really tell them off I'm much more controlled than when I was on TP . . . It's just control. I can control my voice and make it rise. I do shout I suppose sometimes, rarely, but I never bellow, if that makes sense. I don't know how to describe it. My voice is up there, but I can bring it straight down again if I want to . . . When I was on TP I wanted to appear more patient with the child because you can't be seen to explode. So you have to pretend to be patient although inside you're seething. Now I just don't seethe anyway.

It is only at this point, when Adam feels that he has sufficient control over his own reactions, that he reveals how worried he was when he had 'had a fit' with the two boys on teaching practice, and that he had discussed his concerns with some other students. Now he feels reassured that such an event would be avoided, although he still becomes extremely frustrated with Chris on occasions throughout the year and gives vent to his feelings, knowing that the pupil will give little response and appears unperturbed by Adam's enacted anger. Whilst Adam regrets taking such action, he feels that as time goes on he only does this as a last resort, and that for the most part he is positive towards the boy, certainly on a social and personal level, a point which is generally borne out by observations over the year. In part he excuses his actions by arguing that the pupil is a very unusual case and should not really be in a mainstream class. In the spring term, when Chris spends more time with the special needs teacher, coupled with Adam feeling less stressed generally in the classroom, he is able to look back with humour on how he reacted to Chris:

I used to take him outside. I'd have a go at him because it got to a point where he was driving me so mad that I would bellow and I didn't think it was good that every child in the class should be subjected to my bellowing because one child was driving me up the wall. So I took him outside and bellowed and subjected the whole school to it! I walked into the staffroom once and they said 'Was that you?' Even people right down the far end of the school could hear me!

In his first year of full-time teaching, Adam's views of behaviour management do seem to change. He tells of an occasion when, in the second week, he confronts a child who is misbehaving, and realizes that he is heading for a confrontation in full view of the rest of the class. He decides, however, to try to diffuse the situation as the pupil is the 'sort who would really dig his heels in'. Adam realizes that this attitude seems in marked contrast to his views of the previous year but reasons that: '. . . foremost in your mind is that you're going to have these children for a year and therefore it's more important to get a relationship built up, no matter how long it takes, that's going to last that year. In TP you only have six weeks'.

Adam seems to learn quickly that it is not in his best interests to confront some of his 'very bright but cocky' boys, and claims that there are other times when he has to 'subtly knock . . . on the head' problems such as minor bullying. Adam feels that as he has got to know the children and they know what is expected of them, he is able to consolidate his use of humour and adopt 'a quiet approach' to managing behaviour. For example, early in the spring term he recounts:

> I sometimes get a smart Alec. Last week there was one child who decided he was going to be the class idiot, that was the role he wanted to play. He was just being a total idiot and I said after a while, 'I think you better take a note home to mum next week' and he asked why and I said, 'it's about your behaviour. Don't you think you're behaving really badly?' and he said he supposed he was. I said this week was the week where he had to decide whether I sent a note home or not. But before I would just have exploded. Now I would prefer to talk about it quietly. He did look terrified at the prospect of the threat.

At this point he again thinks back to his experiences on the final practice, realizing that, 'On my last practice I was told to avoid confrontation at all costs. I never really understood what it meant.' At the same time, observations of Adam within the school seem to reveal that he also wins the respect of the boys through his sporting abilities, especially in football. On one visit to the school, he comes in from football practice with a group, and there is a strong sense of camaraderie. Generally, observations reveal a warm, jocular but mutually respectful relationship with the children, although Adam reacts differently towards boys and girls. He says that he is still wary of reprimanding girls because he fears that they might 'burst into tears' and appears to lack an understanding of young girls at a social and personal level.

Planning and Organization

As Adam faces the new academic year, he reports that one of his biggest problems was, as he had expected, the 'nightmare' of setting out a full timetable which takes him a 'really long time, juggling things around and fitting everything in with the timetables of the other staff'. Adam feels daunted by the fact that he is to be responsible for the children's progression over a whole year. As the school has parallel classes for each year group, Adam is thankful that he is able to do much of his planning with June, who acts as a source of tried-and-tested ideas. He finds that the planning procedures that were recommended at college, which he had found difficult to make sense of during his teaching practices, now provide a valuable framework for his plans. Together with June, he initially uses flowcharts to develop a notion of the progression of the schemes of work, and true to his own expectations, Adam clearly strives to be very organized and to plan the class's work in detail.

When organizing the class, Adam initially allows the children to sit in friendship groups and, as he observes them, moves pairs of friends to form alternative working groups. Having decided that it is vital that he makes a good impact on the children from the start, he plans his first week's activities, 'so that nobody could really fail them. Obviously some produced better work than others. I just didn't want anyone to fail in the first week or the children would get very tearful and upset. I had to give them an opportunity to please me by succeeding'. In his planning he uses a particular activity that he has used successfully in the past:

> There was my favourite which I'd done at G. [first placement school], observing bubbles. Blowing bubbles and writing up the experiment. Almost from day one a bit of science. They were having to pattern them by doing bubble prints. So by the second day what I wanted happened. I had everyone's work up on the wall. So everyone had something somewhere on the wall. So I made a big thing about 'Isn't our class wonderful!' It was a collective thing, not just mine. That was one of the main things. I was determined to get something up from everyone.

As Adam sets up a pattern of organization for the class, he appears to draw upon a range of influences, including his three teaching practices from which he developed very clear views about the contrasting approaches. Within the school itself, the teachers adopt a range of approaches to classroom organization, and so he is able to observe and discuss various ideas. During the first term, Adam experiments with different forms of organization, even reorganizing furniture a number of times, in order to create the kind of classroom he wants. It appears that he is guided by quite specific images of classroom practice. Particularly when planning practical activities, Adam visualizes events and individuals in the classroom, and so can anticipate problems, taking account of seating, personalities, resources, etc.

Adam clearly wants to achieve some degree of integrated work, but also wants to establish times in the classroom when, for example, he knows exactly what everyone is doing in order to ensure that work is completed. Within a few weeks, he establishes a pattern of 'pretty formal mornings' and 'pretty integrated afternoons'; a pattern of organization he continues to use throughout the rest of the year.

Adam claims that the formal times allow him to undertake such activities as spelling tests, tables tests, reading, comprehension and grammar. When the children have to do formal writing, he likes this to be done with 'heads down so that you can hear a pin drop. I think there are times in a day when you just need that bit of silence really, as a teacher and a child'.

Although Adam includes mathematics for everyone in the morning, during the early weeks he reports that he is unhappy with the organization and that he is finding it difficult to monitor the work. Adam wonders whether this is because he has simply followed what June did when he was there on teaching practice. His own experience begins to expose some of the inherent problems of taking on the approach without necessarily 'having all the skills' to make it work.

> You set up some activities which don't need much writing, so that you can concentrate on your scheme. But then you find that things you thought didn't need much monitoring they just don't understand. So you have forty hands up and you find yourself looking around, looking for somewhere to hide. That might be something that I might be looking to change possibly before half term. I spend most evenings sitting wondering how I'm going to do maths the following day, so that there aren't quite so many hands up. At the end of the day I might well have to integrate maths with something else for sanity. That's the beauty of being a teacher in your first year because you can just try something and if it doesn't work . . . I've been told to give it four weeks or so to try to let it settle down, but if it doesn't work I'll change it, think really hard about it over the weekend.

Adam decides not to change, concluding that, 'The other choice was to have half do English and half maths and swap, which would bring just as many organizational problems.' Instead, he reports that he concentrates over the following weeks on the planning of the sessions, ensuring that he is thoroughly prepared:

> I always do maths as a priority in terms of getting that sorted out. That's the one thing I do every night. Maths book open, that group doing this, that group doing that and I sort myself out. Which children are at a stage when they can carry on and which children need directing.

Such planning allows Adam to be clearer in his organization of the learning environment. By the end of term, he describes the routines he has devised as:

> I'm using more things like calculators, worksheets, multilink . . . I still have them all do maths together. One of the main ways I've done is to start the lesson, they come in from assembly at 9.30 am and I say, 'Reading book open. Quietly read. Group one on the carpet'. Talk to them, tell them they know what they're doing because they did the page yesterday, ask if there are any questions and if not then off they go. Group 2 on the carpet, group 3 keep on reading, then group 3 on the carpet. Now we've got a new concept here, teach it to them for 10 minutes or however long it takes and then ask, 'Think you've got it?' Then off they go to have a go and come straight back to me. So getting up and running is fine, although I still have problems with children wanting marking, but instead of having this ridiculous queuing idea they just sit down with their hands up and if I know I'm not going to get to them then hopefully I've got some extension work up my sleeve and ask them to find out for me in their books or something. It sounds like a cop-out, but at least they're busy rather

than sitting there waiting for me to come and see them. At least their minds are actively working on something.

Chris and another pupil, Charlotte, who also experiences learning difficulties, often act as constraints upon the smooth running of what is already a challenging form of organization, but Adam feels that he has to accept that he cannot give them the attention they require, 'I've still got two children who are extremely slow and who are on books for infants. They need one to one and I cannot give it to them.'

The afternoons are described by Adam as 'pretty hectic'. This is when he usually undertakes topic work focused upon history or science, or practical activities such as design technology or art. For the first term, Adam emphasizes the importance of children learning through 'first-hand experience', and he tries to organize activities which will allow this. He also asserts that he is striving to make the tasks more open-ended, and this also has an impact upon his timing. Below he gives his reaction to an afternoon session which involved thirty-three children working in four groups, one undertaking diary writing for history, two working on science experiments on vibration, involving alarm clocks and tuning forks, and another completing a science worksheet about the eye. Field notes at the time record that the classroom is quite noisy, especially the group working with the tuning forks, who are often off-task and start playing about, putting the tuning forks up their noses. Adam regularly stops the class to reprimand groups, the first time being 15 minutes after the lesson has started. Generally he moves from group to group, talking to individuals or pairs. Chris is completing a worksheet on sound and Adam frequently goes to him in order to keep him on-task. Afterwards, Adam comments:

> Well I expected Chris to be like he was really. The tuning fork people finished again very quickly, quicker than last time, and the stuff they've been writing is OK. The worksheet has very short sentences and I think they're more interested in observing and talking rather than actually writing. But I was just amazed how long it took the Columbus people to settle down. They should by now know what they're doing. They were unsettling most of the class. But apart from that it seemed to go fairly well.
>
> [If I did it again] I think I'd probably have science going with something else, perhaps even maths with some groups. The only thing with that is that you're ability grouping them for science as well as maths then, which I don't like to do. Possibly do it in a morning rather than an afternoon. We've had quite an intensive morning really.

When Adam is asked why he decided to put these particular activities together, he replies:

> Just space and resources really. The alarm clock experiment they were quite happy to do in the corridor on their own, the sensible groups. And the eye sheet didn't have much input from me. The tuning fork people asked questions but they were irrelevant because they knew the answer before they asked them.

> It was bitty really . . . most of my activities last about the same time,
> but these were so staggered — the alarm clock one takes ages and the tun-
> ing fork one takes about 10 minutes. I'm not particularly satisfied with it.

He concludes that in future he will have to make sure that he has activities that do
not require so much of his attention so that he can concentrate on particular individuals or groups.

Adam continues to address such organizational problems, and each visit to
the classroom suggested that his classroom routines have become increasingly
refined. At the same time, Adam still experiments with different forms of organization for subjects he has little or no experience of teaching. For example, Adam
decides to model a design and technology lesson, in which all the children undertake practical work, on the way the male Year 6 class teacher organizes such lessons. The children attempt to design and make weather vanes. However, Adam
abandons the lesson halfway through when he realizes that the children need to use
equipment he hasn't got, and that the organization of the lesson is proving to be too
difficult.

In the first term of his appointment, Adam reports that one of the most satisfying features of being a full-time teacher is having the freedom and confidence to
do activities that are thought of on the spur of the moment. Adam associates this
spontaneity with effective teaching, and throughout the year incidences when this
occurs form significant and satisfying memories.

> The best work has been the unplanned, spur of the moment thing when
> you have an idea. Sitting in the staffroom you get a fantastic idea that
> takes no setting up and it turns out really well. It hit me on the Wednesday
> night to do something the following morning, I came in and did it and it
> was one of the best activities I have done . . . Funnily enough other people
> I've spoken to have said exactly the same thing. Their spontaneous lessons
> have been far and away the most successful. I can't explain that but it's
> just happened. The plates — that was spontaneous, thinking about it at
> breaktime and we did it after break. That's probably the best art work they
> produced. [Last year] I wouldn't have had the confidence to see it through
> because I hadn't written a lesson plan and didn't have it all listed out with
> objectives and if someone came in to observe I would have had to say I'd
> done it off the top of my head. That plate example . . . was totally relevant
> to the topic and the only reason it was a rush job in terms of planning is
> that someone said it was Columbus Day and I thought we should get
> something to make to commemorate it and that was it. I just think on my
> feet really . . . It worked better than anything I'd planned before. I don't
> know why. That's not to say I don't plan, but some of the things that have
> been best have been off the cuff.

Similarly, Adam now has the confidence to re-do activities which are unsuccessful,
which enable him to act almost immediately upon his reflections:

... if the lesson starts going wrong I feel capable of getting it back on track and putting it right. If the children go off and start going in the wrong direction, now it's your own class and nobody is looking at you, you can say 'OK, come and sit back on the carpet. I didn't explain that to you very well, this is how it should be'. I don't mind admitting mistakes ... but on TP that would be an admission of failure. Now if your instructions aren't clear then all you have to do is re-do them and make them clearer. [For example], I said I'd like them to write a poem about one of their favourite animals and we'd talked about poetry a little bit. It wasn't particularly linked, but we'd talked about poetry and I wanted them to do a bit because we hadn't done any. So we sat down and I didn't go into any discussion about what it should be like. They had to do it in rough and I said they should get a friend to read it and give a valued judgment. If they thought it was OK they should write it up in best. It was horrendous, so the next day I came in and totally redefined my instructions and went through examples on the board of how a poem should be set up, not prose, but a poem ... I wasn't cross or anything and I told them it wasn't their fault because we'd rushed it the previous day. I said the ideas they had in their original piece should be set out as a poem and it was three times better, not brilliant but better, because I wasn't afraid to say that we hadn't had enough time to talk about a poem and what it is like.

Children's Learning and the Teacher's Role

Adam's early ideas about children's learning centred upon creating the right atmosphere, using practical experiences, making things 'relevant' and 'exciting' to the child. At the same time, he saw the teacher as a source of knowledge who 'instructs', and it appears that it is through this role that Adam gains the sense of fulfilment that he seeks in teaching. On several occasions during the first year, he attempted to reconcile the role of the teacher with his ideas of children learning through experience and discovery. For example, on his final teaching practice, two boys were undertaking a maths investigation about probability; they were unable to answer Adam's questions, as to what they had discovered, and Adam explained the reasons to them:

I was having to instruct Ian and Andrew when they got their coin-tossing results. I was having to really lead them into why the result was always 50/50. They just couldn't see the connection between one toss having an equal chance, and 60 tosses giving you an equal chance, of 30/30. They couldn't see that. So I had to direct them in that decision, rather than let them find it out for themselves. I do like children to discover things for themselves, but if they're just not doing it and they can understand the concept but haven't quite found the key that unlocks it, then I'll unlock it for them.

Now, Adam begins his first year of teaching supporting the idea that children ideally should learn through experience, but that he, as the teacher, should provide direct instruction when this is needed. Subsequent discussions with Adam indicate that he has clear ideas about the degrees to which these dimensions of teaching and learning can be enacted within the various areas of the curriculum. For example, early in the spring term, Adam explains that he has organized his maths session in a different way to allow him to instruct a specific group who experience difficulties in this area:

> I would normally have a whole class of maths together and then after break we'd do English together, but because the one group had to get fractions across to them — which I think is quite tricky because they're not particularly bright — I thought I couldn't really afford to have other children with queries on their maths, so I had to try and devise an activity which I thought would basically run itself after a brief explanation. Namely the English. Once I'd discussed with them capital letters [the children are given a worksheet which comprises sentences without any capital letters], I really thought they should be able to read the sheet and do it anyway, but I thought it would be best to chat about it. Once I could get them on the English and had the two brightest children on maths carrying on, they didn't require much input from me, apart from sorting out where they were. That freed me then. Also with Chris being out on support [i.e., with the support teacher] it freed me to spend a quarter of an hour really hammering the fractions home for the Dragons [the name given to a less able group]. That was my thinking. The whole of the two sessions were really geared towards that one group having as much time as possible to get that new piece of work across. That's what dictated how the lessons worked.

In science, Adam is gradually able to manage the teaching in a way that he feels allows the children to be more active, and he is able to chart the development in his own teaching:

> They've developed and got to this stage now themselves because to start with I was looking at quite closed experiments . . . They get given the equipment, they're told what they have to do with it and then they just list the equipment and what they did, so they get used to writing it up and then what they found . . . All I didn't say is what they'd find. The next stage [came during] experiments on light and growth. I told them what they had to do, gave them worksheets and equipment and they had to predict what they thought was going to happen and now we're at the stage [with the topic Minibeasts] where . . . They can all work out their own criteria. Obviously we're going to have a lot of discussion about arachnids, insects with six legs, slugs, etc., but at the end of the day they're going to have

to classify them themselves in whatever groups they want and obviously the only way they can do that is to have studied the creatures.

Adam feels particularly proud of the activities he has organized and that he is not just relying on the topic boxes which are there to provide staff with ideas. A sense of satisfaction is implicit in what he says not only for himself but also for the children, and it is interesting to note how Adam seems prepared to manipulate situations to achieve this. Below, he talks in the summer term about how the session in which the class search outdoors for minibeasts has been developed which will precede the classification activity:

> We . . . got the books out and looked at wood lice to see things about them and we chatted about it briefly and decided that perhaps we could do some experiments with minibeasts and today's activity was really to get them thinking as a group and working as a group. That was one idea. And really to see what experiments they could come up with, with the facts they know, what they want to find out and what they want to prove. Why do experiments? To find things out and prove things that we already know . . . so they know woodlice like damp places and dark places under stones, but they have to prove it beyond reasonable doubt. I started off saying 'What do you think you want to find out?' and Matthew did say 'Food' and 'Where they live'. One of them said 'I want to find out how they communicate' . . . There's always that danger when you say 'What do you want to find out?' and they could go and find something totally inappropriate, which is why we started off with a whole class discussion which I generally lead in the direction I want them to go . . . I don't shoot them down in flames, I'll say, 'That's a good idea, but is it practical or possible?' and so you're leading them a bit. So that's as near AT1, 'Planning and Doing an Experiment', as you can get with this age group.

Whilst he feels that his teaching of science is progressing well, at the same time Adam finds that what he is striving to achieve is increasingly compromised. For example, Adam reports that he is continually under pressure from the volume of curriculum and assessment he is expected to cover, recognizing that, in part, this is because he hasn't known how to pace the work over the whole year, something he expects to improve with experience. Although he believes subjects such as science and maths should involve practical investigation, this takes a good deal of time to carry out, and he suspects that he could satisfy assessment criteria for classification, for example, in the topic of Minibeasts, by using a knowledge transmission approach, but this would take, in his words, 'the fun out of teaching and learning', something he resists at this stage:

> In theory it's possible, as far as what the government wants us to do, to sit them down with a textbook and say 'that's the classification. Learn it by rote. Write it down'. Test, pass, done. But that's pathetic and I don't

see the benefit of that at all. As far as the assessment goes, though, that's all they need to know. So if I wanted to I could spend a week with the textbook out, learning them. Not even drawing them, making lists and then giving them a test, but they're not going to be learning by experience at all. The whole fun is looking at them and studying them and that would all be missed.

However, as the term progresses Adam finds that the pressure builds to such an extent that he despairs about meeting assessment targets, finding that he has less and less time to undertake oral assessments by listening to what the children say during group work. To add to his problems, experience also appears to show that children are not necessarily learning through experience. So Adam comes to accept that at times the children 'just need to be told a fact. Sometimes they'll do experiments and come up with nonsense' and he resorts to demonstrating an experiment or simply dictating 'scientific facts' in order to ensure that the children produce the correct writing. He realizes that this does not 'necessarily prove that they understand it', but at least '. . . there's no come back [from parents]'. This final comment reflects Adam's growing disillusion that he does not have the sense of autonomy he had expected to feel in his teaching, and that parental pressure is highly influential in his teaching, because 'They're the consumer . . . On TP you're performing for your lecturer and teacher. Now you're performing for the parents and they're even more important because they can make life really sticky. I'm always conscious when the parents look through the books.'

Late in the summer term, Adam repeats the experiments on friction which he did on teaching practice, discussing how he responds when things do not go as expected, and how he then manages the assessment:

> It was a friction experiment, which I did for my TP perfectly alright. This lot were a disaster. The smoother surfaces were just running along and the rough ones weren't moving. I sat there and said, 'Look, a bit of sandpaper is the rough surface and this is the smooth surface. Which one do you think is going to be harder to move?' 'The rough surface'. 'Why?' 'Friction' and then we talked about it and I said 'Do we all agree with that then? We have discovered that the rougher a surface the harder it is to move the object . . . this is called friction.' Underlined. New line. It's almost as regimented as that. I've done that in some cases because I've thought they haven't got it. So my science has changed, [although] I still do . . . investigation. I love it and they love it . . . I think last year I'd have said [that I assess them] by talking to them, but now I realize you can't go and talk to thirty-two children because there's no time. I usually give them a little test. Sometimes I use it in the assessment folders . . .
>
> We discussed it as a force and I put the question 'What is the name of the force that makes it difficult to move an object?' Answer, friction. Tick. I might have worded it in a [different] way and drawn a diagram 'Which would you think would be easier to move and why?' The bright

ones would say the smooth one's the easier to move because there's no friction, whereas the less bright ones would just say 'The rougher one would be harder.' They might not mention friction, but I know they know about friction, so I'd probably give them some marks for that. But that's where science has changed a lot. Before everything had to be experiment, experiment. Sometimes they just need to learn the facts. They need facts . . .

Sometimes I let them do an experiment and then make sure we have the right facts at the end of it. To be honest it depends whether it's being assessed or not. If it's in the assessment booklet that they need to know according to school policy, then I'll tell them what it is and they'll know it. I make sure we discuss it. They just don't write it down and close the book and that's it. We chat about it. Usually I say 'How would we put that in words?' and someone will start off a sentence and sometimes it will be from them and I'll just clarify it. Some of it, to some of them, is just pure gobbledygook but it [still] would be if they'd done the experiment as well. They're not all going to get it.

Such formal teaching Adam associates with becoming 'tougher', something which has characterized the way he has talked about various changes he has made over the year. For example, Adam reports that with creative writing he had tended, in the first term, to 'go for the ideas . . . now I go back the other way saying that full stops and capital letters must appear in their creative writing. Creative writing doesn't mean that they don't have to remember spelling, etc.' In the second term he realizes that in the children's maths work they have not been setting their calculations out as they should 'because I hadn't been pestering it, they'd just got lazy and I had to redefine what I expect in standards'.

In the third term, however, Adam still maintains that he would like children to experience excitement in their learning. He recounts an experience when he identifies ladybird chrysalis in his garden which he then brings into the classroom, and is able to follow up the children's interest in discussion:

The thing I liked most was that it was a fluke really. I knew they were ladybird chrysalis, but whether they'd hatch out or not was another thing and after about three days I thought perhaps not. So I was ever-so excited when I came in and found them and I rushed up to the staffroom and said, 'Hey, look at this' and they came down and were all really interested in it and I showed the whole class before assembly and they were generally fascinated. Due to me keeping my eyes open and being aware what my topic was and working in the garden I was able to bring in something that they could actually physically watch. I don't know whether they'll ever get that chance again. They might. But I could give them that and I didn't spoil it by saying 'Now we're going to do a drawing and write it up'. We just talked about it and there it was. Everyone in the class was fascinated, so I was being an effective teacher in being able to get resources together, into the classroom and getting it to work.

Developing Subject Knowledge

Prior to the course, Adam's views about history seemed to be heavily influenced by his own experiences of learning history at secondary school. The history teacher he admired so much had projected a great enthusiasm for the subject, which Adam claimed inspired him. Having studied history at degree level, he anticipated that he would be able to 'put a lot of what I've learned into the classes and make them very interesting and hopefully exciting for the children'.

Adam has always believed that story is a useful way to introduce topics, especially in the light of his experiences with picture books early the previous year. Now in his full-time post, using story characterizes the way he thinks about a topic. In most instances he uses popular literature: 'We're doing Rubbish next term, *Stig of the Dump*. After that we're doing Minibeasts, *Charlotte's Web* . . . whenever I do a topic, the first question that comes into my mind is "I wonder if I know a story about that?" It's like an anchor to gel everything together.'

In the spring term, when teaching Ancient Egypt, Adam is amazed by the power that story and drama have in helping children, and he recounts his experiences with enthusiasm:

> For the Ancient Egypt topic I found it difficult . . . to find that initial thing, but the first activity was brilliant. They were mesmerized. We did Tutenkamun and I've got a tape on which I played the story of the discovery of the tomb and when they found the seal I put an imaginary seal on the door and said 'Outside there is the tomb of Tutenkamun and the seal is on here and it's not been broken, so what does that tell you?' and when they realized that nobody had been in there for 3,000 years and I said 'If we just open the door . . .' and they were entranced. I don't know what they expected to see out in the corridor, but it just got them. It really had them on a Friday afternoon — a bad time perhaps to start it. But over the weekend they were looking for tons of stuff on Egypt and I thought the activity had really hit home a bit . . . They have an idea of tombs and mummies, but the idea of wondering what it's really like going in there — I said that you could still smell the perfume in the room from when it was being built 3,000 years ago, because apparently the room still smelt.
>
> I was almost doing drama with them. It wasn't talking about it, it was actually going back in time with me to 1922 when Carter actually opened that door. They honestly seemed to believe for a split second that there was going to be something out there behind the door because I just grabbed them. It's great when you do that because you've really got them and can start to take them where you want to take them.

From this point Adam sees that he will have 'got the interest there' in order then to carry out the rest of the topic which in part must be assessed.

> We're going to finish Tutenkamun and do a newspaper report about some of the treasures. Then we're going to look at an overview of Egypt,

concentrating on the River Nile and I think that's not going to grab them as much as the initial activity, but . . . I hope it's going to keep it going for a bit, so I can plug them with the stuff I've been told to plug them with.

'Plugging' the children is to be achieved through class discussion and group work and 'Unfortunately a lot of that will be a lot of textbook work [because] it's very difficult to do practicals to get the facts in.'

For Adam, history in the primary school is 'just seeing how other people lived'. The concept of time is not perceived to be particularly relevant because, 'To them 1200 AD and 1000 BC doesn't mean anything, it's no real difference to me either, so I don't really concentrate on time lines much. It's more looking at how people lived and realizing that they lived in different ways.'

Ideally Adam would like to do history through story and discussion, so that he could give them worksheets in order for them to work in groups finding out information. Equally he would like to show them 'art and things like that . . . The way I'd love to do it is to give them things they can touch and feel and experience . . . if you [could] actually say "This is part of a tomb" . . . but you can't do that and so a lot of it is theory from books, which I feel I have to jolly along and make as interesting as possible.'

Teaching history is therefore seen within two frameworks, one which focuses upon recreating a sense of the past through story, drama, role play and the use of artefacts; and a second which is concerned 'with the textbook thing, finding the facts out in groups, doing worksheets'.

Like science, maths is seen as a practical subject, best developed through investigations. However, Adam soon finds in his first year of teaching that the exciting activities he devised on teaching practice cannot be enacted on a day-to-day basis in the classroom, and he feels that the college has not prepared him for using a maths scheme. Early in the year it becomes clear that Adam views the maths scheme as a chore. He describes it as 'something you [have] to do [and] once its out of the way . . . everyone can relax and do something else'.

Whilst the scheme is viewed by Adam as 'formal', and is often 'repetitive', he admits to relying on it in order to cope with the wide range of abilities in maths, and to provide evidence of progress for parents.

They love doing maths, but I don't particularly enjoy teaching it. I find it quite a difficult subject really, quite difficult to juggle the groups. Of all the activities, maths is the one where there really is such a wide range of abilities. I think I probably put too much weight on the Ginn [maths scheme]. I concentrate on that and don't do enough investigation on it. It's just number, number. They do some problem-solving but no real investigation. It's very rare that they have to go out and measure the playground or do probabilities . . . I'll be honest with you, it's a survival technique really if you do maths everyday. As long as you've read it thoroughly and then know what they have to do, it's all there on the teacher's page.

Although Adam is sure children learn best from practical activities, as in science, by the second term he resorts to 'drumming rules' when children have difficulties. He accepts that the children 'probably do not understand the concept' when taught in this way. For example, in the spring term, a group of children were experiencing difficulties in understanding the notation of fractions:

> If this square is being equally divided into ten parts, there are so many tenths . . . I just asked the relationship and said that the number of equal parts decided what was going to be on the bottom . . . It's pretty parrot fashion and probably isn't really learning the concept. But if they remember that, it's a stepping stone to working out what a fraction is later on. I don't think they realize yet. I'm sure I couldn't do fractions at their age. I always think that.

Again, it appeared that some of his doubts, and attempts to teach 'parrot fashion', were influenced by his own difficulties with maths at school and how he remembered being taught. Although Adam does not want to teach like this, he feels unable to suggest alternative strategies. With the same group of children, he also reports 'drumming rules into them' when they experience difficulties in simple problem-solving. In the final term, Adam is then surprised, and delighted, to find that this group of children scored well in a mental maths test.

> All year I've been drumming it into them all year. 'I've got six carrots you've got two, how many are there altogether?' Drum, drum and blow me down, I've suddenly started doing mental maths this term. I shout out the questions and they write down, the answers, almost like a test really and a lot of this is on that practical stuff. I was absolutely staggered when we did it yesterday. A child in the Dragons [lower ability group] beat the socks off every other child in this class and I couldn't believe it.

Conclusion

As Adam reviews his development to date, he seems quite satisfied with the kind of teacher he is able to be, recognizing that his teacher image must accommodate an expression of himself in order to be rewarding. He revisits how he reached this point:

> I'm quite happy with a lot of my style because otherwise I wouldn't be enjoying it as much as I am. Basically I have to be really hard early on. I still don't think I was as hard as I could have been but I had to really get them to knuckle under, really drive them so that they knew exactly what I was doing and then I was able to ease back, have a bit of a joke with them, be approachable but still be firm. One of the things I said very early on at that initial meeting was that I wanted to be approachable but

firm, and I think I've got that to a certain extent now. I think most of them would approach me and nearly everyone in the class has had some problem or another. We can laugh, but they know when to stop. I was sometimes very aware of inconsistency. You can come over as being approachable and friendly and have a laugh and then the next minute, as soon as it goes over, it's shutters up. I think you've got to be able to have a laugh with them really because you've got them for a year. I don't want to be there with a constant frown on my face all day.

At the end of the two-year period, Adam feels he has learned a great deal, particularly about classroom organization and management, and although he still clings to notions of children learning 'actively' and 'through discovery', he recognizes that he has compromised his ideals and that his teaching style overall has become more didactic. Nevertheless, he still feels he has much to learn. He points out:

You're constantly learning. My mother said that out of all the professions, teachers are probably the least satisfied in themselves because they know they can always make improvements.

Adam has always accepted that teaching would be hard work, although it is only towards the end of his first year of teaching that he seems to fully recognize how constrained he is as a teacher, and how some of his ideals for teaching and contributing to a caring community are almost impossible to put into practice:

You have to be teacher . . . social worker, you have to look for warning signs if parents are separating and there are traumas at home, you have to take the time to ask, sometimes you have to know when to be sensitive. There are just so many complex roles you have to play often in a day or a lesson with individual children. You have to treat every child differently almost. Some respond in one way, some in another. Also just keep going. I was absolutely shattered at the end of this term and felt tired at the end of every term. The last week was a real drag and you have to get there. Parents Evening is going to be over tonight and then that's it . . . It's just keeping going really. Keeping yourself motivated, and them.

Chapter 5

Case Study Two — Nina

Introduction

Nina is taking the PGCE course, specializing in the early primary years. Her first teaching practice is in a large village infants school, where Nina reports problems in being able to freely observe and discuss the class teacher's practice. She senses that staff are rather uncertain and defensive about their own ways of working, which Nina describes as 'traditional'. Her second teaching practice is in a small, rural, village primary school, where, in contrast, she is placed with an out-going, self-confident teacher, who places great emphasis upon child-centred learning, and who frequently engages in discussions with Nina about her teaching. Other staff within the school are also supportive, and classes are generally smaller than average.

Her third placement offers yet another contrast, being a large, urban, primary school in an area with quite a high level of social deprivation. Nina thoroughly enjoys working within this setting. She establishes good relationships with the staff. The school has a headteacher who is well respected in the area, and is seen to offer positive leadership, and to place emphasis on building a strong sense of team-work. Staff are generally young, aged between 20 and 40 years. Within the infant department in which Nina is placed, teachers team-teach in a large, open-plan area. Some class sizes are quite large. Each class has a separate quiet bay which can be closed off from the main area.

After the course, Nina is unable to secure a post for the following year, and consequently undertakes some voluntary and supply work at her third teaching practice school. Towards the end of the first term, Nina is successfully interviewed for a full-time post there.

Entry to Teacher Education

Nina is a modern languages graduate, in her late 30s and is married with four children. She was educated in two convents, at primary and secondary level. Nina is adamant that she has few memories of her first school, and that she rarely talks about her school days:

> I don't actually think of the school and days at the school. It's funny, isn't it? . . . I don't go back there and say, 'Look this is where I went to school'

as my husband tends to do. I don't talk about it a lot because there's nothing I remember. But if I purposely think back to it, I remember being very happy at primary school, although it was a period outside school of great stress for me. Enormous stress, and yet I was very happy at school. It was a place of great security. And the nuns were very, very kind and funny. They used to make us laugh and they were very caring.

Nina declines further discussion about the 'enormous stress' which she experienced, but feels sure that her perception of the school as a place of great security is not significantly influenced by this, and that the staff were indeed caring and good humoured.

Transferring to secondary level, she recalls a harsh regime in a school run by French nuns, although she valued two German teachers who seemed to provide discipline that was fair and consistent. She enjoyed the subjects they taught, namely German and maths:

I realize that they were good teachers, which you don't appreciate at the time, but you realize afterwards. I enjoyed those subjects. I enjoyed the discipline of them and the fact that these two were always the same. There was never this 'What are they going to do today?' or 'Will they fly off the deep end today?', which there was with some of the nuns. So there was security.

In addition, she liked an English teacher who told stories about her own family, presenting an insight into the teacher herself. In her own teaching, Nina often comments that it is important to her that the children see her as a person, who has a sense of humour and is also fallible. Throughout the two years of the study, she also frequently places emphasis on enjoying children as individuals and being able to talk easily to them.

After A-levels, she went to technical college, gained secretarial qualifications, and then went on to a university in Scotland to study languages. As her father was Italian, she had developed a second language at an early age, and then found that French was also easy for her to learn when she went to school. She spent one year in Italy and six months in Switzerland. After graduating, she dismissed teaching as a career, having only considered teaching at secondary level.

As her husband sought promotion, she lived in several places both abroad and in this country, which prevented her from pursuing a specific career. At various times, she undertook work, sometimes full-time, as a language tutor teaching Italian and French, or English as a foreign language.

Through studying and teaching languages, Nina reports a growing interest in the way language develops and functions, 'I realized that what fascinated me was language in general. I collected them . . . the similarities and expressions and the way it joins together . . . really fascinated me.'

As she had her own four children, Nina recalls that her interest was deepened by a realization that language seemed to occupy a crucial position in their cognitive development. It is this intellectual interest which eventually draws Nina to consider primary teaching.

Images of Teaching

Prior to the course, Nina appears to have an image of teaching which incorporates three aspects: the personal, the professional and the academic. It seems that she is already sensitive to the complex interplay between these. For example, the personal qualities which Nina identifies are seen as 'emotional' and she postulates that there 'must be something very concrete which is the centre of all this . . . [linking] the personality thing, the professional aspect and the academic aspect. How to put them altogether into one . . . I think that's what makes a teacher in the end . . . I'm aware that I've got to put all these three into something that functions efficiently'.

Within the personal dimension, Nina hopes that facets of her personality will find expression in her teaching, so providing her with an emotional satisfaction. These qualities include 'a level of tolerance, an ability to cope [in pressured situations], a sense of humour, a willingness to learn'. At the same time she hopes that she will not show the intolerance which she recognizes within her relationship with her own children, 'I fly off the handle sometimes.' Although, she is fairly confident that this occurs 'within the confines of home', she is not totally free of doubt.

She reports that she can be very organized while also being able to accept situations over which she does not have full control, a quality Nina associates with being flexible in the classroom. Nina imagines that this will be similar to her experiences when she was running a catering business from home for which she had to be very organized, though her home life during this period was, as she described laughingly, 'total chaos'.

Tolerance of seemingly chaotic situations is also reflected when Nina watches three video extracts of classroom practice early in the course. One extract is generally seen by other students as an example of disorganized practice with children learning very little. Nina, however, offers a very positive interpretation of what she feels the children are able to achieve, as well as the teacher's overall approach which she describes as child-centred. It appears that the images of the teacher, her relationship with the children and the language she uses are, in many ways, reminiscent of her own style of parenting. Whilst she hopes that her own classroom would be quieter, and that she would make sure that children were listening before she spoke, she still feels that she would do much the same, and particularly values the teacher's ability to put the focus upon the children and not be the dominant personality in the class. This final point indicates her view of how the teacher transacts authority in the classroom, and appears to relate to the way Nina attempts to manage her teaching during the two years of the study.

Within the 'professional dimension', the teacher is seen as a very powerful force in helping children to succeed. From the discussions of her experiences as a parent and as a voluntary helper in her children's school, there emerges a strong orientation towards child-centred education and a belief that the teacher's role centres upon an ability to match and differentiate the curriculum appropriately for each child:

> What I think the teacher has to provide is enthusiasm and the spring-board for the enthusiasm . . . because once they [the children] can absorb something it just goes on. I think that stems from the teacher . . . I think a teacher must be willing and ready to learn along with the children and to tailor the material to the children as much as possible. It's something that worries me and I think it must be terribly difficult. It's one side of it that I'm a bit anxious about. The ability to have a class and tailor material for the whole range of abilities in the class. I think the teacher has to be incredibly sensitive to what's going on and to provide the right stimulus at the right time and to put the right amount of pressure on at the right time and take it off at the right time.

An image of the teacher inspiring children seems strong, and appears to evoke a powerful sense of vocation for Nina. Being with children, deriving enjoyment and enthusiasm from learning, is expected to provide considerable job satisfaction. In talking about this image of teaching, Nina reports that her own child had loved being with a particular teacher the previous year. Now, having recently helped with her class, she is filled with admiration for her, and claims to aspire to emulate her practice. She recalls her son's experience of his final term:

> My number three son, who was in his top infant class last year, came home in the summer term doing snails. He went round the garden getting dozens of snails. She'd already worked out that every child's garden was riddled with snails and the next day every child in the class came back to school with a pet snail and they did snails. They did maths, everything with these snails. He learned about how they worked. One of the things she did was races with snails and she knew what she was doing and throughout the whole thing he was fascinated, as were all the others. They were all absorbed by these ridiculous things in the garden. I felt real admiration for her. But she was enjoying the whole thing as well. I think she thought that the class was such that she'd pick something like that. And something that would appeal to disgusting little boys. She had this great ability to grab the children's interest. I'd like to be able to do that.

Within Nina's views of the professional aspect of the teaching role, there also appears to be a strongly held belief of social justice, and Nina professes that the teacher should help children to acquire 'a picture of themselves which is a good picture that they like looking at, that they know what they're good at and they know how to overcome the difficulties'.

Nina's early thinking about the 'academic dimension' appears to hinge upon the powerful influence of language in children's learning, and she is unsure as yet what part the teacher plays in promoting language development. Already, however,

Nina is able to distinguish between different kinds of language activities which occur in classrooms:

> I'm sure it's very important to learning, the way they learn their language influences the way they actually learn, but what I need to do is clarify my role in that or my prospective role in that. I can see it quite clearly pre-school, I'm not aware of it yet actually in school. Obviously [there's] the language work, but I'm talking about a more pervasive level.

It is Nina's interest in language that also draws her to contemplate teaching Reception children, a position she has previously thought of as little more than child-minding:

> The one thing that's changed is before I started I thought I'd never ever want to teach a Reception class, and now I think I'd love to teach them. I think because of the language. I think I probably could at the end of the day deal with the runny noses and doing up the shoes and taking them to the loo.

At the end of the first year, she talks enthusiastically about the profession, liking what she terms its 'wholeness' and 'busy-ness'. It is important to her that she can enjoy a relationship with the children that is satisfying at a personal level, whilst at a professional level she is responsible for managing their learning which she visualizes as occurring within classrooms where children are bustling, enthusiastic and active. Equally, there is considerable academic challenge to be derived from understanding subject knowledge which must then be made relevant to children's education: 'I can go as deeply into it as I want to and then bring it down to their level academically. That's the real pull . . .' Summarizing her motivation to teach, she says: 'I like the fact that it incorporates all of me and everything I've been and am, and that I can use my whole self . . .'

Year One — Learning to Teach

Nina had previously dismissed the idea of training under the articled teacher scheme because she wanted to be a student: 'I didn't want the responsibility for the children's learning before I knew what I was really taking on.' Nina felt that the PGCE course would allow her the 'time to learn how to put theory into practice. How to teach and how to learn what I'm going to teach in the most efficient way'.

Early in the course, she compares her experiences of learning to teach with her learning during her degree studies:

> I'm aware that it's completely different and that I'm working at a different
> — I can't say level because it assumes that one is higher than the other
> — but in a different *sense*, in that it was me and the language, me interacting

with one other thing. [Now] I've got to take into account this whole body
of knowledge and then look at the little bodies that are wandering around
doing it. But there's a third party involved and because of that I think the
academic level is not as high as that which I used to aim at at university.
But I suppose that's natural. I know there's a difference because I can feel
it. I feel I work in a different way, that I think in a different way.

By the end of the first term, however, Nina is elated. She has particularly enjoyed
the English and maths sessions in college. She enthuses that the English tutor had
'everyone on the edge of their seats' and that the sessions confirmed and extended
her understanding of the importance of language development and literacy: 'It was
what I had always wanted to hear. One afternoon . . . I sat there and thought "I
should have done this years ago."'

Whilst she had, in fact, expected the college to teach her more 'facts', Nina
has come to the conclusion that this is unnecessary: 'What I need to be shown
is how I can learn them and then teach them and learn through teaching them.'
Although her ideas appear to have shifted, in fact this is consistent with her views
about the value of her degree studies which she expressed prior to the course: 'It's
how you acquire the knowledge and that's what a degree gives you more than anything. Whatever the subject. You eventually learn how to learn. And how to apply.'

After several visits to the school, Nina anticipates her first practice and she has
clear ideas about what she hopes to learn. For example, she is aware that, unlike
experienced teachers, she does not have a whole picture of the curriculum, the children and how they learn, and that this prevents her from being able to act spontane-
ously in response to a child and so promote learning effectively:

> I think one of the things I'd like to learn is how to pick up children's
> responses — it's not until I come back and think about them and it's too
> late that I realize what was going on. That must take years, but I wish
> when they say something I could think 'That's it. That's what they're
> doing.' But I miss it and I notice I've missed it a couple of times, even
> on the two days. I've missed the cues that they're giving . . . I think that's
> from lack of understanding on my part. And this is where I think the
> learning theories come in.

At the end of the three-week placement, Nina clearly makes connections with
previous ideas that she has expressed, her learning within college as well as her
developing ideas within school. Early in the practice she is asked to write a story
with a group of children who, although able to articulate good ideas, have a lot of
difficulty in writing. Nina is initially resistant to the teacher's suggestion that she
acts as the scribe for the children, believing that the children should do the work themselves in order to learn. However, after seeing the quality of the children's stories,
their enthusiasm and enjoyment, Nina accepts that this is a very useful language
activity from which the teacher could then develop writing activities including word
processing. Excited by her new insights, Nina reports:

I saw this enormous gap between what they can actually put down on paper at that age and what they can say. I hadn't realized it was so enormous. I think there was a top group in the class and they were much better at it, but I then actually began to wonder whether this same gap existed. Whether, because their writing was better, I assumed that they were expressing themselves through their writing and then I began to wonder if they would be expressing themselves in a completely different way . . . I didn't go much further than that.

Nina's last comment typifies the discussions of her emerging understanding of classroom practice. It seems that she readily accepts having partially formed ideas, and is confident that ultimately she will make sense of what she sees. Later in the practice, Nina applies her newly developed ideas and challenges some of the things she is asked to undertake. For example, she is adamant that there is no value for the children in having to write a story after a language activity which involves examining 'funny shaped parcels with funny things rattling inside' and then brainstorming to produce vocabulary. Nina's views appear to have shifted so far that she now indignantly attacks the teacher's ideas and does not appear to consider that perhaps the teacher had different purposes in mind for each activity:

I had pages of words which I'd written down for them and there was one group which was particularly poor at language and when we got to the end of it — three-quarters of an hour talking about it — I would have been quite happy to leave it at that point. But she insisted that they write a story and none of them could write it. She insisted they write a story using these words and they found that far too difficult. I felt it worthwhile as a [oral] language exercise. They'd used these words, listened to them, heard the ones that sounded the same and I felt it was a success up till that point and I wanted to leave it. But there was no way. She wanted something written in the book. That smashed the whole thing for the children because they weren't interested at all.

Over the practice, Nina notices that she is willing to tolerate a greater level of noise and disruption than she had expected: 'It doesn't bother me that they shout particularly if they're lining up.' When she had initially visited the school, Nina was struck by the low level of noise and lack of 'rowdy behaviour' which she associated with children learning and she commented on the good management of the teacher. Observations of Nina at the time and over the subsequent 18 months confirm that she does not appear unduly concerned by noise levels and a fairly high level of off-task behaviour. Nina gives the impression that she is quite easy-going, and that she consciously resists becoming an authoritarian teacher.

In common with many students, Nina identifies incidences when she is able to spark an unknown interest or to 'reach a difficult child' as being high points on the practice. For example, she talks with enthusiasm about her interaction with one child who was inspired by an object she had taken into school in order to make a story interesting:

I never heard him speak, he'd never uttered a sentence. I tried to encourage him to ask his friend to pass a rubber, but he couldn't put the words together. He didn't want to do anything. He was naughty and miserable and really didn't want to be there or like what he was doing. Anyway it had been his birthday the day before and in the morning I asked him something about it and he just didn't tell me. Nothing came out at all. In the afternoon I read them a story called *The Christmas Train* about a little girl who waves a lantern to stop the train from crashing.

I took in the big railway lantern that's out there [outside the house] and Jonathan knew what you put into the lantern, where you put it and I couldn't believe it . . . he knew where the station used to be, what kinds of trains went by. He knew all about how the thing worked, how steam trains worked and it all came out . . . It just astonished me and it really threw me how much he knew. I had thought that he was a dead loss, and I could now shoot myself in the head for it. I know that's a lesson that you can't do that. He was fired by this. So if I've learnt nothing else I've learnt that from my TP.

The first term concludes on a high point, as Nina feels that her skills and knowledge about teaching are developing from a fairly harmonious interplay of theory and practice, and that she is continually excited by the things she is learning both at college and in school: 'I'd be sitting doing something and all that had been thrown at me [college studies] suddenly came back to me and I hadn't expected it to be so relevant.' In the second term, however, prior to her next teaching practice, Nina appears weary and dejected. She has not enjoyed the second term period in college, and feels that her understanding of teaching has not increased. She becomes anxious about this since she anticipates that her responsibility for children's learning when she is in school in the second term will be much greater. As a result, her confidence, even in the skills and knowledge she thought she had acquired, plummets. She explains:

I think it's partly because the course itself is so impersonal. I think that's part of the problem and it hasn't been particularly interesting this term. There's been nothing I've related to at all and I think that's partly to do with it. I know a lot of people have had problems with the course this term because it hasn't measured up, and I don't know if that's the way it's affected me, but it makes me think I can't do it. I just have no confidence going into school . . . I'm very, very apprehensive about approaching many of the subjects, particularly the subjects we've done this term. I can see as I plan out the work that I'm pinning my hopes on maths and language and thinking that if every child progresses in those two at least I'll know that what I'm thinking is right.

Everything has just seemed so . . . it's terribly difficult to put into words, but it hasn't had the impact that last term had. If I try to quantify what I've learnt in the various areas I can quantify what I've learnt about teaching children. What I didn't know beforehand. Things that didn't enter my head. Now I know that's the way they have to do it and the same applies to language. Even to art. I hated the art course and felt totally intimidated, I hated it, but even so I can see that I've learnt something about teaching children art and I can't say that about design and technology. I don't know if I learnt anything. I don't know what it is. That's been the main back-stepper. History and geography, I don't think I learnt anything. I picked up the odd fact but not about how to teach. PE [physical education] lessons have ostensibly been quite good, but there's something missing. There's a basis missing. I don't know whether it's because I haven't got the basic skills.

From the start, Nina has been concerned about the lack of seminars and opportunities to discuss ideas. She regards these as valuable for her own learning, enabling her to explore and reflect on issues in depth with a tutor and other students. For Nina, the interpersonal dimension of seminars is an important aspect of learning. In their absence, she reports feeling quite isolated and frustrated because 'as far as my learning as a teacher is concerned, I don't have relationships in college which affect that, apart from friends. There is no talking it through with feedback'.

It also transpires that Nina has found the pace of the course during the second term too slow. In addition, she reports being uncomfortable about her next placement which is in a school that she describes as having a 'homey attitude'. The small, village, community school seems to be associated in her mind with a stereotype of intellectually unstimulating, nanny-like teachers, and seems to offer an ethos in which she anticipates feeling distinctly uncomfortable:

> I'm not a country person at all. I don't like the palsy-walsy attitude. Not that I don't like the teachers being friendly, they're incredibly friendly and very nice . . . It's something to do with a certain amount of anonymity which I need to maintain, and I feel more at ease in large communities than in small country villages.

Nina, however, appears to settle well in the school, and claims to be learning a lot from the class teacher. She frequently reports that she is happiest when 'everything's going on at once' and repeatedly asserts her preference for a busy atmosphere within the classroom.

Nina is disapproving of the widespread practice of ability grouping that she sees in her first school. In her second practice, however, the class teacher uses mixed ability grouping, although occasionally she will separate the Year 1s from the Reception class for some activities. This strikes Nina as sensitive teaching with the teacher putting children together who might mutually benefit in some way, and Nina observes several activities where she believes this works well. She is particularly struck by one example when the teacher boosted the confidence of one boy, who had difficulty reading, by pairing him with another child on a computer task at which she knew he could readily succeed.

During the second practice it appears that Nina's fears about her teaching are being addressed in a very positive way by the class teacher. Nina's personality is such that it seems she can readily and openly articulate her concerns, without giving the impression that she is incompetent, or lacking in ability. Nina reports that the class teacher encourages her to focus upon specific aspects of teaching when she is observing, and claims that the teacher 'taught me how to watch . . . One of the things was that she told me to watch where she put herself in the class, how she moved. We're told these things in college but it's decontextualized'.

Nina reports that the class teacher believes student teachers learn through their own experience, and she therefore encourages Nina to try things out for herself. Nina appears anxious in doing so, but feels that she is learning many valuable lessons from her mistakes. She likens the experience to learning another language: 'the thing learning to teach reminds me most of was learning another language. Initially you think "Panic, panic. I can't do this," and gradually you relax a bit and take a step at a time and you gain confidence to fall flat on your face'. 'Falling flat on her face' occurs several times for Nina, particularly with regard to maths when she misjudges the children's ability and assumes more knowledge and understanding than they have. For example, on one occasion she asks a group of Year 1 children if a piece of Plasticine still weighed the same when only its shape was changed. Nina is somewhat amazed that one boy denied that the weight was the same 'till he was blue in the face', and she is confused as to how children develop conservation of weight and what her role in developing their understanding might be. Expressing her surprise at the mismatch between her assumptions about children's abilities and what they can actually do, and how they seem to learn, characterizes many of her reflections throughout the two years:

> I don't know whether they learn it by touching it and feeling it and holding it. I don't think they learn it from seeing it on a picture. They have to do it. That's one of the things that I've learnt in a big way. They don't really learn very much from me speaking. Comparatively, they learn very little from me speaking or seeing it on a picture. They learn it from doing it. Sometimes they don't even learn it from that.
>
> I think my role was to ask the questions that would give the answers to know their understanding to enable me to go onto the next bit. However, I'm very aware that I'm not very good at asking the questions yet. I asked three questions where one would do and sometimes I word them incorrectly and don't get what I want out of it. I feel I should ask one or two essential questions and get the answers I need to know. My role is a little confused at the moment.

After the practice, Nina reports that her confidence has been sufficiently lifted and that she is now ready to take on board the challenge of her final practice within a large urban primary school, which uses team-teaching, and an integrated approach. Nina finds that the expectations are much greater within this school; that all activities are carefully planned and have a purpose, and she is excited by what she perceives as a high level of professionalism within the school. She is able to sharpen her ideas about teaching by comparing her experiences:

> Really it's theory into practice on this one. The management side of it. It's suddenly all fallen into place and I've realized it's very hard work. I don't want to say anything that is critical of another teacher but Mrs H. [second practice] gave the children something, but I see the way the college says to do it is the way it's being done in [this school] and it's good for me to see it being done in that way because I realize it's in fact an extremely efficient way of teaching a large variety of children, that it works. It's just an enormous amount of work. It's so enormous I just don't know where to start. Every activity has to have an aim or an objective within it. I know that. But in the other schools, there were a lot of activities that went on that didn't have an aim or objective and they didn't fit in anywhere in the pattern. They kept the children occupied while the teacher was doing something else. Now that doesn't happen there. Everything they do is done with purpose, even if they can go and choose. She does accept that the little ones choose what they're doing occasionally. It's not pressurised from their point of view, but from mine.

She does, however, question the way the school teaches English and is bemused 'because there seems to be a lot of copy writing and emphasis on correct spelling with 5- or 6-year-olds' which surprises her because 'there's a lot of handling stuff, construction of toys, sand and water play, it's all brought into the learning and they do it with a purpose. There's a lot of unwritten maths activity, so it surprised me that this was the approach to writing. I don't know whether the parents demand a certain level of spelling and that's what they think learning to write is'. Within college, a developmental approach to writing is advocated, which emphasizes communication rather than strict adherence to rules, and this has always married well with Nina's beliefs about young children's language. On her second practice, such an approach was used, and Nina reports that children of the same age produced very imaginative work. It does not seem to occur to Nina, however, that contextual and environmental factors, such as different catchment areas, may affect practice.

Here the role the class teacher adopts differs from the second practice and Nina feels that this is what she needs. She admires the teacher's business-like approach, and soon decides that she would like to teach like her. Having regained her confidence, she feels that she can now cope with working with someone who seems less tolerant of mistakes. She senses, without any resentment, that the class teacher feels that her plans are sometimes not up to standard because she frequently ensures that Nina is clear in her thinking about how the lesson will proceed, and that she has the resources to hand. Nina is appreciative, however, of her class teacher's frequent support:

> We were doing a shape activity with wooden bricks and the whole class became so noisy because the children were knocking them on the table. So

> she said 'Sit them on the carpet' and that's the kind of thing I didn't
> realize — that the carpet was available for sitting on. It was just such a
> simple thing. When we're planning it, she'll go through that. Now, I
> hadn't planned that activity with her for one reason and another . . . To a
> certain extent she's leading me through. We plan the day and she'll say
> to me, 'The activities are all right but you can't have those two going on
> together'. Then she'll wait for me to say why not, and it's the leading
> through. If I come to a dead end she will show me the way out. Occasion-
> ally she'll say, 'Do this with them. This is the way to do it.' Now that's
> happened once or twice. I do get the impression that she thinks her way
> is better than mine. It doesn't bother me though.

Nina also reports a difference in the way she is able to deal with her own mistakes. She recalls a time mid-way through the practice when she was aware that a
session was going wrong, and she was able to let events run their course, to stand
back and reflect on what was happening, and then to have the confidence to discuss
what occurred with other teachers:

> I was aware that the session was going wrong and I tried to think, 'Forget
> about this. It finishes in 15 minutes. Just leave it going wrong and watch
> and see what you've done wrong.' I don't think I'd have been able to do
> that [before]. I think I would have tried to salvage what was left. But I left
> it and thought they could do it again.
>
> I sat down with Jane and Kate at lunchtime and we talked about it
> and part of the problem was my position in the classroom. The other part
> of the problem was the nature of the activity I'd given the other children
> I was not teaching. It was one that needed someone watching over them.
> The other question about it was what were they learning from one of the
> other activities that was going on? I was just using it as a babysitter. I saw
> that and I picked out the fact that this one group weren't really learning
> anything because there was nobody there. The other group kept coming to
> me. But they said I was sitting in the wrong place . . . It was during this
> 10-minute period that I realized what was wrong. But I need someone
> when I say, 'That activity went wrong because the work I prepared meant
> that they had to keep coming to me so I couldn't teach the children I was
> with', to say 'Yes'. Just as I need someone to reassure me that what I did
> was right.

What also emerges quite strongly during this practice is her style of pupil management and the way in which Nina uses humour. On visits, the atmosphere was
generally noted as 'happy', 'bustling' and 'quite noisy' which is how Nina has often
stated she hoped her classroom would be. It was also noted that Nina enjoys a
good relationship with the children, she watches the children's faces, really listening to what the children have to say, and generally creates a relaxed but stimulating atmosphere in the classroom. When she is with the children on the carpet,

Nina holds the children's attention well, and is calm and quietly spoken. She gives very clear instructions, and checks that the children have understood their tasks before they are sent off to their groups. However, when the classroom activities are actually under way, there is the sense that, although the children are never out of control, Nina is not always on top of what the children are doing, and on a number of occasions, the children have done a task incorrectly or started to wander off-task. Her response to such events is to use a form of humour which seems to be intended to counterbalance her exasperation or annoyance, such as 'Oh, Michael!' or 'And what do we think we are doing?' accompanied by a wry smile. Nina is generally able to make her exclamations good humoured, such as the time she reprimands a group of children who are sprawled across a table and she tells them, 'Come on you lot, *off* the table!' On this occasion the children react immediately. At other times, they appear to be unsure whether she is telling them off or not, particularly when it may not be quite so clear to the children that they are doing something wrong. As a result, the children do not always respond to her requests or directions first time, and consequently she has to repeat herself which again contributes to the noise level.

Her use of humour in control, which often relies on quite a high level of linguistic understanding, seems to have originated from her relationship with her own four children, which Nina occasionally talks about:

> . . . if I tell my children to be quiet, on occasion I will shout at them in Italian to be quiet. They know that when I shout in Italian to be quiet it's not deadly serious, but if I then go on to shout in English they know it's serious . . . My children know that I'm half-joking when I shout in Italian.

There are also moments when Nina's irritation is barely disguised, and she does give vent to her annoyance. Nina recognizes that this facet of her personality shows itself within her teaching, and it bothers her as she realizes some children can be upset by her occasionally fiery approach, a point which had emerged in her second practice, and which she refers to at various times throughout the two years when she consciously stops herself from over-reacting:

> When I was in H., there was . . . one very sweet girl [who] tipped a pile of earth over the table. I was up to here and I shouted 'Oh Lucy!' and she burst into tears. I felt awful and thought I'd never do it again.

Throughout the final practice, when she now takes responsibility for the whole class, Nina's greatest challenges lie in organizing and managing group work. The children are grouped according to ability, a practice which Nina had previously criticized because she felt that individual needs could not be met as the children were seen as a homogenous group in all subjects. Now her views have shifted quite noticeably, and she re-evaluates how effective the teaching and learning had been in her previous school. For the first time, she is required to produce rigorous and detailed plans, as well as undertake regular assessments. Through this process she realizes that, for some children, she is building a 'detailed picture' and so her ability to match and differentiate appropriately is significantly improved. Nevertheless, Nina still feels that she has much to learn because she finds having to plan for, and teach, four groups of children, for whom she aims to provide purposeful activities, where she can teach one group and give varying levels of independent work to others, extremely difficult.

> On this TP . . . [planning has] become much more involved and complicated because of the demands of the teacher. On the last TP . . . I don't think I did think about it to the same extent. I certainly didn't put it down on paper in the same way, about who was going to be doing what. Now I'm becoming aware of what individual children are going to be doing. But the work is really intensive . . . I feel I can't do it enough because I don't know the children enough and in the cases I do do it, I know the children and their individual needs. I think it's demanded of me because they do plan for individual children and because of the structure of the planning and the way the children are grouped and the way the whole school operates, it's quite feasible to do it. In the other school it would have been much more difficult to plan for individual children, simply because they weren't grouped in the same way. Here, I make a core activity and adapt it slightly to individualize it, but that wouldn't have been possible in the other school . . . I think I've still got a lot to learn. I'm not very good at working out how long children take to do things and this kind of thing, and how to blend the activities. I'm also not very good at using the teaching activities to their full. I realize that teaching time is limited for each child. Each child gets a small amount of time and I want to maximize that. I've still got to learn how to do that . . . The more strictly I plan, the more teaching time I manage to give to each child, but I also find that . . . [I am] more careful . . . in considering the activities that I'm not teaching . . . if I consider it very carefully I can give them activities that they can actually get on with. Otherwise, if I don't plan it properly, they have to get up every 30 seconds and come and ask me, then it seems that they forget how to get on with it for themselves.

As a teacher of young children, Nina is expected to utilize an integrated approach to the curriculum. Before joining the course, she had felt that this was a good way to structure the curriculum since her own children had often been excited by integrated topics at school. However, at the end of the first year, having taught a topic on minibeasts, she now begins to question what an integrated approach actually amounts to, whether it is always justified and whether it genuinely leads to children's learning:

> I get very confused about this topic approach. It doesn't do a great deal for me. When you talk about integrated learning you mean that the children understand that the learning in one area has relevance to other areas

of the world. So if they learn about minibeasts, which is what they were doing, this has relevance to the soil because some of them live there, to man, and that's an integrated approach. For me to then say that it has relevance to creative work because they can write stories and do paintings is stretching the meaning of integrated a bit. I don't think that is actually integrating . . . And I do think that in the areas where learning is truly integrated it is only sensible to teach children that way, but I don't think it's as widespread as it's made out to be. I think there are some areas where it's not actually integrated in the pure sense of the word. It's integrated because the teacher presents it in that way, but in my mind it's not part of the same . . . It's partly due to a confusion about what it means. In my mind, when I think of beasts and soil I think about where they live, what they eat and how they affect me, which is integrating it. But I don't think how I can paint them or what colours they are. So it's not integrated. It's me using it as a vehicle for another subject, but it's not an integrated curriculum. I don't think, 'I'd like to paint a butterfly'.

. . . if you were doing light, there's a lot of knowledge you can gain about light and the way it works from artwork. And that's an obvious integration of knowledge. And observational work is always there. That applies across the board and it's only one aspect of art. But it's not being true to the spirit of integration if you call the whole thing integration. If I apply integration to doing artwork with light and colour, etc., and if I apply that same integration to when I'm painting minibeasts, I don't think it has that same value of knowledge being gained about the subject they're studying through doing it. I don't know how much knowledge of beasts they gained from doing that wonderful artwork.

Year Two — Being a Newly Qualified Teacher

Nina begins the next academic year without a job. She undertakes voluntary work within the school with the Reception class, working with the same class teacher as before. Whilst she is anxious about her prospects of ever being employed, she feels that she benefits a great deal from the return to teaching a single group of children without having the responsibility of the whole class:

I have time to think about it before I do it, while I'm doing it and after I've done it, which is because I'm not thinking about the three other activities going on in the classroom and the rest of the children and what I'm going to do later on. I think I can actually learn quite a lot . . .

At the same time, observing other teachers allows Nina to compare her style of teaching with theirs. She realizes that her own teaching is somewhat intense:

I don't know whether it's in my head like that, but it all seems slightly frenetic when I do it, and yet it seems terribly relaxed when anyone else does it. I don't know if that's me or whether it's because the activities I'm giving the children to do are too intense. I think I probably have learnt that in these two weeks. I don't need to pressurize all the time. I keep thinking it was because I was doing a TP and I had to show them what I could do . . . I think I overestimated totally very often what the children needed to do and I thought I had to keep them doing activities that were directly linked with the NC [National Curriculum] all the time I was there, which isn't necessary.

Working in a supportive role also enables Nina to observe how staff introduce Reception children to classroom activities, and how they aim to build up the skills and routines that the children will need later in the year:

I think the main thing I've learned or seen in action is how much it takes to get Reception children into gear really . . . All of us spend a lot of time teaching them how to do things, how to wash their hands, put the toys away, how to play with this game, so that they can actually do something. There's very little that goes on initially that has to do with academic subjects. They do very little reading or writing. It's more manipulative things. They use the time to judge where the children are. I've never seen it clearly before . . . I think I would have over-estimated their ability to cope and do things. I think last Wednesday, Jane was sitting on the mat with a group of them with the train set and she was showing them how it fitted together and how they played with it. Now I think I would have said, 'There's the train set. Go and play with it'. She said I couldn't do that because they don't play with it properly and then you're stuck with that problem for the rest of the year. They'd just fool around. I don't think I would have realized how crucial that was. The other thing that was interesting is that they spend half the time doing a particular activity. Whereas when I was there in the summer there were four or five Reception activities in a day, they're doing four activities in a morning because they can't concentrate that well. That was quite enlightening. I would like to teach a Reception class.

Nina claims that her observations are now more finely tuned and that she can make much more sense of what is going on in classrooms generally. From her observations, she can infer the purpose behind activities, and is in a better position to identify the ideas and activities that she would like to use herself. For example, she makes notes of the teacher's ways of interacting with the children on the carpet and adds these to her own repertoire, recognizing their importance for management. When she visits her children's school as a parent helper, she can also more readily appreciate what the teacher is attempting to do:

The children were playing games, which was fine, and the teacher was reading with each individual child throughout the afternoon. I started to look at the games they were playing and it was all good stuff. But to an untutored observer it would have looked as though she was giving them games to play so that she could get on with the readers, which she was to a certain extent. But they weren't playing games that were unrelated to things they had to do and learn in the immediate future. They were given huge buckets of pine cones and plastic mice of different shapes and sizes and they were sorting. There wasn't anything you could remotely criticize because they weren't wasting time. Had I been a parent a year ago looking through that window I would have been horrified. But not now. So I think I look at things completely differently. I can see that they have to have these skills so that they can do things.

Towards the end of term, Nina is successfully interviewed for a full-time post, and so begins the spring term team-teaching another Reception/Year 1 class, which is partly shared with another teacher. Nina describes the organization:

I start off the day with my registration group, which is Year 1 and Reception. Mary [also] has a mixed class. It's really a pastoral class more than anything else and then we swap so there are certain periods of time [3 weeks] when I'll be taking the Year 1 class and she'll be taking Reception and at other times I'll be taking Reception and she'll be taking Year 1.

The first visit to her new classroom takes place within a month of the start of the spring term. At that time, Nina seems very much at ease. She appears to have a good relationship with the children and with staff. Her classroom, as always, is characterized by quite a high level of noise and movement. Her activities are well organized and the children are busy and involved in the activities that have been set for them. Nina gives the impression of allowing the children a good deal of freedom and does not feel that she needs to exert a high level of control.

Professional Relationships and Support Networks

Throughout the rest of the year, Nina acknowledges the important role her colleague, Mary, plays in her development. Working in adjacent teaching areas, the two are able to discuss problems as they arise, and Nina feels that, as they are teaching the same children, she is not encroaching upon Mary's time, and that Mary actually enjoys talking over problems with her. As Nina had recognized in the first year, talking through problems and ideas is very important to her as verbalizing helps her to learn.

She has ready access to a very experienced teacher's craft and subject knowledge, the complexity of which she quickly appreciates. Being able to check out her understandings with an experienced teacher greatly adds to her confidence. For example, in thinking about teaching science to young children, Nina confidently asserts that unlike English and maths, there is little to be gained from recording, either from the point of view children's learning or for assessment purposes. Nina explains why she feels so sure about these views: 'I'm able to go and say to Mary "I think such and such" and she'll say "Yes, that's right". So that's what she said about the recording!'

Throughout the remaining two terms such discussions and advice are referred to constantly, and her official mentor, Julia, the class teacher and head of infants with whom she worked previously, provides her with help and guidance about such matters as school policies and longer term assessment plans.

At the end of the year, Nina speaks very highly of the support she has received within the school:

> Magnificent. That's the best thing. Initially my first call of support is Mary who will talk to me about anything and everything I've done. She'll talk me through it and why it might have failed and if I think it's a complete disaster she'll reassure me. She encourages me and hints at things I hadn't any idea about. The nursery nurse is very helpful and will talk about anything we've done with the children or whether I could have done it a different way. She's really experienced, so she's a second support, and then Julia, if I have any other problems . . . of assessment, etc. . . . she's the one I'll go to. The head is very supportive but I've never had recourse to ask him anything because the support system further down is so good. It's magnificent in this school because there's always someone to talk to. The special needs coordinator is always ready to talk about the children you think might need help or if they're having problems in a particular area. I can't fault it at all.

Nina reports that she feels extremely comfortable within the school, and it has never really worried her that within an open-plan setting any mistakes can be seen by everyone. From observations and notes made during that time, Nina's relationship with the other staff appears to be strong. She greets other staff warmly, smiles easily, and readily joins in staffroom conversations. She appears to be well accepted by the staff. In her teaching, she tends to be fairly self-critical, and so invites staff to give advice which she can be seen to try to act upon, even when it seems quite personal. For example, near the end of the two terms as a full-time teacher, she is advised that it is not appropriate to let the children sit on her knee at registration. Nina, without any appearance of resentment, seems genuinely grateful for this piece of advice, and changes what she does in the classroom.

Nina feels that she can be herself, even to the point that she is not concerned that she is sometimes lax in her control of the children and has to shout when they become excited:

> I just feel very relaxed. I felt all along that it was alright for me to make mistakes. I think because it's so open and any mistake I've ever made has been for everyone to see, so there's no point in getting embarrassed. Because the school is that way then it's expected that you make mistakes and it's

a way of learning. So that's one of the things that has made me relax. If I was in a classroom where the door was shut and nobody every knew I'd made a mistake, or heard me shouting at the children, then I'd feel very embarrassed. Yesterday I was yelling at this child because he'd done something he shouldn't and the headmaster walked past and for a split second I thought 'Oh God', but then I thought he'd heard me shouting before so he was used to it. And he's heard all the other teachers shouting, as I have heard. I know there are days when I'm very lax in my control, but because it's open plan I know that other teachers are lax too. Nobody is expected to be perfect and that's good for you.

Children's Learning and the Teacher's Role

Prior to joining the course, Nina had expressed a strong orientation towards child-centred education. She viewed the teacher's role as one of providing the appropriate conditions and stimuli for individual children to learn. As Nina began to work in classrooms, she again emphasized the role of the teacher in relation to children's learning, and identified specific skills, such as helping children to make sense of their experiences through promoting talk, and being able to ask the 'right questions' at the 'right time' — skills which she realized she had still to develop:

> We were doing this maths thing with them and there were two or three times in that when I thought 'mmm' but afterwards, thinking back on it, I realized that I didn't know how to respond. They were talking about what they were doing and as far as I was concerned at the moment they were chatting, but they weren't actually chatting. I didn't know that and I was inept really at the time. I think that ability to pull out the bits that are incredibly relevant is something I need to learn. And learn to be able to do it on the spot, not two weeks afterwards.

In her final practice and in her full-time post, Nina retains this view of the teacher as facilitator. This is also reflected within the school's existing system of classroom organization, in that the children are divided into several small groups for large parts of the day, with the teacher attaching herself to one group at a time in order to undertake a specific teaching task, typifying the approach widely used in early years education.

As Nina continues to use this form of organization for her own class, she seems to develop a greater sense of ownership and purpose. She becomes increasingly confident in her questioning and responding to children and is clearer about her intentions when she aims to interact with one particular group. For example, in the summer term, Nina discusses geography work she has just undertaken with a group:

> There was . . . writing about postcards, which was part of the geography because we'd done all that work on the landscape and we've been doing

masses of geography and environment. So it was in the context of that that it gave an excuse for some writing and also for them to look at things and they can understand what they're seeing. There was one picture I held up this morning that was very obviously a river. Two children said it was the sea. And when I asked those who thought it was a river why they thought it wasn't the sea, they said there were trees on the side and there was no sand and there were two sides to it. That kind of thing. It was that that I was looking for as well as the writing.

Even though Nina feels that she has developed the skills which allow her to respond quite well to the children, she continues to be perplexed when they seem unable to learn. When children fail to learn or are unable to tackle a particular task, Nina partly blames herself because she is sure that she often 'overloads' the tasks as she still cannot 'break down concepts step by step'. By the end of the summer term, however, Nina has begun to look for other reasons, speculating that aspects of the National Curriculum lack relevance for some children, demanding skills and knowledge even in the earliest stages which some children do not have. She often also attributes difficulties in learning to the limitations in children's language which she thinks are frequently underestimated:

I had never realized that many children had such limited language. I knew that their language was a vehicle for every learning that they were going to do and I can see that it is. Sometimes I think I need to sit and teach these children to talk before they can do anything else. Before they learn to read or write or any other literary thing. Maths, I feel they can cope with, but science, history, geography — I wonder what is the point of trying to teach these children . . . I can't see the point of trying to teach them to describe a time in the past when they still can't describe themselves. They're not able to talk coherently about something they're very familiar with. That's what I should be teaching them. To talk rather than about the past and the world around them. [But] I've got to teach them history and geography and science. I have no option. I find it very difficult though. It gets to a point where . . . the activity is hindered because they find it difficult to talk and they don't know about the subject. The children who are articulate and find it easier can learn about the subject because they can express themselves and say something . . . I do the best I can if the children have the language, but it sometimes pains me that the children who have the language have access to everything and yet the ones who haven't are denied access. They can't articulate what they're seeing. They feel, but getting their opinion is another question.

Nina's experiments in teaching drama help her to think of ways of making history and geography accessible to the children, and these lessons also lead her to gain some further insights into the importance of practical experience in children's learning:

I suddenly realized for the first time . . . that drama for those children is a very effective way of learning and afterwards they showed that had been the case. All the little nuggets of information I wanted stored were stored as pictures in their mind because they were doing it. I realized that had been an effective piece of teaching, planning, everything. I thought I'd remember that and do it again and we did that last week with the castle and it worked again. So I thought I was right. It was particularly good for those children . . . because they're the Year 1 children and . . . although they have to learn things like history and geography they haven't yet got the skills of story and reading and writing and taking information from books. One of the ways they learn is still by touch, by doing things with their body. One of the best ways of teaching them their letters I've found is having the letters there, solid plastic things. It has to be tangible and I think that's why it works. It's at the level they're at and they can actually understand what the whole thing is about.

Towards the end of the study, Nina starts to piece together her views and experiences. She concludes somewhat dejectedly that many of the children in her school begin their school lives with serious disadvantages. School, she argues, can never compensate for the vast experiences which children need to acquire at home. In the final interview, she reflects on her ideas about teaching and re-evaluates the role of the teacher:

I thought that the teacher was more important in the child's learning than the teacher actually is. I think the parent is more important and crucial. The children who learn most easily are the children who have parental backup. The ones who achieve and progress and learn quickly are the ones who've had a lot of input before they came to school. It seems even children who are not particularly bright but who have a lot of parental concern or interest achieve more than brighter children who have no parental concern at all . . . To a certain extent I have to try and put in what is lacking. I have to give them some reason to want to achieve, which generally means self-motivation . . .

So I think for children who have a lot of background and experience outside school, school provides a very structured environment and a place in which they can then learn to be part of society. For those who don't have any input at home it has to provide something that home should provide as well. So it has to provide the story-telling and then lend an ear when they're crying, and understanding, going shopping, all this kind of thing that doesn't always come from home. Does that sound terribly callous? I worry very much that I do the children down. But I feel that unless I accept them as they are then I can't teach them. If I say, 'Yes, you have bags of imagination and you're motivated and have had everything necessary at home,' then it's a bit unfair to them because they're not like that. I don't mind how they are, but I have to accept them as they are and start from there, not treat them as I would like them to be or how someone else is.

Further Constraints on Nina's Teaching

As she gains experience as a full-time teacher, Nina becomes more confident in her opinions about curricular issues, and is able to evaluate various materials and approaches used within the school. Whilst some of her ideas are still only partially formed, she is much more sensitive in her second year to the constraints which temper what she would ideally like to achieve in practice. For example, early in the summer term she voices her misgivings about the *Letterland* system which is used for teaching phonics. Although she hasn't fully articulated them, Nina expresses quite strong concerns, influenced partly by Mary, about its 'lack of relevance', arguing that she cannot see the value of isolating sounds in such an artificial way. However, she is not able to offer evidence that children are not learning from the system, and accepts that some do seem to benefit. At the end of the day, she is not prepared to challenge the existing practice and accepts, albeit without conviction, that she will teach *Letterland*:

> The *Letterland* system I really don't like, but it's used in school. The argument for it is that it helps the children remember sounds and letters. I don't know whether it generates an enthusiasm for these characters which they then cannot apply to the sounds as part of the language. I'm not terribly keen on systems that isolate sounds. I've no idea why you have to call an n a 'nu' or Naughty Nick. I don't like it . . . I just think that they make no sense — a Kicking King or Impy Ink. These children haven't the foggiest idea what ink is. I had to bring in a bottle of ink to show them. Yellow Yo Yo Man . . . I don't like it [but] I have to do it. I have no option and I wouldn't change it. I have no desire to change the system, so I'm happy to do it, but I do it without any feelings.

However, Nina is more resolved in her objection to the daily silent reading time at the beginning of each afternoon, which the whole school is supposed to follow:

> Mary laughs at me but I don't see the point of that silent reading. I don't see the point of that at all. I never did . . . Because there's not enough structure to it. I really don't think it's relevant to Reception children or even Year 1 children.

On this occasion, her opinions are sufficiently strongly held that she has formulated an alternative plan as to how she would use the time: 'If there was time and space, which there isn't . . . I'd select books for them and I'd also have an area where they could go and write and draw and sit quietly and talk to their friends . . .' She is not able to put this into action, however, partly because she feels the pressure that this is a whole school policy matter, partly because of the lack of available space, but mainly because of the enormous demands that managing group work places upon her time and energy. At the end of the year, Nina still experiences these demands:

> I've got so many other things to think about. The most difficult thing is to find an activity, because when I teach I want to be like I was this afternoon, have their total attention and I want to be able to give them my total attention. There are very few things that the Reception children can do without standing up and coming up to me and then I'm taking my attention away from these children who I'm trying to teach. That's what I find most difficult, finding activities that aren't nonsensical, that have some learning in them, that they can get on with and do without coming up to me every two minutes and asking about what they should do . . . The top half of the class isn't bad and if I ask them to sit there and I'll come to them, then they'll do that. They'll get on and do what they can but they don't come to speak to me. But there's very little the tiny ones can do without actually coming to me. They get frustrated. I give them something like a maths thing and they get frustrated and bored and they start chatting.

Critical of the silent reading policy, on occasions she defiantly carries out activities like story-telling instead, which gives her some satisfaction that she is retaining her integrity and using the time in a more productive way, although she is somewhat concerned what the head might say if he saw what she was doing:

> I will do something about it, but at the moment, fair enough. I don't like that at all. I like that least, having this 20 minutes. It's considered sacrosanct, and yet we're allowed to shove it out of the way to go and do PE [physical education] or something. I'm not allowed to use that time to read them a story and sometimes I do and I sit there quaking in case Jack comes in and catches me . . . !

Subject Knowledge and Developing Understandings of the Core Curriculum

During the final two terms, Nina's reflections about her own subject knowledge become more and more sustained, and her ideas about the relationship between language and learning in different subject areas become more developed. In discussing the mathematics curriculum in the spring term, she comments:

> The other thing I find with maths is that the articulate children appear to be better [than they actually are]. They can actually cover up their lack of understanding of number concepts by the way that they can understand instructions or all the rest of it. Ben . . . I sometimes wonder if he's understood these maths concepts, but he appears to because he's articulate. It's

very fuzzy in my head at the moment because it goes round so much. I spend a lot of time talking to them and initially I felt terribly guilty about it, but now I think they need it, especially the little tiny tots. They need to be asked a question and for me to elicit a response.

One of her prime concerns in mathematics is pitching tasks at the appropriate level. Sometimes she claims to be 'completely skew-whiff' in her understanding of the complexity of the tasks she sets. For example, she discusses a money activity developed from a visit to a local museum:

We'd been doing the local area and they went to visit the sweet shop at the Black Country Museum, so we made a shop and they take it in turns to go into the shop and while they're there they have to make a list of three things they've bought and how much it costs them. They make up the prices, make the sweets, decorate the posters. So I felt that [the top] group had to take it a bit further and I wanted something down in a book. So I gave them prices and said, 'In separate weeks you've got three sets of 20p coins and the first week you go into the shop and buy two things, how much does it cost altogether?' I did it with them. 'And how much change do you get from 20p?' . . . 'The next week you go and buy something different.' We did have the problem that there were only five things to buy and they had to work out if they could have a different combination. So one week they could buy rock and chocolate, and the next ice-cream and chocolate . . . then I talked to Mary afterwards and she said it was level 2 stuff and I didn't see it in terms of levels at all. I thought it was one of the simplest problem-solving activities I could give them. But then we looked through the books and she was right. Through talking to her, I realized I'd put one step too many in. I could have asked them 'You buy these things. They cost 16p. How much change do you get?' or 'How much does it cost you to buy these two things?' but to ask them to do the two was one step too many at this stage and it was this that was flooring them.

Throughout the two years, Nina remains perplexed by her seeming inability to match tasks appropriately, but continues to analyse her mistakes, and steadily appreciates that teaching and learning mathematics is more complex than she had originally imagined. She wonders whether her inability to apply what she has learned from one situation to another is similar to the children's experiences in maths, theorizing that each time the children face a problem in a new context, they do not recognize which number operation they need to apply, thus implying that they have not yet fully acquired the concept.

I must learn from my mistakes. I had, but the thing I find difficult is that if you give these children numbers under ten you think you're giving them work that isn't worth doing, so the numbers they deal with are between ten and twenty. Now if I gave them a page of subtraction within 25 or 30, most of them would rattle them off with no problem, but I didn't understand that there was such a leap between doing a problem-solving activity and using numbers as numbers. Richard is wonderful as an example of that because he will fill in pages and pages of the maths book as if there's no tomorrow, but once you ask him to apply it, he can't do it ... They're having to apply their knowledge. They have to take the experience they have and apply it to something else. It's not just using their experience straight. It has to be something to do with the development of their concept and this ability to be able to take a fact and generalize it. I can't learn from one activity not to set the same thing the next day. I think they must be able to do it and they can't ... It's only within the past few weeks in talking to Mary that I've realized things like that are actually problem solving. In my mind it's an addition ... or a subtraction. 'If there are nine gobstoppers in the jar and a boy buys four how many are left?' To me, that's a subtraction and not a problem-solving activity because I haven't really understood the nature of problem-solving activities for young children.

Nina discusses several maths activities during the spring and summer terms and each time she reiterates her discovery that maths 'progresses in very small steps and although the concept of number can come there's a vast amount that has to be done before that concept of number is understood in all its elements so that they can use and apply it'. By the end of the year she is relieved that she 'has maths more under control' but is still amazed at the length of time it has taken her to master this, and the difficulties she has encountered on the way. Nina tries to pinpoint the influences upon her understanding and, in doing so, reveals the complexity of knowledge growth and the variety of factors that have at different times shaped her understanding and practice of mathematics teaching:

I keep reading that little book we were given — Pamela Liebeck — and I do read that over and over and that takes my mind from the children to the theory and joins them together, but even in that the steps are very big. You can't obviously put everything in the book, but I found that I try to keep that in my head. The children influence me a lot because I thought when you teach a child number 7 or number 6 that they knew it and the next day you could do the next number and I couldn't understand why it didn't work. I've learned a lot and I realize they have to have seven of everything five thousand times before they have any idea of the concept of the number 7. I learn from the children doing things, from my own mistakes and Mary. She'll say to me, 'That's a bit too hard for them.' I still haven't come to terms with problem-solving activities because what I consider an activity is actually level 5 or something.

... a year ago I would have said [college] had played a very important role [in developing my understanding of maths]. [But] At this stage I can only see what I've learned in the past two terms, so to say that it's not played a role is unfair because there was something very important going on while I was doing the maths at college and I learned a lot of things that I hadn't understood at all. But at this stage I realize that what was lacking was the idea that, first of all, children go forward so slowly in maths — not all children, but they can go very slowly. Secondly, how basic was basic. I don't remember at college ever being talked to about how to teach young children the pre-maths concepts like sorting and colour, etc. I might have been and I've forgotten all about it, but I don't remember it. So I had no idea that before they could actually start to count they had to do all this pre-learning skills.

Nina claims that it is her experiences of mathematics teaching that have also mostly influenced how she approaches science, since the former has helped her to appreciate the importance of practical activity. Here she discusses her science teaching with the youngest children in her class:

I'm very aware at this stage, at Reception, that the science is almost all investigation and seeing what they can see of shapes and how it feels and what happens when you touch it, what the things are made of and how they work, rather than trying actually to acquire knowledge about them. If they do acquire any knowledge they'll forget it. Most of them will. It's not the kind of thing they can retain for a long time, so it tends to be more hands-on stuff, try it and see how it works, all this kind of thing.

Nina also talks of how language enters into science, as she feels it does into other areas of the curriculum, and explains how her emphasis on language is partly derived from the role she sees language taking in her own learning. After a science activity in which the children played with a variety of springs and toys containing springs, she comments:

A lot of it wasn't science but language. It's not that they don't know springs stretch, it's that they can't say it. They're very good at deducing things and they could see that the tighter the spring the more difficult it was to pull apart. There were other things involved but they can't see that when they're 5. I personally think that's probably enough at 4 or 5. I don't think they need to go any further. They knew [the spring] bounced. They had a go at that, they had a go at toys . . . what they worked out was that the harder they pressed the further [they] went. They put this into words and tried it out and did it again . . . They were gaining an understanding of the way that things work, forces basically. A greater understanding than they already had . . . they're almost compartmentalizing their knowledge that they've gained from the world around them. I think this is one of the benefits of having a topic system, that they can actually put these things they know from their own life experiences into a useful box and say 'Yes, I know that'. It all tallies up eventually . . . I can think of Ryan, for example, and I don't know what his experiences are, but he was able to bring a spring out of the box and he tried to open it. He said, 'I can't open it.' He said he didn't know why he couldn't stretch it and the girl next to him was Lianne and she was stretching hers. He said it was because hers was all round and his was all apart and he'd worked that out for himself, so his knowledge of how things work was actually quite extended there . . . when I do things like that I find when I've put them into words I can understand better. I don't know whether I just assume that if other people put it into words they can understand. Because of that, I assume that when Ryan puts it into words he understands it better.

By the end of the year, Nina is more confident in her view that, for young children, the science curriculum must involve verbalizing their experiences, and so making sense of them, and that some of the knowledge of science that she feels she is expected to teach can actually only be learned at a later stage:

I think with young children, [science is] a lot about language and how they can verbalise it. Sometimes I feel quite ambivalent about the whole thing because the last science activity I did with them was material, so we had a whole collection of different kinds of stone, pumice, etc., and they were allowed to feel them and the children who appeared to be successful in understanding the differences were those who could tell me what the differences were or who could talk about the characteristics of the particular materials. There are children whose language experience is very limited and I don't know whether they experience the characteristics and can't put it into words or they don't experience them at all. One little girl picked up a stone and I asked her to tell me what it was like — it was a smooth, cream coloured stone and that's what I was looking for — and she said it was soft because that was one of the few descriptive words she had. I think I'm actually teaching these children language rather than science at this point. Science is for the ones who have the language to describe it really, and I worry a bit about that.

Conclusion

As Nina reviews her professional development over the two years, she is generally satisfied with her progress, though she feels that learning to teach has been a slow and gradual process. She still reports being uncertain about several areas of her practice, but she gains a sense of achievement from much of her teaching, especially in the field of mathematics. She feels she now understands young children well, and has a much fuller appreciation of how they learn. It is in seeing children learn that she obtains much of her satisfaction: '. . . a sense of the children having made, however tiny, a step forward and being aware that their learning has progressed. Usually you can see it afterwards. Someone will come back and you realize they've learned'.

Although Nina is confident that she is able to perform in the classroom, she says that, 'I wouldn't yet describe myself as a teacher. Not yet. It's too early for that. I still think about how I teach'. She still regrets that she is 'ratty with the children', although admits that she is sometimes 'quite fierce on purpose. I'm selectively fierce because that's one means of control that I have. I have others too [but] it's the one I dislike most, so that's the one I notice most'. She wishes that she could 'be more exciting and less ratty. I'd like to do more exciting things. I always feel the activities I do are quite lacking in imagination really and it takes so long to think about them. They're not really like I am. They're a bit boring and I wish they weren't. So I'd like to change that.' Lack of time for planning, coupled with the pressures of covering the curriculum, managing a class of very active young children, and adjusting to school routines, seem still to be viewed as obstacles preventing Nina from being the teacher that she would ideally like to become.

Chapter 6

Case Study Three — Beth

Introduction

As an articled teacher, Beth's host school is a large infant's within a socially deprived catchment area. Parental support is variable. However, staffing tends to be fairly stable, with the majority of teachers in their 30s and 40s. Whilst the head is seen to provide strong and progressive leadership, it appears that differences exist between the staff in terms of personal philosophies and ideologies. The school enjoys close links with the college, and frequently has a range of students placed there. Built in the 1960s, the school shares a site with the junior school and classrooms are spacious, and self-contained.

During her time in the school, Beth works in several different classes, and in the spring term of the second year, she undertakes her teaching practice in a Reception class.

In the first year Beth spends four weeks in another infant school within a very supportive, middle-class catchment area and, in the second year, is placed within the junior classes of the primary school which her own children attend and where she had undertaken voluntary work in the past. Again the catchment area is principally middle-class with good parental support. In both schools, staff appear mutually supportive and a positive atmosphere prevails.

Entry to Teacher Education

Beth, in her late 30s, was born and raised in Holland. She has pleasant memories of both school and home, describing herself as an 'outgoing and easy-going' child who enjoyed a close relationship with her parents. She recalls their supportive approach to her upbringing:

> My parents were both tremendous listeners and they always gave me an amazing amount of free rein to experiment with my life, but they've always been there so that when I made mistakes they didn't say, 'Well we told you so, you shouldn't have done it.' They listened to why I'd done it and we worked it out together. I felt I had their support and learned an awful lot through that, through being able to make my own mistakes.

Although she describes her schooling as formal, she respected those teachers who talked to children as individuals and made her feel valued — characteristics which she associates with Dutch people:

> I was lucky in that I lived in Holland and I think people are quite open
> and talk about things a lot and you always felt that you could talk and be
> honest about how you felt and how you coped with things.

This level of responsiveness to others is something she yearns to achieve in her
own teaching, and is seen as an intuitive quality.

At 18, when Beth wanted to attend art college, she recounts that her parents insisted that she should learn several languages, with the view that she might
take up a career as a secretary in a multi-lingual company — an occupation which
they regarded highly. She lived in Brussels for a year to learn to speak French, an
experience which she did not enjoy:

> I was desperately unhappy because I'd had no say in this instance. That's
> why it threw me terribly . . . because all of a sudden I was treated like a
> child who was told to go and do something. Before, I had been allowed
> to be my own little person and develop like that. I hated it.

Beth moved from Belgium to Spain where she lived happily with friends for six
months, learning Spanish. Following this, she studied secretarial skills and languages in Rotterdam for a year, and then came to Oxford as an au pair, a job she
'loathed'. Finally, she persuaded her parents to allow her to study art in Oxford,
since she could also improve her spoken English. Here, she met her future husband,
and so settled in England, initially working as a secretary (whilst her husband then
trained as a teacher) and then as an interior designer for a housing firm. Whilst she
had her family, she undertook part-time secretarial work, and also helped at her
children's school, working with small groups of children. Entering a primary school
for the first time since her own education, Beth reports being filled with admiration
for the head, approving of her philosophies about education, as well as the ethos
achieved within the school, which seem to resonate with her feelings about her own
upbringing:

> She believes very strongly that children should learn to love learning, so
> not to be told to do things so that they know things. But that they should
> try and find out for themselves and they should want to find out.

In time, the head and other staff encourage Beth to apply for the articled teacher
scheme, and continue to support her during the course. It is to this school that she
returns for her second placement, and at the end of the course, she is successfully
interviewed for a post there.

Images of Teaching

There are two main aspects of teaching which characterize the ideas and images of
teaching that Beth talks about at the beginning of the course. A parental, caring, and

affective aspect is seen as largely intuitive, consisting of offering children security and a trusting relationship through which they have the confidence to learn, and such images contain a strong moral element. These images seem to have developed partly from the memories of her own childhood, her own style of parenting, as well as experiences as a helper in school. Beth feels comfortable with this aspect of teaching and sees teaching as offering an expression of herself, since she is a very warm person who genuinely likes children. It soon emerges that the need to be encouraged and reassured is very strong for Beth, and this is how she envisages her own learning being nurtured, 'I tend to be the sort of person that needs to be told, "Yes, that's good, fine."'

The second aspect of teaching which she focuses on is discipline, which appears to derive from Beth's understanding that the teacher will have to be firm at times in order to maintain control. However, her ideas about discipline do not appear to relate easily to her self-image, and Beth is unsure how this aspect of the teacher's work will be reconciled within her own practice, as it seems at odds with her personal beliefs and ideas about relating to children.

In thinking about her qualities as a teacher, Beth values highly her rich and varied life experience (including the times, away from home, when she felt lonely and unhappy), believing that this allows her to 'appreciate' things from different perspectives. For example, she reports that her art background has given her an appreciation of the aesthetic appearance of a classroom, as well as an understanding of the intrinsic nature of art, particularly its emotional dimension:

> I think it gives children a chance to really experiment and also to let their feelings out. Nobody tells them, 'That's not neat enough or on the line enough or that sum's not right.' They can do something that nobody can criticize because it has a meaning for all of them. Whatever they're doing, it's something they can have confidence in and they can do it without worrying about what it's going to look like.

Such views are generally reflective of her beliefs about education which contain a deep respect for the individual, and Beth asserts that her primary aim as a teacher will be to equip children,

> ... with a belief in themselves, that they can do what they are asked well, that they feel confident. Obviously you have to teach children to learn to read and write, but it has to be done in a way that the children want to learn ...

Beth admits that her ideas about education have been influenced by her husband, Daniel, an English and drama teacher who is seen by others as an effective, dynamic yet sensitive teacher, popular amongst the pupils. He is described by Beth as someone who 'believes' in children. Over the two years, Daniel, and two particular friends who are also teachers, are referred to by Beth as major sources of support in two important ways: first, they give much emotional support, reassuring

Beth that her ideals are worthy and attainable, while recognizing that Beth is very self-doubting and lacks confidence in her abilities to achieve the high standards which she sets herself. Second, they help Beth to make sense of the difficulties she faces in learning to teach. For example, when Beth first started the course, she expected to be able to talk 'naturally' to children because she liked being with them so much. By the first half-term, Beth finds that, to her frustration, talking and responding to children in a purposeful way now seem to be complex skills which she does not possess and must learn. She reports that it is through talking to others that she can begin to identify what the skills are and how she can learn them:

> It's little examples like when I'm doing story time and I've got the children there and ask them questions and there's one little girl who goes on and on and I don't know how to cope with that . . . She's just talking, the kids are switching off and I don't really know what she's talking about. And things like that. I feel that I don't really know what's going on. Yet when I look at it afterwards I am now beginning to be able to analyse what's been happening and put into place what went wrong and what was happening. Through talking to people who know about these things they put it into words for me and I can then understand that this is a very natural progression that everyone learning to teach will go through. This interaction between children and teacher, that there is some way of making things flow and work and you have to learn. You can't just do that naturally. Some people can, but some people can't. And you can actually learn how to cope with situations. Before it would all have completely overwhelmed me and I wouldn't have known what was happening and I would go home thinking, 'I could never do this. How could I possibly expect to do this?'

Year One — Learning to Teach

Beth's early impressions of her host school stand in sharp contrast to her image of her children's school. She notes that the children are not valued in the way she had expected and which she has come to associate with child-centered, discovery approaches to learning. She does not feel at ease, and has difficulty seeing herself in the role of the teacher:

> I find that so hard at the moment because I really did have a different idea of it before I came into the school . . . My initial idea was a feeling that it would be much more stimulating in the actual classroom: that I would see them mucking in, finding out for themselves, and I find it is all so 'sitting down and putting their heads down and trying to write and read'. I don't find that very stimulating. So I'm totally confused. It's all so suppressed in a sense I feel.

She recognizes that the schools have very different catchment areas, and that the children may come with very different needs, but claims that she is disturbed particularly by the way some teachers discipline the children. To Beth, teachers appear to step in too quickly to reprimand them, and there appears to be little empathy between teachers and pupils in some classrooms. Beth is concerned that she feels so critical, and tries to understand her feelings, as well as to make her views on discipline explicit:

> I know that you need a certain amount of discipline because you lose children. I'm not going to sit in the classroom and talk and have children not even listening, because what is the point of doing anything? But I feel that it is a natural thing that should come forth from your interaction with the children, and that you will know yourself how much to give. I can't see it as something to be set in advance. I think that your person should react to all the children as well and how different they are and then you set up that communication, rather than in advance saying, 'I'm going to do this and this is the way it is' . . . It's a big school and the discipline is right there from the top down because there are 320 children and I suppose you have to have rules and regulations. But I think it's quite strongly emphasized. It's unsettling for me because I've never thought of it like that. I actually like children very much and I know that you can't just like them — you have to be able to help them to listen to you, to have your attention, to be interested in you. But this pure discipline thing in black and white I find very hard.

At this early stage of the course, she reports that she is observing a lot, and that she feels quite helpless at times when she does work with the children because the practice within the school seems at odds with the philosophies of the course. However, some experiences in the classroom serve to reinforce her view that she can communicate with children through her personality, and so manage their behaviour in a very positive way. For example, she recalls the children's reactions to her after telling (rather than reading) a story. Even though she was very nervous during the session, she felt that she had captivated the children's interest by giving something of herself:

> They all came up afterwards and touched me and wanted to shake my hand and say, 'We'll see you tomorrow.' So I think it made them see me as a person in my own right perhaps, not someone who was just reading a story. Someone who was trying to communicate. I noticed really strongly that they all came up and touched me. Just touched my legs and said, 'See you tomorrow,' and they've not done that before. Perhaps it's a communication thing, that you're showing some of yourself to them as well . . . I could only work like that, truly communicating. By truly sitting down with children and listening to what they're saying and replying and working things out together and I think also just listening is incredibly important.

Children have to say what they are thinking and feeling, what goes on in their little heads.

For Beth, this session exemplifies what she hopes to achieve in her future teaching. However, she also recognizes that, to date, she has only worked with groups of children, and she postulates that her views and images might change in the light of further experience, particularly as she contemplates controlling misbehaviour within a whole class.

I see this more on a group level really. I'm not really seeing this as a class because I haven't done that. So I might change completely once I've been in class. I might see that it's complete bollocks. All my theories about going to do this and that might be rubbish.

Within a few weeks, Beth's views have shifted in the light of further experiences, especially when she takes the whole class for 'story time'. Although she is able to hold the children's attention during the story, she is unable to keep the children under control during the discussion, and she recognizes that she needs to be more assertive:

I feel confident about story time, about the actual reading of the story. I feel I have learnt how to bring the story across, the children are interested when I read, they don't switch off because they like to listen. You have to choose a good book obviously, but also it's the way I read it. I'm sure that helps as well. I'm quite lively and they are interested in that. I still am mastering the sort of linking processes of story time, when the story finishes, how I best pose the questions so they don't shout out at the same time . . .

I think you have to recognize that you have to be positive and also assertive and that you cannot all the time take everyone else's feelings into consideration . . . You're just going to have to make statements, and you're going to have to act, and you are going to have to be assertive, and the children have to learn that you are the one that is pulling the strings and setting the pattern, that is, telling what's happening. I'm not saying thereby that you don't understand what the children need or that you're not observant of what they will need and want, but you have to come across quite positively and securely and assertively to set this framework within which you can start working, which is something that perhaps I knew was happening but couldn't put my finger on. There's so much going on and it's still so bewildering.

At this stage, when Beth talks about managing children, she compares her teaching to how she acts as a parent, and feels frustrated that the strategies she uses with her own children do not seem applicable in the classroom. The matter of discipline troubles her a great deal. Beth suspects that it will only be a matter of time before

she experiences loss of control, and reports living 'in fear of pandemonium breaking out'. When it does occur, only days later, Beth is in a class where she hardly
knows the children or the routines, and she is shattered and demoralized for weeks
after. At the time, Beth gives only scant details about what actually happened: near
the end of the day, she is left with a class whilst the teacher temporarily leaves the
room; when the teacher fails to return, Beth has to organize getting the children
ready to go home. Beth often cites this episode as a low point in the course, initially
preceiving this as an example of her own weakness, whilst trying to be philosophical about her learning experience:

> . . . my organizational side is very bad really. I didn't know the children
> or their names at that time and liking them wasn't enough in that situ-
> ation. I realized that something else had to be brought in and yet couldn't
> do it at that moment. That's why there was a terrible situation because I
> panicked completely and that was a real low point. It gave me a huge setback
> in confidence. I went right down . . . It still upsets me and I'm only just
> beginning to think that I've done some other really good things with them
> since then that have worked. You have to learn to fall and get up again.
> That's how you build a base on which you can draw to deal with different
> situations and children. All that makes a difference . . . I think it's mainly
> the bad situations that teach you a lot about yourself. I don't know why
> because we always try and be positive. I think mainly they've been situ-
> ations where I've been in a panic and I've had to just act on the spur of
> the moment. I've learnt an awful lot. It made me stronger in a way, going
> through that situation. But what I'm still battling with is that I don't have
> it clear in my head how it works really. I don't want to be someone who
> is really negative. I can't . . . I think I'm trying to say, 'How do you know
> when you have to be really firm and strong?'

Over time, however, she relives the incident again and again, in part evaluating
what happened against a growing understanding of the complexities of managing
children. Eventually, in the final interview, she rationalizes that the teacher perhaps
placed unnecessary stress on her:

> She said, 'I'm dying for a pee, can you just take the class and I'll be back
> in about ten minutes,' and I'd never even been in front of a class before
> and here I was. It was about 2.20 pm and at 3.00 pm the bell was due to
> go and she just didn't come back. She didn't tell me what the routine was
> or anything, so I just decided to tell a story and got them on the carpet and
> told a story because I didn't have any books with me. I just told this story
> from the top of my head, because Peter [tutor] had just done one of those
> stories at college and I used that and at 2.55 pm this mother came in who'd
> been baking with a tray full of biscuits, and they all wanted a biscuit and
> I had absolutely no idea how to organize this so that it would run smoothly.
> They all started talking and I just didn't know what to do, so I sent them

off to get their coats and when they came back in I said they could get a biscuit, but of course they all came back in at the same time and they all grabbed the biscuits. There was a throng of children and this poor mother with all this chaos and I felt worse and worse. Then I thought I had to do something, and so I shouted at the top of my voice, 'Right, now you can go and line up by the door and nobody is going home until we have a neat, straight line by the door.' They did and it was fine later, but I was totally out of my depth and didn't know what I was doing. It was awful. If I'd been a more positive person I would have said, 'Gosh, that was a really good learning experience and I learned ever such a lot and I really wasn't too bad dealing with the whole thing. I did all the right things and they went home and their mums got them intact. OK, it was a bit noisy and rowdy and perhaps slightly disorganized, but so what?' But of course I thought I had no organization, couldn't control the children . . . and I felt totally shattered by that for a long time.

Beth is continually faced with dilemmas as she tries to accommodate discipline within her ideas of sensitive, child-centred teaching. Increasingly she talks about the need to assert her authority whilst being convinced that this can be achieved in a positive way, yet she seems to have so few images of such teaching on which she can draw, and lacks confidence in her own ideas. At the same time, she feels under considerable pressure to adopt the approach she perceives exists within the school. It seems that she does not have a role model with whom she can identify in the early weeks, and so feels unable to discuss her concerns with other teachers, which leads to much frustration and a sense of isolation. Yet Beth is able to reflect upon her experiences with insight:

I had another incident yesterday and I was in Year 1 and they were prac-tising their Nativity Play and I was sitting next to this mat with a whole load of really naughty girls and boys. I was thinking 'I don't want to be here next to this lot because I don't know what to do to keep them in con-trol.' But I thought I shouldn't be defeatist. I had problems thinking what sort of person I was going to be with them. Whether I would say, 'Don't do this, don't do that.' The teachers were there and it was a very difficult situation with them being other teachers' children. You don't know how far to jump in. It's a very superficial and difficult situation. I just decided I wouldn't be rotten but tried to get them to sing, and smile at them instead of being cross. And some of them were amazing. I explained things kindly to them and afterwards one of the girls came up and sat on my lap and said, 'You know I'm really naughty sometimes,' and I said, 'We're all naughty sometimes, but you've been very good today,' and she gave me a huge cuddle and went off. I thought then that surely there must be something in the positive approach. Of course it won't work every time, but that's why I find it so hard. The strictness and the positive approach. Possibly when you've your own class you're more in control of the whole situation.

They're your children and you know what's called for and you can tune
into the different children. When you're just a student and not really the
teacher of the class you don't even know half the children well.

It seems that a significant part of Beth's difficulties in learning to teach lies in her
relationship with her mentor, Elaine, an experienced teacher who is due to retire the
following year. Early in the course, Beth has clear ideas about what she wants from
a mentor which includes being given honest advice and criticism, being listened to,
and being cared for on a personal level. Yet Beth feels that her 'emotional needs' are
largely unmet by Elaine. Additionally she had envisaged that she would work with
a younger teacher whose ideas were more in sympathy with the college course. From
the start, Beth is uncomfortable with Elaine's teaching style which she describes as
traditional. Beth is rather disturbed that she should feel so negatively about an experienced teacher's practice when she is so inexperienced herself:

> I think she lacks a bit of imagination. But what do I know, coming in with
> outside ideas? It's not really fair of me to say that because I haven't really
> done it. I haven't been there keeping all twenty-eight of them amused all
> day long . . . It's something that fills me with dread in a way, so I shouldn't
> be criticizing. I should be saying, 'You're doing very well.' I'm sure they'll
> all go out reading and writing and putting it on the line following her struc-
> ture . . . [but] I feel that a lot is overlooked at the moment by concentrat-
> ing on putting it on the line. I think you're forgetting a lot of other things
> that children can do . . . I feel I am critical and I can't understand why I
> am. I wonder if I'm being over critical.

In addition to talking through her experiences, Beth believes that in order to learn
to teach, she must be allowed to experiment, so that she can learn from her mistakes. Yet she feels stifled in her mentor's classroom because she feels obliged to
adopt Elaine's teaching style and approaches. At times, she reports actually feeling
frightened of Elaine, who can appear brusque and somewhat severe. On the other
hand, from the mentor's perspective, it seems that Elaine is surprised, even perhaps
exasperated, by Beth's lack of confidence and reticence to take the initiative.

Beth realizes that she must resolve some of the problems within the relationship, and after the third week, she plucks up the courage to discuss her emotional
needs. She reports that this leads to a great improvement in the relationship, as each
is able to understand the other's viewpoint:

> I'm having a lot of good help and support from my mentor at the moment
> because [before] it was not good and I wasn't happy about it. I had a
> really good mentor time with her and told her how I felt and how she
> intimidated me and that I felt very ill at ease with her and her confid-
> ent, organized manner, and that I was frightened by her. She was totally
> unaware of that because she actually had a very high opinion of me and
> wanted me to do so well and was perhaps over anxious on my behalf and

therefore immediately jumped in when something was happening because she wanted to protect me rather than me thinking it was her personality. She wanted to show me immediately that that wasn't the way to do it. It was because she was so concerned. So now I know her real feelings and I understand the way she's behaving because I know why she's doing it. Before I only guessed what she was doing. [Now] she's giving me interest in me as a person, concern about what's happening to me and also my home and whether all is well with my children and my husband.

Although Beth reports a significant improvement in their relationship, it seems that her enthusiastic claim that a mutual understanding has been reached is probably over-optimistic. It soon becomes apparent that, in fact, several issues remain unresolved. For example, Beth still feels very uncomfortable working with Elaine. In turn it appears that the mentor feels the same, because for the rest of the term and the subsequent one, Beth spends all her time working in other classrooms. Not actually working with Elaine also seems to affect their relationship, since Beth is unable to discuss shared teaching experiences with her. From talking to other articled teachers, Beth is aware that this is viewed as an invaluable part of mentoring. However, she is able to discuss ideas with other teachers who are often more sympathetic towards Beth's views. For example, she spends a few weeks with a Reception teacher, Shirley, who encourages her to try ideas for developmental writing. Beth reports that such experiences increase her confidence:

I've worked with one particular class, with a teacher who is very supportive. She likes language and is very keen to help me. We share a lot of things about development. That's what I've been focusing on. She's given me a lot of support and she's given me her children to work with. She says I can do whatever I want to do and can talk to her afterwards. That helps build up my confidence.

Elaine and Beth continue to have weekly mentoring sessions which Beth finds useful because she is given valuable advice about organization and she values Elaine's honesty and structured approach to their discussions. Generally, Beth accepts that what she receives from her mentor is somewhat 'patchy' in comparison with the other articled teachers, and that she must take responsiblity for getting the help she needs:

I sort out my own tasks and I tend to go and talk to the people in whose class I am. She has introduced me to everyone though and made it possible for me to do that . . . [although] I find it a bit of a shame because I have to rely on other people to support me in that sense. Like Shirley, who is not being paid for it and who is not really my mentor. I feel guilty sometimes asking for her time. But you need some sort of classroom feedback as well and she needs to see me in action.

Beth's experiences within other classrooms are quite mixed in terms of building her confidence and self-image as a teacher and she faces many constraints. At times, she reports that she is unable to undertake her tasks properly, because she is often faced with the dilemma of trying to implement them in formal classrooms where the children seem unable to respond — for example, when she attempts to encourage developmental writing. Additionally, Beth often feels that she is not really in control of anything herself because she has to 'fit in' where she can. She is also frustrated on occasions when she starts work with children and is then unable to continue because staff are ill, or they change their plans. Equally, Beth reports that there are times when she has to work with such 'difficult' children that she loses confidence, and the sight of her positive ideals, and this seems to sap her energy levels.

There are, however, a number of occasions when Beth carries out work from which she can see what children have learned, and experiences a great sense of achievement and satisfaction. For example, towards the end of the first term, she collates the work she has gathered for her focused study on developmental writing and, in doing so, she sees evidence of how much one particular child has learned:

> I had a lot of work, gathered over four to five weeks, and I saw this wonderful development happening and it was fascinating. Talking to the children, giving them confidence, making them feel they can write and it doesn't matter what it looks like. There was one little girl and I sat down with her the first time and she wrote nothing at all. I said, 'You can do it, take your time.' She did nothing and I ended up writing a sentence for her and she copied it beautifully. She did beautiful drawings. And I worked with her a bit because I liked her so much. After two or three weeks she was putting all these lines on the paper and it was becoming writing patterns and the next day I was sitting with her and she was writing all these letters, page after page. It was wonderful to see how she had gained in confidence and would have a go. She actually knew a lot and she saw that. That to me was wonderful.

Beth reports that, in some classes, she observes good practice where she can actually see the children are learning. Her observations in one particular case also appear to provide her with an activity framework for maths which she later makes use of. What she observes also serves to support her early beliefs that children learn through doing and talking:

> I also have observed some nice teaching activities in the infants. Sitting round the table talking about shapes, blocks, some thick and thin, and how the children themselves establish what the difference is between them. Their own learning comes flowing out having talked to each other and together they come to their conclusions. All those little things are incredibly valuable I think . . . they reached conclusions by themselves . . . with a bit of help and encouragement they then take it from there and you could

see them thinking, using their minds, and coming out with things they didn't know before they started. It might have been there but they hadn't voiced it . . . I think I find it's incredibly important that children learn through experience, through hands-on experience, try things out, feel them, touch them, put them on top of each other, stack them, drop them, make mistakes and learn through actual doing, being, experiencing. And in that way they can learn.

The college input in the first year is consistently seen by Beth to provide invaluable support and encouragement, which comes not only from the tutors but also the other articled teachers. The very personal nature of the sessions is valued highly. Sessions usually include a time for reflection, including discussion of the students' experiences during the week, and Beth gains emotional satisfaction from talking about her situation and re-living incidences, and also through the vicarious experiences offered by others who, for example, sometimes share her frustrations or have been able to carry out tasks successfully and so gain confidence in a particular approach. Additionally, the college provides theoretical understandings onto which she can sometimes map her practice and, generally, Beth finds the sessions stimulating. She is, however, critical that there seems to be too little input in terms of organization and management. In common with other articled teachers, she feels that she needs more help in organizing a class, more techniques for behaviour management and that the college should be providing more support in those areas. Overall, however, Beth believes that she is learning to teach through a mixture of practical, if sometimes 'harrowing' experiences and theory.

By the end of this first term, Beth reports an increase in confidence, although she admits that she is only just beginning to feel like a teacher: 'I don't feel quite so petrified walking through the school having to pretend I'm a teacher. I now feel I'm beginning to start to go into the role a little bit more.' She is still quite reticient to take on responsibility, but feels that at least she now has some control over her own learning, and is able to take a longer term perspective. For the time being, she sees herself:

Just taking it easy, making it easy on myself and not trying to do everything at once, taking it a step at a time and not feeling I have to learn to be a teacher in three weeks. I'm really recognizing that . . . I am actually very gradually building up confidence, so it is coming. So that's giving me trust to know that I have to take it easy and it will come . . . I'm not quite ready [to understand how to teach] English, maths or whatever . . . I think the priority is gaining confidence . . . I'm only doing a little whole class work because I want to show myself that I can do it and [yet] there is this other approach that says I will do it when I'm ready for it, not just to prove it tomorrow so that I can then relax. I will be ready for it and then it will come. It's very hard to keep telling myself.

Early in the second term, she exchanges schools with another articled teacher. Now Beth reports that she feels very comfortable and extremely positive because her new mentor shows confidence in her, and helps her to focus on specific aspects of teaching, such as planning and children's learning. From a visit made to the school during this period, Beth certainly appears much more at ease and smiling. Whilst it is noted that Beth is still very much focused upon her own performance, she seems less afraid of making mistakes. Observation of a science session with a group of Reception children reveals the new found confidence with which Beth explores ways in which she might improve her teaching and so encourage the children's learning. Below Beth discusses what she learned from undertaking an investigation into the 'absorbency' of a variety of materials on previous occasions and the changes she proposes making for the next group. Notes record that the experiment essentially involves stretching various materials over jam jars, holding them in place with elastic bands, and then pouring water onto the materials to see what happens. Beth's intentions for the experiment again reveal a strong allegiance to a child-centred approach, and also reflect her understanding that science is about letting children find things out for themselves. For example, before the lesson, Beth says:

> What I want to do this session, following on from the last one when I did materials and water, [when] there was a very competitive spirit in the group . . . I wanted through my questioning for this not to happen again. I felt I had perhaps paid too much attention to waterproofness rather than any other attribute of the material. Somehow it didn't quite work. My questioning was much better but I still felt that it was some sort of competition to find the most waterproof material. This time I'm just going to find a lot more exploring going on. I just want them to feel the materials and then choose and put it round the pot themselves and see if that might help . . .
>
> I want them to get a good idea what happens to the materials and see if what they thought was going to happen does happen by pouring water on. So I will talk to them a bit about predicting and then see if it coincides with what they thought . . .
>
> I don't want to talk about waterproofness so much . . . Only after they've done the testing we could perhaps talk about that. So [instead] of giving them input beforehand, it's going to be the other way. I'm going to leave them to it with the materials. Obviously I'll have to help them devising the test but I'll see if they can come up with something as well. Can they make the connections themselves? . . . [I think if they] test out their [own] ideas . . . it will make sense to them. If they're testing out my ideas they're not going to make sense of the outcome. It might not be what they were thinking. It's what I'm thinking of. So I want them to have their ideas, test them out and then consolidate at the end or extend their knowing through having tested what they thought.

Observation of the session seems also to reveal that Beth is quite intent on being very positive in her responses to the children. She lets the children play with the materials, all the time responding enthusiastically to the children's comments, often asking questions such as, 'What do you think will happen now?' After the session she says:

> I wondered whether I really sounded like [I was] answering the ques-
> tion . . . talking non-stop to them without letting them explore. I think I
> was doing that a lot more in the last session. It's a very difficult balance and
> I don't know if I was doing it right. I was trying to allow them the space
> and to help at the same time, to point in the direction.

Beth describes Sandy, her mentor in the second school in which she is placed, in glowing terms, claiming that she is helping her to focus on specific aspects of teaching, as well as encouraging her to make decisions about what she could do with the children:

> She has made me aware. I have looked at things . . . I've discovered all
> sorts of things I could do. She's had confidence in me to take the class and
> to do these things with the class, so she's given me confidence. She's been
> extremely positive in her feedback, so she has not said, 'That's rubbish,
> that's wrong.' She's been very positive, but very constructive. She hasn't
> beaten around the bush, so she's told me exactly what's what. And she's
> just been a lovely person, very kind, and I feel I can ask her anything, and
> she's very professional. Extremely professional.

Beth can now see that she does have certain teaching skills and that she is able to plan and carry out various types of activity. However, she is also aware that there are contraints which she must address. For example, she comments on the very different nature of forming relationships with children in specific contexts and the problems this creates for behaviour management:

> I have felt that building up relationships with children is incredibly import-
> ant . . . The children get to know you and you get to know the children. I
> had that . . . a bit more at [host school] in a sense because here the children
> have very many different people in their class. There it was just their own
> teacher and me. Here they had three different people [classroom assistants
> and parents] this week and . . . Sandy is the fourth. So that is different again.
> They are adapting to lots of different people, so I feel I have to work harder
> here to keep the balance because I can't just rely on the children knowing
> me and me knowing them. It's not very clear. This relationship you have.
> This looking at children and them knowing what you mean. I can't do that
> here because they have so many different looks that they have to con-
> stantly reinterpret who the person is, how far they can go, etc. But I feel
> at [host school] that I can build up a strong relationship with that class.
> I could manoeuvre them. But here I'm still fighting a bit with that and
> finding my feet a bit. But I'm doing it. That's how you learn, by doing it.

Beth claims that the skills she has developed have greatly boosted her confidence and that she can actually see herself as a teacher and that she can even envisage transferring her new found confidence back to her host school:

> I feel even better about going back to the other school. I feel partly it was me not being confident and seeing things worse than they really are . . . I'm going to be in this class where teachers are doing the SATs and I now feel confident enough to say, 'Try me. Let me have a go at planning a bit for the class and taking them and seeing it through.' I'll ask her if I can do that. Before I wouldn't have wanted to put myself in that position. Now I'm myself suggesting that I should do it.

After returning to her host school, Beth maintains a friendship with Sandy, and continues to meet or phone her regularly throughout the rest of the course. Now she works in a Year 2 class with the deputy head, Chris, and again her confidence is boosted as she reports being encouraged to be herself and to establish a close bond with the children, although Beth admits that she is still doing a lot of observation. Although she continues to make mistakes, and to be acutely critical of herself, this does not seem to disturb her as before, since Chris is very positive about her strengths, and spends time with her, helping her to see things in perspective. During this time, Beth is observed taking an English session which involves the twenty-five children writing thank-you letters. Beth and the children have been planning the redevelopment of the school conservation area, as part of a focused study for college, and recently have been given advice by a local conservationist, Mr King. Before the session, Beth talks clearly about how she has planned the work, what has influenced her ideas, what she wants the children to learn, and, as can be seen below, how the session is to be organized:

> I'm going to start off with calling the [afternoon] register and then we'll all sit on the carpet as I want us to write a letter to Mr King who has been involved in our conservation area project. This has been part of my focused study. They're wanting to do it up because it's a bit of a mess and we've designed what we would like to do. Mr King was the kind man who came to have a look and talked to the children. So we're going to write a letter to him to thank him and tell him what we've been doing so far and tell him what's going to happen in the future. So I want to start off as a whole class, ask them first of all if they know what a letter is and how you start and end it, what you put on it, and then I want to talk a bit about what they're going to put in it, not just 'Thank you' and then nothing. But telling him something about what they've done and so forth. How they're using the books he gave them. And then I'm going to send them off and make them do a draft letter. I don't want them to do it neat straightway. Once they've done the draft letter, I will want to pull them all back in again, feed back by letting them read out some of their letters and hearing what they've come out with, which letters are good, which didn't work and why, and

then emphasize again that you have particular points you have to adhere to in a letter. Then I will send them off with a partner to do a neat copy and I'm going to send them off with one of the pair being quite good at writing and they'll work together with another who may not be as good, so that they can help each other. One can do the writing and the other can think about it. I don't know if I should specify that. Chris suggested I do that, but I'm not sure because I want them to work together. Presumably they will sort out themselves . . . into dominant and less dominant partners.

Beth has not undertaken such work with children before. She attributes her 'framework' for the lesson to the lectures in college, when the students carried out a drafting activity themselves. However, Beth seems unable to make decisions about how she will develop this framework to suit the specific context in which she is working. She is unsure, for example, about how well the children will work together and cannot decide whether to follow Chris' advice to specify which child will do the writing, which offers more control, or to allow the children to be more independent as she would prefer. Equally, she seems to be hoping that because there is a genuine reason for writing, this will give the children the motivation to do it well and to work cooperatively. Such expressions as 'a beautiful letter', 'motivation to do it right' and 'they'll both want to succeed' seem to reflect her beliefs that children respond to teachers who believe in them.

In her planning, Beth has used ideas and advice from a number of sources, including National Curriculum documents and a book, written by a college tutor, on children's writing. Beth's ideas about the role she will play during the session are consistent with the desired image of herself as a teacher. She anticipates that she will initially act as a facilitator for the whole class by drawing out information from the children and then putting it in a clear format so that the children will know what is required of them. She then hopes to simply oversee their work.

The session itself runs for just over an hour, and during the discussion on the carpet it is noted that Beth is extremely nervous. When the children enter the classroom, they are quite boisterous after a wet playtime. She begins in an assertive manner, and seems to be acting upon advice to set the ground rules and to keep reinforcing these when necessary. For example, she repeatedly says, 'I want to see you sitting on bottoms' and 'Hands up, don't call out'. When, after 5 minutes, a number of children become silly, she stops the discussion and reminds the children how she expects them to behave on the carpet, and this is repeated 3 minutes later. Minutes after this, one boy — who has managed to work his way from one end of the carpet to another, poking and prodding various children on the way who, in turn, call out indignantly — is told to 'Stand up, and stop being so silly!' Isolating the boy is partially successful but the group is still restless. After 25 minutes the children are sent off to their groups, whilst Beth appears very flushed and ill at ease, although she has managed to carry out what she intended to do.

During the next part of the session, Beth continues to remind the childen that they do not need to worry about spelling because their 'ideas are more important'. This, however, does not prevent children from following her around the room, asking for words. Several children are off-task and rather silly. After 40 minutes Chris returns and quietly joins the noisiest group of children and their behaviour improves significantly. The lesson is concluded on the carpet with some of the letters being read out.

After the session, Beth feels exhausted and dejected. Although the session essentially ran according to plan, she reports that she found it very difficult to handle the children. Having previously undertaken a reportedly successful whole discussion with the same class, she had expected a similar response, and she tries to analyse why this did not happen. Beth seems particularly ashamed of her negative response to the child who was misbehaving on the carpet, and whom she again speaks to very sharply when the children are writing. She is confused that she resorted to the kind of approach she dislikes so much:

> I was very nervous and I think it showed and the children picked it up. The children were quite high because of the rainy day and no outside play. I knew that and was worried, and they knew that. It was a vicious circle. I wasn't relaxed at all and I'm sure they could tell. Had I been more relaxed, it might have been better. I tried to put my teaching points across, but am not sure how many actually came across. I tried to involve all the children, but some weren't that interested and it was very hard . . . Don't ask me how I could have done it better, because it was rather instinctive. I was floundering a bit and it came across I'm sure . . . Later on when they'd all gone back [to their seats] and they were doing their rough copies . . . Gary had really bugged me during the whole feeding back session. I was really quite weary and it looked as though he was writing absolute rubbish, but in fact when he came to read it back it was fine. Because it looked like rubbish I said, 'What is this rubbish you've written?' and I thought 'How could I say that!' and when he read it to me it made such sense. I thought he was just winding me up, so I was taking it personally, which is ludicrous. But I think that's because I was nervous and he hadn't been a very easy boy earlier. I didn't handle it very well. I found it very difficult to know what to do with those boys who were playing up at the beginning, whether to make them stand up or how long you let it go on or how much you accept. What do you do? You can't just threaten. It has to be interesting for them . . . they were so lively, it's hard for them to sit still.
>
> When I did the seeds growing in pots with them [a previous lesson] they were so keen and interested and I had no trouble with the whole class feedback at all. Whereas this one obviously didn't catch their imagination so much, so they weren't as naturally inquisitive and I had to use more strategies that I hadn't really got . . . It was pure instinctive floundering . . . It really wasn't a strategy. If it had been it might have been much better. Saying that, I don't think it was totally a waste of time. I managed to keep them down, it would get out of hand and then I would get them back for a little while. I did manage to pull it back . . . I stopped and that was a strategy. I wanted them to know it wasn't acceptable . . . I thought I had

them all fine, and then worried I would lose them again. So I got so nervous again. If you think it's going to happen, it does.

I wasn't myself and they were a little bit surprised in a sense because they see me as a much calmer person in that class context and I felt I wasn't the same . . . and they noticed that and started playing on it. I've built up a good relationship with Carla, and at the end she was just doing her own thing and seeing how far she could go. Before she was doing lovely work for me because she knew what sort of person I was and trusted me and was herself. I felt that came across quite a lot, that I saw her slipping away . . . possibly because I wasn't feeling relaxed. My voice must have been much higher than normal. You can't hear that yourself, but I'm sure it was. Chris says that he can always tell when I'm nervous because of my voice and that I should breathe deeply.

Later, Beth points out that some children completed little more than copying 'Dear Mr King' because she had not used the appropriate words to explain what she meant about drafting. It appears that having been so convinced by the lectures about the power of drafting, she fully expected that they would automatically write without difficulty. Similarly she is disappointed that several children did not seem to be writing with a purpose at all.

Beth decides that she has tried to 'pack too much in, in too short a time' and that she ought to have broken the session down into stages, starting with a discussion about what had happened, followed by a session to write the letter.

In the following week, Beth claims that her teaching is much more successful, and in one particular session, she is able to enjoy what she does because, 'I was just being myself. I didn't aspire to anything, there was no-one watching . . . I was so much more relaxed and people respond to that. If you're edgy, they pick it up. We finished off some things and had lovely talks about it and things worked really naturally.'

By the end of the year, Beth feels she has learned a lot, though she is aware that, had she had a different mentor and a different host school, which embodied practices and beliefs which were more akin to her own, she might have learned even more. Beth comments:

I think if I'd been with a different mentor I think I would have been different. It really hit me when I came here, the discipline and the squashing, and I . . . do it myself now. It's rubbed off. I think you need a certain amount of discipline, so you need to be precise and concise and say what you accept and what you don't. But then you must allow the children to be themselves as you would like to be yourself . . .

I still am edgy with my relationship with the school. I don't feel I'm honest to them in a way and I'm not sure they're honest to me either. I don't feel I fit in there yet. I've battled with that quite a bit. I do think I'm perhaps highly critical.

Beth has always shown great respect for the headteacher's ideas and philosophies, but she remains convinced throughout her time at the school that these are not being reflected in the ethos and practice, and the high level of variation in teachers' practices has made working in different classes especially difficult for her.

> There should be a common theme. It's chalk and cheese. They have meetings together and yet they still go their own way. Like the writing. They have a totally different approach in the different Reception classes. It's terrible. There's no pleasure from it — it's all worrying about spelling, etc., and yet when you read the school policy on writing they say that writing should be a pleasure and children should be considered as very valuable with a lot in there already . . . I find that quite amazing that it's in all their documents and presumably it's something they've all talked about, but you don't see it in the classes. Perhaps it's inevitable.

In the final interview of the year, Beth reflects on her learning to teach. She reports that the college tutor has been very supportive, empathizing with what she was trying to achieve. She has also valued the focused studies which encourage the students' own reflections upon their experiences. Beth reports that she learns a great deal through these because, 'as I'm writing them down, I'm seeing all these things I could have done at that time and I didn't do'. Beth anticipates that in time, with practice, she will be able to think more on her feet. She asserts that she is still determined 'to be herself' and that there are things which she will not accept, such as putting children down. She feels strongly that authoritarian strategies should only be used when it is necessary, but realizes that this is not what she actually achieves in practice:

> That's my big thing. I'm so anxious that these things [misbehaviours] will happen and I won't have the right response. Instead of relying on myself to deal with it when it comes up or when it doesn't, I go very nervous and edgy just in case it goes wrong. Once I relax it's so much better. I enjoy it and the children notice that. I don't know why I can't be like that all the time.

Year Two

Beth begins the second year on a note of considerable optimism, looking forward to her full practice in the spring term with a much clearer idea of what she can achieve, and the help she will require. She feels confident and resolves to set her own goals and satisfy her own standards. She sees this as an important step forward. Many times over the year, she has suffered crises of confidence, to such an extent that she reports, 'I just lost all my belief in myself through doing things and constantly getting jumped on. Everything I did was wrong. So I lost my belief in my honest, happy personality.' She does not anticipate using her mentor very much during the year, and she is reassured by the knowledge that she can turn to the deputy head should she need to.

Beth claims that she can increasingly make sense of what she has learned in lectures and her reading, and so incorporates this more readily into her teaching. This has developed through experience in classrooms — for example, after the letter writing lesson in year one when Beth felt that she had 'suppressed' various children because she was afraid of losing control. She comments:

> I read a book and as I was reading things became much clearer. One of the most enjoyable occasions is when I've done something and I sit and read a book and then suddenly realize how I could do it or approach it. It really broadens my mind. It's often just pure coincidence. It was a book on education . . . about behavioural patterns and how people are in class-rooms and how they interact with the children . . . I suddenly thought I wasn't allowing Emma to be her own person . . . because I was frightened of losing control. I didn't have the confidence.

Since what she reads she can now visualize in real life situations, Beth claims that she has so much more accessible knowledge which she is able to enact within the classroom, so feeling 'empowered'. This, in turn, means that teaching has taken on its own intrinsic rewards since previously what she read so often only had mean-ing 'in retrospect'. For example, for the first few weeks of the second year she works in a Year 1 class, with children she has known since their Reception class, and reports a considerable level of satisfaction when she finds she is able to think on her feet:

> I'm going for it and trying it out, so that feels better and I'm doing things that I've read about. And it doesn't seem all that difficult. I was doing religion on [the teacher's] timetable and she gave me a 20-year-old book to read. So I chucked it under the chair and the children and I had a wonderful discussion of what they thought God was like and where he lived and it was wonderful. I tried to draw him on the board as they told me what he looked like. And I was really pleased that I'd done it myself without a 20-year-old book. And it was actually quite easy. It wasn't a question, they didn't feel I was quizzing them or finding out how much they knew. It was just a talk.

Beth is very aware, however, that she still has much to learn, and comments on assessment and record-keeping over a period of time as areas that concern her particularly as she anticipates her responsibilities during the teaching practice in the spring.

These early weeks of the term are not, however, without stress. Again, Beth reports being at odds with the teacher with whom she works, as she perceives a sense of injustice on the behalf of herself and others. For example, Beth reports:

[For] the last two weeks I've been in another class and I see all these things where I wonder how they can do things like that. I'm just a critical person, I can't help it . . . I feel I'm not being allowed to be myself and consequently suffering because of it. I think I'm just over-sensitive. I'm sure I react very strongly where others might not. Yes, it's a lovely class but the teacher is just acting in a strange way. She's constantly on my neck. Whatever I do, I do it wrong, and whatever I don't do, I should have done. [Also] There was one little boy crying and he came up to me and I worked out what was the matter. It had to do with the new nursery nurse we had in the class and it had upset him. The teacher came up and asked what was going on and I explained and she said, 'Right Peter, what's the matter?' and he had to go through it all again. Poor little lad. She didn't hear him properly, so she asked everyone to be quiet so she could listen. The poor nursery nurse felt awful that she was the cause of his grief and the poor child had to tell his story again. So it's that type of thing I get the whole time and it drives me bonkers. It's making me angry even now while I'm talking to you. I have to bite my tongue.

Early in the new academic year, Beth is to transfer to a primary school in which she had worked on a voluntary basis for six weeks. On the one hand, she anticipates the move with great excitement since the school had been so influential in shaping her ideas of good practice. On the other, Beth wonders whether her 'ideals' might be tested since she is returning with so much more experience and insight: 'I feel I'm going to get a more realistic idea of the ethos of the school. Is it a dream I'm having or does it really exist? That's what I'm really looking forward to finding out . . . I want to know if I'm right in being biased.'

However, Beth quickly feels at ease in the school and during the placement she works with Barry, an experienced teacher, in a Year 6 class. Beth claims that she is looking forward to the stimulation of working with older children:

I'm going to work with juniors and it's a totally different way of working. They're much more equals and they have so much more to say. You can discuss things on a more equal basis. They will give you back a lot more. With infants you give a lot and you get a terrific amount back, but not in the same way as with juniors who can mull it over and can come back with their own thoughts to look at it again. I'm looking forward to the interaction with the juniors. Getting more of an equal rapport back.

In this setting, she is able to try out many of the ideas suggested in college and her reading. In particular, she enjoys undertaking redrafting work, and observation of this session reveals the ease with which Beth is able to work in a team teaching situation with Barry with whom she reports feeling 'very comfortable'.

Again Beth is able to observe the teacher's style and to evaluate this against her beliefs about good practice:

> What I like about it is its informality. It's very natural the way Barry is in his class. He's very much himself. There's also a bit of waste in some ways, in that time gets lost quite a bit. So I would want to be a bit tighter on that ... I feel children learn a lot more through being able to get hands on experience of things, rather than saying 'You will do this now this way.' They have to find out and are able to explore. I feel it's very justified.

To her surprise, she also thoroughly enjoys teaching maths during the placement, reporting a significant growth in confidence through planning a series of maths lessons on shape with a very competent and experienced maths specialist. The experience not only serves to reassure Beth of the valuable emotional support gained by working with a like-minded colleague, but also allows her to develop a greater understanding of how to structure children's learning experiences, and from this she formulates a model which informs her future planning:

> I went away at half term and wrote down lots of ideas to do with shape and space for juniors. So I got lots of books out and it was like a brainstorm. I wrote down lots of bits and then I went to see the teacher on the Sunday before the term began, and we got together and did our ideas together on paper. Then we talked about the best way of starting the subject off and how to get to the next stage. Because of her experience, she put in a lot more than I did because I'd never done it before. I worked well with that and agreed with her. I wouldn't have done it so well if I hadn't been in agreement with what she was trying to do. I could take her ideas on board though as if they were my own ... I knew precisely what I was doing. [It was] structured ... first we do this, we have five minutes introduction ... how the introduction went is obviously up to the children ... then after that we give them tangrams. They did some practical cutting out and sticking and getting their tangram ready in bits. Then they went off to sort using their own criteria. There was room still for the children to do their own thing, but it was in a timed, organized environment, unit. Then we get together, hear what they've sorted and why ... everything was planned precisely with scope for the children to do their own thing within that.

By the end of the first term, back in the host school, Beth is aware of having broadened her experience of teaching, but she is concerned that she is not as well prepared as she had hoped for taking responsibility for a whole Reception class next term. Beth is also clearly unwell and showing signs of stress, which she recognizes may affect her view that, 'I haven't been very happy because I feel it's been very disjointed ... I haven't really done a lot of whole class teaching, so I'm feeling a little bit apprehensive about the teaching term coming up'. Although the term has brought many positive learning experiences, Beth still seems to experience various pressures in her relationships with some members of staff in the host school. Commenting on her contacts with a parallel Reception teacher [who is about to leave] in preparation for her teaching practice, Beth says, 'She's created all sorts of horrible fusses and has been very unkind. I find that very hard to cope with because I'm so tired. It upsets me terribly. When someone is nice to me . . . I just burst into tears. I think I'm a bit over-tired.'

At the end of the fifth term, Beth reports further on her uncomfortableness within the school:

Partly because I don't feel like a teacher still, and because once I start teaching I think I'll probably feel better. It's not the sort of school that makes you feel comfortable. So it's only through doing the teaching and realizing that's what I'm here for, not for any other reason, that I'll feel more comfortable.

Behaviour Management and Relationships with Children

During her teaching practice in the fifth term, Beth attempts to reconcile her views about pupil management with her experiences of teaching. Beth is still convinced that many classroom behaviour problems can be resolved by the skilful way in which teachers respond to children at the time, and she perceives herself as lacking the ability to think and respond quickly in an appropriate way, especially when she feels stressed.

Early in the practice, Beth is observed to experience discipline problems when lining up the children at lunchtime and at the end of the day. Observations reveal that the children appear to expect this to occur and are always ready to rise to the occasion! Beth's reaction is to raise her voice or shout at the children, usually with little effect. She is deeply unhappy with this strategy, as well as her image of herself during the interaction, yet she is unable to enact alternative responses to the children's behaviour:

On the carpet I don't find it so hard, but it's the lining up when you lose them I think. I do lose them and I haven't found a good way yet of dealing with it and I lose my rag and start physically pushing them into line because I get so cross and shout and it has absolutely no effect whatsoever. It just has the opposite effect. They don't even listen! I sometimes hear myself and its awful. I'm shouting and nobody is taking a blind bit of notice.

Beth realizes that in times of stress she relies upon strategies she has seen in action and which seem to be the first thing that comes to mind, as in the previous year:

I can't just say, 'It's not working, so I shan't do it any more.' It's a gradual process. But what I'm doing now are little games to get their attention. I've done that quite a lot. I call out names of animals and if it swims they have to do this with their arms. That's a new game and that really does seem to help because they like to do it and they listen. I do songs now as well, but there's something about when your confidence goes. It's funny, but you do these things, see it all falling to bits and you start shouting. You say instant things that you think will help instead of calmly thinking 'Let's think of something else to do' and as you do more things and actions, they become part of your repertoire and come out easier [but] I still freeze up and forget things.

Although examples of management difficulties become less frequent as she continues to develop her strategies, Beth continues to experience times when she 'freezes up', but she takes comfort from the thought that when she has her own class, day-to-day experience will allow her to resolve her difficulties.

Children's Learning and the Teacher's Role

Beth stresses from the start of the course that children should learn through experience, by making mistakes and learning from them, and that the teacher should act as a 'facilitator'. Initially she reports that she cannot find evidence to support her views within the practice she observes in her host school. In turn, she is frustrated because she finds it difficult to accommodate what she learns in college and from other articled teachers in her early teaching. When she transfers to C., in the first year, and G., in the second year, she is relieved to find practice which reflects her basic beliefs about teaching. Over the two years, Beth's ideas about children's learning appear to remain unchanged in essence. For example, in the final interview, Beth talks about how children's writing and their understanding in maths develop, which she feels is exemplified by what she has observed in the first year at C., an infant school:

> At C., actually they think along fairly similar lines to me and these children are really in tune with that way of thinking. And that is that you must allow children to develop by themselves and that they come out with their own ideas that they can go and strengthen and you look at the redrafting process and then they go back. And this whole thing was working before my very eyes and I thought it had been the right thing to believe in all along, rather than other methods of teaching which I've seen in operation where children are just talked to about writing, having to be neat and have finger spaces in between, the spelling has to be correct and they're not even looking at the content. It's just to look neat and not be misspelt and then it's alright, no matter what it says . . . The same with maths. Really thinking about concepts and trying to get those across in many different ways before you take children on. So you try and approach addition in very many different ways to give the child the experience to make the concept their own. So they learn automatically and gradually what it's all about.

Beth has constantly held the view that children will learn from experimentation, and from being able to express themselves. Throughout the first year, she appeared to give little regard to the conditions under which this occurred, except that she felt that the classroom environment must offer security, allowing children to 'achieve independence that comes with being happy and feeling secure'.

When Beth transferred to her second placement school, early in the second year, she was more settled in her teaching style, and her experiences seemed to serve to sharpen her ideas about certain aspects of her practice. For example, the joint planning she undertook with other teachers convinced her of the need to 'structure and organize' learning experiences in order to enable the children to learn.

Planning and Organization

In Year 1 it appeared that planning was largely used to give Beth a structure to work with so that she knew what she had to do. In Year 2, she emphasizes the children's learning and, just prior to her teaching practice, Beth conjectures how she will apply the ideas she has gained from working in the junior classes to a Reception class, contrasting these with the practice she has observed in other Reception classes:

> In Reception, I look around and the children are playing with pegs after register and before assembly. They're just playing and that's all they do. I would much rather have more things for them to do, plan it, have 5 minutes on the pegs and then go somewhere else. It's very much, 'You're in this section of the room and that's why you can play with that and that, and you just sort it out for the next hour.' That's because the teacher has to teach with other groups, but I would like to think more deeply about why those children are playing with the pegs and what I want them to get out of it. The same with the sand and water and playhouse. I would also like to see me thinking about it in a structured way and therefore making changes so that it's not always the same.

Beth resolves to bring more structure into her planning in order to ensure that all the activites in the classroom maximize the children's learning experiences. A visit to Beth's classroom early in the practice verified her determination to implement such ideas. Her activities were well-planned and thought through in terms of children's interests and learning. Children moved purposefully around the classroom and Beth herself seemed to have a clear conception of what she wanted from them.

Initially Beth reports using worksheets for those children she is not immediately working with, and then abandons these because the children cannot work 'independently' and they do not provide concrete experience. She therefore spends a great deal of time planning and preparing toys and games and construction tasks in order to produce quality activities.

Beth claims she does not have any models of organization within a Reception class from the school which she can draw upon because the Reception classes have in the past worked so differently. She most readily identifies her current organization with that of Sandy, with whom she worked in her second school in the first year, who had six groups within her class. Beth has three groups, but each day she subdivides these into two to produce six 'small' teaching groups. Beth reports, however, that managing so many groups is very hard especially in the transition period:

> After a quarter of an hour, really they should all be swapping and I find that hard to think about . . . and am still struggling with that. I'm getting better though. You actually have to get up and say, 'Please would you swap over with the robot makers, and the puzzles can now go onto the tracing on this table' . . . [Moving the children round] is the thing I must be more aware of, otherwise the children get bored if they're too long in one place.

Beth persists with this difficulty, however, and a visit to her classroom later in the term reveals that she is much happier with her organization, and, although she looks exhausted, she feels she has developed the routines and relationships that enable it to work. Beth claims that she is moving towards the balance she is striving for, that is to have a well-planned learning environment, which comprises of worthwhile activities, and to allow the children to be independent in their learning. Below Beth talks about this balance and the constraints she has had to face in order to achieve it, including her own fears about losing control, the children's emotional needs and previous experiences in classrooms:

> I feel much stronger . . . because I feel I'm growing away from that closed way of teaching. I do let children go sometimes where they want to go. There are designated areas, but if they want to go and do something, then I will let them if it happens to fit in with everything. I do think you need to hold on to the structure all the same, because otherwise the thing might just fall apart and it could be very chaotic for the children if one day you say 'Yes' and the next 'No' about something. That's very hard for them to understand as well. But on the whole I'm often telling the children to go and help each other, which is something they were just not used to doing at all. Nobody had ever asked them to do that. They're responding to that and I like to see that in the classroom. Some children can do some things and others cannot. So they can help each other.

Conclusion

Beth's ideas about education are very child-centred, and at the end of the first year she was reassured by the college component of the course, which seemed to reflect her views on teaching and learning, and gave her a sense that what she was doing was right. This was particularly important for Beth, given that her observations of practice in her host school seemed to be strongly at odds with her own views.

At the end of the second year, Beth reported that she now felt like a teacher. Having had the opportunity to evaluate the children's progress during the teaching term, she could see the evidence of the children's learning, and could feel more confident in her own teaching ability. Beth is particularly proud of the progress the childen have made in their development of writing, and artwork. Evidence gathered which focused on the latter was presented for her final project work, which was judged very highly by college staff.

As she reviews her development over the two years, Beth fully recognizes the extent of her own anxieties, and how this has impinged upon her ability to act within situations which challenged her views about education. It also becomes clear during the latter part of the course that Beth has now reached the conclusion that many teachers will not or cannot engage as critically as she had expected with their own teaching. Beth attributes some of her frustrations in the past to her expectations that they could. She also recognizes that her attempts to discuss issues with other teachers may have been perceived as threatening, particularly since she tends to appear very intense. In addition, Beth realizes that her own uncertainties about herself as a teacher may have been disconcerting to others. Her comment during the final interview suggests how Beth still greatly values discussions about teaching, but has become rather more selective in her choice of whom to talk with:

> I talk with my friends. I have a friend who is a teacher and talk to her an awful lot . . . I've talked to lots of people at G., [second placement school] about teaching and had really good discussions. I've been going to staff meetings there and it's wonderful because people aren't frightened to speak out. They were discussing the new IT [information technology] policy and their aims, and they all said, 'Why is that in there? How do I have to interpret that? I don't understand it,' and people would talk about it openly. It's a real educational discussion going on and I think you learn an awful lot from it. When I was there in November, I talked a lot and we go and have coffee together still, and I talk to them about it. I try and take every opportunity with people I respect to talk about things to do with education.

Beth looks forward to her further development in the next academic year when she will take up a part-time teaching post within the school where she had been placed at the beginning of the second year. Her immediate goal is to increase her confidence and to become much more relaxed in her teaching. She admires and seeks 'the total unflapability that experienced teachers have. They take it all in their stride and I want to be more like that. I still live intensely, every moment of it. You can't keep up with that'.

Chapter 7

Case Study Four — Maggie

Introduction

An articled teacher, Maggie, is placed at a village infant school which has a 'family centre' attached. The quality of housing in the area is quite poor, and unemployment is high. The school consists of the original, small Victorian stone building along with several mobile classrooms in the playground. Inside, the rooms are well maintained and bright with displays. There appears a strong, caring ethos amongst the teaching staff, who are mainly aged between 30 and 50 years. The school actively promotes a sense of community, parents are readily welcomed, and support staff are valued and respected. A similar age to Maggie, her mentor is a calm, quietly spoken teacher with many years teaching experience. She is highly regarded by colleagues and others.

In Year 1, Maggie gains further experience in a large, modern, village primary school which has several classrooms feeding into open-plan work areas. Maggie reports that noise levels can be high, which she finds distracting. Staff within the school are generally in their 20s and 30s, and Maggie comments on her mentor as 'young and outgoing', favouring a lively, group work approach within her classroom.

In the second year, Maggie spends six weeks in an urban primary school. Here she finds the staff less supportive of each other. Her mentor during this time is a young, male teacher.

Entry to Teacher Education

Maggie is in her early 40s and comes from what she describes as a 'diligent, working-class family'. Her own schooling spanned a variety of institutions, an infant school followed by a primary school, transferring at the age of 9 to a Roman Catholic school, after the religious conversion of her parents. She then gained entry to a grammar school at the age of 11. Maggie seems to have performed well at school, but reports being aware of coming from a poorer, 'tougher end of town' from the others in her class. She attributes her success to the high expectations of her parents, and her own determination to do well. Her experiences of the grammar school, however, have left her with a distaste for selective education:

> We were streamed. It was an awful school really. The top class were
> expected to aim to go to university. The next best thing was that you might

get a place in a grot-bag training college, and hard luck if you did. Then
there was the poor old typists and the riff-raff . . . and they weren't expected
to achieve anything. As far as I could see there was no input for them either.
They knew they weren't going to get any O-levels, and so did we; and
they didn't!

Maggie appears to maintain an acute sense of injustice that many people close
to her were branded as educational failures after failing the 11 plus exam, yet later
went on to be successful in their own way. These experiences seem to be linked
to Maggie's strongly held beliefs that schools should value all children, and that
education is the key to self-development:

Education is the most important thing in the world in a way, because it
gives people the tools to change their lives, to give you the opportunities
to have new experiences and gain new knowledge; and knowledge is power
basically. Power over your income and your social level and the people you
mix with.

Maggie frequently refers to 'social class' when talking of her own background. She
views herself as 'a working-class person in a middle-class background', and her
identity seems to be defined with reference to the two cultures. She recognizes the
problems of having 'acquired a lot of middle-class values, without really liking the
middle classes very much', but at the same time expresses resentment towards what
she sees as the parochial, anti-academic features of working-class society:

I suppose ultimately [you] just choose the bits you like. There are some
very good positive working-class aspects, of friendliness and so on, they're
straightforward, their lack of pretence. But there are middle-class people
like that as well and I like the better, cultural aspects of middle-class life
and the fact that the middle classes might not be so inclined to sneer at
your interests and so on, whereas you wouldn't dare mention to certain
working-class people that you could spell, because it would be seen as a
negative, creep-type thing.

Going to university is seen by Maggie as an important milestone in breaking ties
with a working-class culture:

On the first day at university I was left there and my digs were across
town and I thought, 'I'm going to walk there.' Now for me to walk through
a town with lots of people was a big deal. So university always had
two functions for me, getting an academic qualification and growing socially, because my family background was quite repressive really. I used
to go out, but not very much, and my parents had strong, old-fashioned,
working-class ideas. Going to university, I had this image of me sticking
my head up through the clouds. And it was just like that. All the different

societies, the film society, the fencing club, Chinese meals, I couldn't believe it.

A significant memory of her time at university involves the breakdown of a personal relationship during her final year. She explains that as a means of coping with this, she returned for a time to her Roman Catholic primary school, which she has always associated with warmth and security, and undertook voluntary work. Her recollections of the understanding and caring approach of her old headteacher, and other staff, appear to relate strongly to her ideas about teaching:

> I think I always felt secure there and was really choked to leave. When I was there someone recognized the quality in me — they had a Chess Club there and I played . . . and he [the headteacher] put me in charge of this. I organized all these kids and gave them instructions and he put me in charge and I loved it. Just sorting them out. This was when I was 11. Maybe it was that, recognizing somewhere where you'd been appreciated.

After graduating, Maggie takes on a succession of fairly low-level clerical, manual and care assistant posts where she is working alongside others with minimal qualifications. After bringing up her family, she trains as a playgroup leader. Maggie's own family has endured considerable financial hardship over the years, partly as a result of several business failures. Maggie gives the impression that whenever she has experienced self-fulfilment, it is short-lived, only to be undermined again. However, she reports achieving a great deal of satisfaction in her work as playgroup leader and is eventually persuaded by close friends to train as a teacher. The articled teacher scheme is particularly attractive to her, because of the financial incentive and because it also allows her to be placed in a local school. Training as a teacher also seems to be perceived as the final step in her transition to a middle-class culture:

> I can't wait to get into this teaching thing where you can use long words and people don't think you're trying to impress them . . . You just hide your light under a bushel really in the interests of just keeping friendly with people and not intimidating them and frightening them . . . It's their problem now, not mine. So they take me as I am.

Images of Teaching

Maggie has quite an elaborate conception of teaching and of how she will learn to teach. First, she sees herself having to engage in a rite of passage into the professional culture of teaching; learning to be accepted as a teacher, acquiring a teacher identity. Second, she is aware that she will have to master a variety of techniques and strategies that experienced teachers possess. Third, Maggie perceives an intuitive/emotional dimension to teaching, which incorporates the development of a 'feel for teaching', demonstrated, for example, in being able 'to judge the mood of the children'.

Prior to the course, when Maggie talks about herself as a teacher, she distinguishes between the person she is at home and the more 'professional' person that she hopes to be in the classroom:

> I think I will be patient initially. Professionally I'm patient. I think this is going to be a great split between home and work and I'll have to come to terms with that. I've always found that difficult in playgroups. There you are going down and giving all your time to other people's children and then you come home moaning and groaning at your own and you get ratty with them, and that seems to me a paradox. And here I am going to be going to school and being brilliantly professional with all these children, hopefully, and then I'm going to be coming home and chewing the ears off my own. So that's an ongoing problem. I think the thing is . . . it's relatively easy to be controlled at work because it would be inappropriate to be otherwise.

For Maggie, becoming a teacher involves becoming a different person to some extent, and learning to mix with people in a different environment.

As far as teaching strategies are concerned, Maggie has memories of one particular primary school teacher whose practice she would like to emulate, recalling 'her smiling, her sense of humour and twinkling eyes', but she sees herself spending much of the time during the early part of the course 'soaking up' the techniques and strategies that teachers employ and putting them together in a way that suits her own way of working. The accumulation of techniques and strategies is a feature of learning to teach that Maggie frequently refers to.

The 'feel' for teaching that she believes to be important seems to be regarded as partly a matter of empathy and partly a matter of experience. Despite her lack of confidence, Maggie reckons that she has learned a lot about herself and other people from her previous employment; she believes she 'has a way with children' and is really well suited to becoming a teacher.

Year One — Learning to Teach

At the start of the course, Maggie's concerns focus mostly on how other people will respond to her, and particularly whether she will be able to strike up an appropriate relationship with her mentor. However, she soon reports that Sarah is not only an extremely competent teacher, but is also a skilled mentor who is very sensitive to Maggie's anxieties. As she is 'just being bombed out by the whole thing', she is relieved that Sarah concentrates on simply getting her used to the children and the classroom routines. Through her observations and discussions with Sarah, she begins to make sense of the context in which she is working, starts to take note of several of Sarah's teaching strategies and develops ideas about the way she might project herself. A few weeks into the term, she seems enthusiastic about her own progress and comments:

> [Sarah's] calm. Everything is structured. These children have no struc-
> ture in their lives. Whether you would do the same with middle-class
> [children], I don't know, or more able children. She makes them sit in
> a circle and sit up straight. We have six or seven children who are with-
> drawn because of language delay. They're very difficult because they're the
> youngest. The oldest is the statemented child and [Sarah's] the only person
> who could cope with him to be honest. The chances are that he won't end
> up in mainstream education. She knows exactly what she's doing . . . and
> they're different with her than with anyone else. In fact she was out this
> morning and the Infant Welfare Assistant said it was awful. Command and
> control is all really . . . She's said you have to overact and I've picked up
> a lot from her. She'll say, 'Children, I can't go on. Look at Mrs R. Look
> at my face. Is my face happy?' and they all say 'No,' and it's brilliant. I
> can learn from that and copy that to a certain extent. I'm sure I'll develop
> my own strategies as well, but it gives you something to work on.

Maggie also seems to be acquiring an understanding of how various subject areas are presented to young children, noting how Sarah structures and manages different kinds of activity:

> She introduced number . . . and I wrote down everything she did and it
> was so structured . . . On the first day or day two of school even, a frieze
> with numbers went up. They were at their height and she introduced them
> to numbers. She had strings and she pulled a string out and she picked a
> child out — the most troublesome. You see you learn that as well. This
> child was first to get the string and one button. 'This is one and I'm going
> to thread it on here' and she had him on her lap. So not only are you
> learning number, but you're learning how to cope with this wretched child
> who'll disrupt everything. So she went round ten children with ten things.
> So they learn that one is one person. She has lots of games that go up to
> five and she picks up five little rabbits. It's singing — so it's varied. It's
> language and loads of games holding hands up and singing. Some of the
> children couldn't hold their fingers up when they started. So she's intro-
> duced concepts like that and all along it's been like that. Then it was the
> concept of [making a] 'set' . . . She would get the entire group to sit
> down . . . then for half a dozen children she would give them a bag and ask
> them to feel what was inside. Then get the things out to see if they were
> what they had guessed. She uses cards for counting with a large circle
> drawn on it. Then she says, 'Take one object from your bag and put it in
> the circle and then point to it and say 'ONE'. And then empty the circle
> and put things away.' Then she goes on to two . . . Then she made them
> touch them because feeling is a crucial part of knowing what the twoness

of two is. She took that up to about four, I think, the first time with her group. And each time the circle was emptied, so that there was no room for confusion. So she clearly defined exactly what it was she wanted to get over. She knows exactly what she wants to get over.

The last activity is one that Maggie tries out herself with another group. Through actually doing it and then discussing what happened with Sarah, Maggie reports that she is able to learn from her mistakes. She points out that when the children started to get bored with the activity, she decided to change the objects in order to sustain their interest. However, some of the large objects did not fit inside the circle and in her discussion with Sarah afterwards, they consider that this 'added an extra dimension that throws things'. Maggie also relates how they 'talked about whether children were receiving what you were trying to teach them. She spoke about some-one using objects of the same colour with children. Then children thought blue was three, for example. So that's another element of confusion. That was mentioned on the course as well.'

Such examples of Maggie being able to match what she has learned in college sessions to her experience in the classroom seem to contribute to her growing sense of excitement and control. A few days later, Maggie recounts how college sessions on language development and getting children interested in reading have helped her to understand particular classroom experiences and to decide on appropriate actions:

> I read a story to a group of children and I thought it was totally unsatis-factory. They were mucking about, it was an informal situation. They weren't in a circle. It was meant to be a bit of relaxation in the home corner and I thought it was a dead loss. But the next day there was one odd child . . . who was reading to her doll, and she said, 'Could you read me a book?' and I said, 'Yes'. I was doing something else but she went and got chairs and the book and she had the book that I'd been reading to them and she'd been mucking about. And she started telling me about it. So even without appearing to pay any attention she had been and that was learning. I've been doing some reading outside about paraphrasing what children say not necessarily being a good idea. So I let her go on. She ran out of steam. An awful lot of children in the school have poor language. It's not imposing. It's using the right moment to give her some words. It's this thing of leading them. My book reading has been really brilliant. It's pulled together college and school . . . Things are more meaningful the more you've done . . . Working backwards seeing the theory there.

However, after the first few weeks, Maggie expresses frustration with the college input, perceiving that the philosophy of the course is that students should 'find their way to the light' whereas she wants to be given 'the shortcuts' and a 'few stated rules' about how to teach. In common with other articled teachers, she feels that the tutors should give more guidance, for example, about behaviour management. Sessions which do provide activities for the classroom are seen as very useful. In particular, Maggie finds an early lecture on emergent writing to be particularly helpful, because she is given a framework for how to actually teach the activities. Soon after, she visits a school with her mentor to see such an approach being used, and reports the value of being able to put 'theory and practice' together. Her understanding appears to be particularly helped by the discussion afterwards with Sarah.

Maggie reports that using a journal has also been useful to her, and during this first term she makes many notes of what actually happened during the day within school and college, giving her reactions to what she has observed or done. For example:

> 1.10. Very down this day — not sure why. Possibly college — felt a bit negative. All the students were in [start of the main college term] — they are *young*.

> Sarah has started activity sheets for each child to assess their abilities and make sure they all experience everything. I'm doing a spatial block-game — there are five different colours and five different heights to be arranged like a staircase. Some children can do it anyway, some learned how to do it and some are still learning. Hetty who could write letters, but not in any order or line, finds it very difficult.

> It's good for colours and language — tallest, shortest — and science, I get them to test the result. Used the words — 'does it work? Well, test and see. Can you walk your fingers up the staircase?' Got a bit low — felt I wasn't making it interesting enough.

> Tried all twenty children with this over three days — satisfying as they had learned something — spatial awareness.

She also notes down ideas from 'model lessons' which she hopes will be useful for the future.

Despite her initial wariness about fitting in, Maggie soon develops a great affinity with the school, accepting that its ethos and practice are to provide the best opportunities for the children, many of whom experience emotional and learning difficulties. Her diary writing reflects a growing admiration for the people she works with:

> Sometimes I'm amazed at the talent of some of these teachers. And I'm amazed at the ground that's been covered . . . the children and the systematic way in which the teachers cover it. You can see their plan when you look back over it. When they're doing x topic there are strands within that and you can see how it all connects up.

Maggie also claims that by reading back over the successes in her teaching, she is able to find consolation in her writing when she is feeling low: 'I'm constantly on a seesaw about whether I'll make it or be able to do it. To read something like that I realize I can do it.' Certainly within the first term it appears that Maggie's development has been characterized by a series of 'ups and downs' which, on the one hand, give her feelings of success and control, and on the other, seem to rock her confidence.

For example, Maggie's confidence is boosted when Sarah invites her to work with her at a parents' evening early in the term, treating Maggie like a colleague and an equal. At the same time, being accepted by parents gives Maggie significant feedback that she is able to be a teacher. On another occasion, Sarah leaves her to talk to a parent while she photocopies some information, and Maggie appreciates the deliberate move to let her act as the teacher while Sarah does the 'menial task' herself.

Towards the end of term, Maggie has charge of the class for a day when Sarah is away, and she reports that this gives her a 'tremendous boost' because she is able to put into practice the strategies she has previously noted, such as placing a mischievous boy close by her during circle time. Having also coped with organizing the class during a fire drill, Maggie feels reassured in her ability to carry out the teacher's role.

Yet there are many times when Maggie reports having 'backward slides', and losing confidence. For example, when she visits another school to observe practice in the later years, she reports, 'I felt quite ill this morning . . . going into this classroom I felt quite demoralized seeing how brilliant this teacher was. I was overwhelmed with admiration for them and I can't conceive of myself yet being able to do that. That's very worrying.' She also reports several occasions when her planned activities do not interest the children or where she has lost control of some of the more boisterous members of the class. She rationalizes that she must keep such blows to her self-image in perspective, particularly when it is close to Christmas and the children are understandably lively.

Maggie's notions of what is good practice in terms of managing behaviour seem to be greatly influenced by her strong sense of social justice, for she repeatedly claims that if children feel encouraged and valued they will be able to learn. She comments: 'I just feel that I would like the children I teach to remember enjoying school or the classes I was in. That's what I would like them most to get out of it. Everything else follows on from that.' She is drawn to ideas about positive behaviour management which she encounters in her reading and observations in schools. She believes, however, that using a positive approach is not her natural inclination, and consequently she derives considerable satisfaction from the times when she feels sufficiently in control of herself that she can enact appropriate strategies: 'I find sometimes I'm thinking "Be quiet and sit up straight," and I remember to turn it round and get a good response and then I'm pleased.' Her thinking about discipline is further influenced by observing less effective practice which she not only distances herself from, but also compares with more positive ways of acting in order to refine ideas for her own teaching:

I've seen some very bad ways of going on with children in the command and control aspect, shouting and keeping on. I put that down to poor organization and not using a circle [i.e., putting children in a circle] in particular, not gaining control and spending some time on that. Then having the session constantly interrupted. I wouldn't do that and have sometimes been in other classes and I've been amazed that I've made it work. I kept control. It amazes me that other teachers don't seem to know this, especially when they've been trained, but I suppose it's a technique. If you haven't come across it . . .

Maggie perceives that her teaching progresses by seeing 'where the gaps' are and 'tackling them'. She expects to learn through more practice, for example, in getting control of the children, being observed and criticized, and generally being given 'tips' and 'hints'. In addition, she feels that she needs more knowledge about what and how she should actually teach, particularly in how to teach reading.

At the end of this first term, Maggie reports that she is no longer so drained and overwhelmed by everything, and can now think further forward instead of simply coping on a day-to-day basis. She is generally pleased with both the course and her school experiences, and claims 'everything's gone pretty well'. The articled teachers, she says, have discussed their concerns with the tutors and feel they have more say in what happens on the course. Also Maggie reports that she has got to know her own tutor better and that she feels able to talk to her. More importantly, Sarah's help and support has been crucial in building her confidence, and she continues to hold her in very high esteem. In the first term, 'mentor time' is often used to visit other schools, but generally they hold weekly meetings which are very organized with a clear agenda, including time to talk over any personal matters that may be bothering her, as Maggie has many stresses to cope with at home.

Maggie claims that Sarah's skill as a mentor lies in her ability to respond to her student's evolving needs. Maggie describes the strategies that she believes Sarah has used to build her self-confidence:

She has to be positive for me all the time. Very positive. That's the main thing . . . pushing, quite a lot of shoving went on, as gentle as possible. She's just an excellent teacher and that's how she gets the best out of everybody. She values you for what you are. I subscribe to that and partly why I want to do this [teaching] is having a lot of negative experiences in the past. I think that's an awful way to go on and that there must be a better way. Sarah embodies that in a way . . . she values where you are . . . Then she's very tactful and she gives you pointers and things to think about, which is marvellous really. She's very experienced and is deputy head. So she has all these interpersonal skills which she's been using with adults over a period of time and I'm sure all this helps. And she's very perceptive . . . When I'm pushing myself and thinking 'I must stick at it,' she knows and she'll say, 'Would you like to take the afternoon off?' She doesn't make decisions for you. She's very good like that. She's like that with the children. She gives them the choice all the time. So she's just one of these rare people I think. Very well chosen as a mentor. Very genuine too. Took great trouble to be positive. We do get on well, but I think if we didn't hit it off personality-wise, she wouldn't be any different. She would be as straightforward . . . Nothing's too much trouble . . . and if I say 'Thank you for that,' she says, 'Oh, that's what I'm here for' . . . She's very self-confident herself in a quiet way.

Maggie finds that the staff are generally very kind towards her and that she trusts them, although she suspects that one teacher resents the idea of an articled teacher being in the school, and seems rather 'off hand'. Maggie resolves that she will 'work on' their relationship. She says that several teachers have allowed her the opportunity to try ideas out, and to make mistakes without this being viewed as a sign of incompetence. She believes that if there were any real problems with her teaching, she would be told. It is important to Maggie that she is able to offer something in return, and she is clearly proud when other teachers compliment her ideas, displays or teaching skills, and this appears to affirm her self-image as a teacher.

Early in the second term, Maggie transfers to a junior school for a four week placement, in order to observe later primary practice, and to do some teaching. When she is interviewed after two weeks, she seems depressed and quite agitated. Indeed, on both occasions when Maggie works in other schools, she experiences times of great stress and insecurity, losing her sense of 'being a teacher', experiencing great difficulty in adjusting to the new environment.

Maggie describes the modern school as a 'bit of a showcase', consequently receiving many visitors which seems to disturb Maggie. She also feels disorientated for other reasons. The school is an open-plan design, resulting in 'phenomenal' noise levels. At the same time, Maggie feels exposed by the openness of the shared work areas, which means that her teaching can be watched by other people. She also has little time to acclimatize to working in one class before moving on to another, 'I've been with Year 3, then Year 5 and I've been with Year 6 and it's been brain numbing.' She has difficulty coming to terms with the various routines and systems within the school. For example, Maggie perceives that, unlike the infant classes she is used to, there is little whole class discussion, nor teacher 'input' while the children are working in groups, and she cannot understand what role the teacher is taking, or where she might fit in.

Maggie is particularly disturbed by what she sees as the lack of support from her new mentor, Sally. They have few mentor sessions, which are occasions where Maggie has come to expect guidance and a focus for her observations. As a result, she feels that she has been 'spinning round with no direction'. Although Sally is quite young, she does not seem to empathize with Maggie's concerns as a novice teacher. Maggie also appears to feel intimidated by her confidence and liveliness. Usually, Maggie values being able to put ideas from college into immediate practice, but because the context in which she is working is so different, she avoids situations where she feels she might not be able to cope. For example, Maggie comments on her refusal to take PE and dance lessons:

I was just more thrown than expected with all these new variables. The task we had didn't help because it was PE. There was no way I would go into a new school and do PE with an age group vastly different from one I'd had anything to do with. I don't think it's safe. I didn't feel confident . . . It was just like starting all over again really. I felt I needed to get to grips with the children and . . . the way of working was so different. There were too many variables.

In the third week, Maggie starts to form a clearer picture of what is happening. She identifies that the junior teachers seem to direct the children's learning less, and tasks are often open-ended. In turn, the children seem to be much more independent and able to sustain an activity for quite long periods of time. When she works with a male Year 6 teacher who is particularly skilled at 'intervening absolutely minimally', she finds his approach exciting because the children are on-task and clearly enjoying their work. From this point, Maggie increasingly stresses the importance of not 'spoon feeding' children and allowing them to take control of their own learning. She thinks about how she might adopt the observed practices in her own teaching. Simultaneously, she feels inhibited by what she can actually do herself in the class at the time, because she is unfamiliar with the age group, and much of her time seems to be spent observing. Contrasting her two experiences of school, she comments:

> The experience I had previously seemed to be very much that the teachers knew all the answers really, whereas genuinely in the primary school I felt the teachers didn't know where the children might end up and weren't floored by that either.

> In the infants school, perhaps because it's a special needs school, there's a tremendous effort for children to find things out for themselves [but] they [teachers] really know what they want the children to know at the end of it. It's much tighter in a way, partly because these children start so much further back down the line. It's almost a luxury to let them flap around and find their own way, so they tend to be more directive. In [the primary school] they seem to have got more skills and ability and they were able to be set off on something and keep going at it . . .

> To my mind it's easier [for the teacher]. There's less pressure and you don't have to be instantly and constantly there with the children as you do with infants. There's no let-up with the infants. Whether that's [infant school] in particular or all infants in general, I don't know.

When Maggie returns to the infant school, she works in a Year 2 class with Ann, an experienced teacher who is about the same age. The curriculum focus in the college course is now science, and this presents an opportunity for Maggie to try to make activities more 'open-ended'. To fit in with the class topic on Buildings, Ann suggests that Maggie takes some sessions on electricity, and Maggie opts to organize some activities on simple circuits with groups of children.

Maggie is very wary about teaching science, and confesses to not having a clear picture of how science should be presented to very young children. She claims that through her reading and talking to other teachers she is beginning to 'tune in', but still finds it difficult to plan the session as she does not really know how the children will respond and has few ideas about what she wants the children to learn from an open-ended investigation, or what her role will be in managing this. Below, Maggie describes how she planned and implemented the session with a group of three girls and one boy:

> I spoke to them in a circle; we spoke about power and we've been building into it, sources of power, the torch. I used that because it was something familiar. Then I just threw the stuff at them just now and said, 'See if you can get the thing to light' ... I hoped they would find it interesting. I didn't tell them what they were going to find out. I hoped they would find something out for themselves genuinely by actually using those materials. I didn't sling it all on a table right away. They just had the batteries and bulb things and connectors with the clips on — the leads. And they started with that and spent quite a long time on that.

After Maggie has repeated the experiment with several groups, she talks about what she has learned, connecting her experiences with her reading, and the children's own ideas, from which she is able to conclude how she might improve the activity and her teaching to make it more exciting and relevant:

> That's the value of doing things with a lot of children. You get all these different experiences. I might have thought that was an absolute doddle if I'd just rested from my first experience where the children fairly easily achieved the required aim ... [although] I wouldn't say categorically that they all know you have to have a circuit to have a light bulb work, and a battery and so on. I think they'd be able to go and get the stuff to make a light bulb work and know what was required, but not necessarily why ...

> The way I would like to [develop their understanding] is with them in a circle and you pass a squeeze round and when the power gets to you to smile. I read that somewhere and that seemed like a good thing because you can model something like that I think. Then break the circuit and see what happens and get the bulb to go out, as it were ... It's a difficult concept to grasp — the pulse of electricity. It's just difficult. Then how the battery itself works and the idea of it being a store. We did touch on that with the second group. That batteries [in their toys] don't last for ever ... I guess that's from home experience. I didn't think about toys actually. I never thought about that and yet it would be much more appropriate. Maybe that would be a good thing to do. Perhaps one could bring in toys and show them the metal bits. One feels one's way into this. You have blinding flashes. I've experienced that when something's come into my mind. I've been talking to them and there's been a blinding flash of something

that would be really good to say to illuminate whatever I'm trying to get over. It doesn't come in planning. It comes as I'm doing it.

Maggie increasingly stresses the intuitive and creative aspects of teaching. When she is feeling positive, teaching is seen as a creative expression, and during the second term she feels that she is moving beyond the 'modelling' stage and can now give something of herself, feeling more in control as a result: 'I'm not play acting any more. You get into the role as it were and then you become it.' Maggie comments further about how she is learning to teach:

> I watched Sarah do a maths lesson and I modelled what I do almost exactly on what she did, because I was wanting to see how the children were with this approach, also wanting to assess the children too. So it was easy to use an existing framework rather than be thinking about extending myself . . . But I have done a similar thing with other children and have added a bit. She provides me with starting points. They're all starting points. I shall forget what I learned from whom ultimately. It's like a mosaic. It will all merge. As it is, something triggers my memory, ways of doing things, or even a few words and they stick in my mind. So on that basis they must be reasonably memorable. So I remember to use them. I've incorporated what's gone in.

> I think [feeling confident] boils down to the fact that I've been going round watching different brilliant people, brilliant in different ways, but what actually happens in the end is that you start to give something of yourself. It's you, nobody else, and it's something that comes from within and you start to produce that with the children. It's not any particular knowledge.

Although Maggie is pleased with her progress in many ways, she is frustrated that her knowledge of what to teach is still partial. She sees both her mentor and the college playing important roles in providing structure and support:

> I've been greatly helped by my mentor who breaks things down into bite-size bits . . . I'm obviously still at the stage where I'm working things out for myself. There are the children's needs and there are my needs. One is here for the children, but I need to find out certain things so that I can direct the children. So there's me collecting information and at the same time I'm trying to progress the children and challenge them and it's a bit feeling the way, and you can't see the wood for the trees sometimes. And that's where my mentor has helped me. She breaks a problem down and gets to the nitty-gritty and she says, 'What you need to do after that is . . .' and she gives me a plan, a track. I would have thought that college could have done things like that because I don't suppose any of us need a course in basic maths, even quite advanced maths, but what we do need is

a schema, an orderly way to progress children through these things. It would almost be helpful if the college were to provide you with a plan of work so that it would give you a starting point and you could try it and if it didn't work it's soon apparent and you move on. But it gives the steps for you. Maybe I'm expecting too much. I have worked up till 11.00 pm every night this week, but I'm not prepared to live like that. I don't necessarily want to use a bought scheme of work either because I think they're turgid. But I need a working aid of some kind from college . . . it's all a bit fragmentary somehow. Maybe this is a symptom of the stage I'm at. I haven't got a totally coherent picture.

At the end of the spring term, Maggie reflects upon these many aspects of teaching, acknowledging that learning to teach is complex and very demanding. Having to teach before she has a clear picture of what she is trying to achieve, how she will act, or how the children might react, has been particularly stressful. In her thinking, she sees a likeness between learning to teach and housework:

The stages I've gone through are . . . comparable to . . . doing the housework. There's a certain stage just before the housework is finished and the house is immaculate, when everything is all over the place, everything is pulled out and in piles everywhere, but it's only a relatively minor job to get it all back again. The major job has been done. I feel that's how I feel about teaching. There have been so many inputs, so many things to cope with, different aspects, parents, teachers, children, me and adults in the classroom, the content of what the children are going to do, controlling the children, all these things. I've really felt, 'Will I ever get together with it?' and so on and all of a sudden it seems to be coming together. It's lovely. My confidence has grown as well. I just feel like a different person really.

Maggie is particularly satisfied when she is able to relax with the children and have fun. Unlike other students, she is reticent to talk about 'being herself' in the classroom because she feels that the person she is outside school is not exciting and her home life is often hard and lacking in fun. Being herself is therefore not what she wants to achieve.

In the summer term, Maggie is observed during a whole school 'science day' when she is again building circuits with groups of children. Interestingly, she does not make use of the ideas she had suggested after her earlier experiences, such as looking at battery-driven toys or making a circuit by holding hands, seeming reluctant to deviate from the activity framework she has already used. Maggie comments on her day's work and on the benefits of having previously undertaken a similar activity:

The main thing about today was that I'd done it before, so I felt quite *au fait* with the materials. They were available, there was half an hour to check them and they'd already been used by some of the children. I came in and my planning was to introduce them to the materials and language, which they may not be familiar with, and to give them words like batteries, crocodile clips, circuit, light bulb, and try and get them to construct a circuit themselves using manipulative skills. I thought they would find the crocodile clips difficult to handle. I wanted them to learn that you needed a circuit to make the bulb or motor work and also that metal was the conductor of electricity and other materials weren't. When they'd constructed a circuit we would introduce other things. It's all individual work, there was enough for each child to proceed at their own pace . . . Some had no difficulty and were able to manipulate the clips onto the battery. You'd get a battery with a clip from one terminal to the other. So I'd ask if their bulb was working and suggest joining the light bulb in some way and they'd have a go and try it. Is it working now? What else can you do? That sort of thing. It rolled on and they were talking to each other. One child would achieve it and there'd be excitement and other children would look to see what they'd done. But some children were struggling themselves and I would offer help in the clipping, the mechanical thing, but not the thinking. I'd ask what they wanted to do and if they couldn't manipulate it I'd do it for them. I tried to maintain it open and not spoonfeed them, or provide solutions for them, no matter how frustrated I might become. But it was usually possible. They found it hard, particularly girls, unfortunately. I was very aware of gender, but again a lot of boys were quite *au fait*. I'd try and notice who was getting on and then incorporate another thing. After we'd done a light bulb, we'd do another piece of equipment. In the meantime they'd try and connect the bulb to plastic to see if it worked. It was all leading them on. They would get the switch in and they got quite interested in the motors because of the noise they made. Then I'd try to get them to hold up their things so that you could see the circularity of the circuit. I'd try and get each child to do that, and notice it formally, and try and get the word out of them. After a bit, some would lose the thread and would try and construct the circuit without a battery . . . As a new teacher I tend to think that if someone has had enough after 5 minutes it's a reflection on me. But I don't feel that any more. I might try to extend them a bit, trying to judge if they've taken in enough for that stint, or whether I need to help them if they're frustrated. If I think they're frustrated I try and help them sort out their thinking, or it can be just this manipulative thing . . .

I was clearer in what I was going to say too. I had more firmly fixed in my mind what I was trying to do I suppose, and the language I wanted to get across. I just stuck to that. I didn't talk so much. I let them get on with it. But you're on the go all the time with eight children because one always has a problem.

At the end of the year, Maggie again talks about how she is learning to teach, realizing that she now must focus more upon what the children are doing and how they learn, which she expects to be able to do when she does not have to think so much about her own teaching, especially her management strategies:

> Ultimately it will be like driving a car. Then when I'm not thinking about myself at all then I'll be focusing entirely on the children. That's one of the good reasons why this is two years. I couldn't have got to there in a year and assimilated and internalized it. I do internalize a lot of things now . . . when I went out to my primary school the children were mucking about, and I wondered what to do, and the teacher came back and I thought, 'Thank God for that'. I'm not like that any more. It's just that moment of self-consciousness and getting over it. Some people may never feel like that, but it was a thing for me . . . And also picking up on everything all the time is hard too. Picking up on children galloping about. It takes a lot of effort. I personally don't care about things like that, but I recognize one needs to in school if the school is going to function.

Maggie again reports that Sarah's role is changing and that she relies on her less and less for guidance, although they still 'chew over' any difficulties she has. Maggie feels that her college tutor's role in her development has been minimal, and generally seems unsure about what the college should offer her. She often feels that her assignments and practical teaching are given only bland comments, 'I suppose they're trying to minimize the pressure in what is a highly pressurized situation in many ways, but it would be useful to know. You can only be laid back so far, I think.' On the whole she feels that school is far more important to her than college, although she accepts that she would feel differently if her relationship with Sarah was not so good.

Year Two

Maggie looks forward to the autumn term with a determination to project herself more and to act with greater self-assurance both in school and college. In college sessions, Maggie is very sensitive to the changing relationships within the group, and it seems that a number of tensions have arisen. For example, some students are seen as vociferous and rather domineering during group discussions. While this tends to have the effect of silencing Maggie, she resolves that this term she will be more assertive.

She has also made the decision to start the new academic year at her next placement school, as she wishes to see how the teachers settle their new classes and establish classroom routines. This time she is to work mainly with her new mentor, a young male teacher whom she already knows as a result of observing his science teaching the previous year. She also spends some time in other classes.

Although Maggie feels that now she should be able to adjust to different routines and make new relationships without difficulty, adjusting to the new school presents several difficulties. Many of her fears and concerns are similar to those she experienced in the first year. Once again, Maggie appears to be filled with self-doubt, she views the teachers in the school as professional and self-assured, against a view of herself as lacking in self-confidence and not yet belonging to the profession. She comments on the awkwardness of her first day:

> On the Sunday night, before term started, I felt very edgy and wasn't expecting to enjoy myself. There was going to be a staff meeting the next day, new group, new staffroom, and afterwards on the Monday, I felt very tired . . . I'm not very fond of groups of staff or staff meetings. Teachers seem to me to be immensely self-contained somehow. They're not necessarily very chatty. I've also worked in social work where people are inclined to think 'Oh they look a bit lonely,' and they'll go and talk to them. Teachers aren't like that. I don't find them very sociable to be honest. I admire them for being self-contained. I think they think about what they need to be doing and they probably haven't got any space for anybody else. They probably think everyone else is all right, doing their own thing. Most of them don't see that as part of their role. But by no means all of them, otherwise one wouldn't have this mentor system, because mentors are people who consider that to be a large part of their job. I wondered how much of that there would be and whether they were really a nice, happy team and whether they would be welcoming. Part of it is what they're like and how I'm going to fit in and part of it is with regard to how they see me and whether they'll accept me.

During the placement, Maggie talks again of feeling 'de-skilled'. She wants to contribute to the Year 6 class in which she is mainly working, but finds that her previous experiences are not particularly helpful to her. She feels she is starting over again, 'learning so much'. She finds her new mentor 'quite cool, personality-wise' offering her little emotional support. She feels helpless as she senses a range of constraints which prevent her from acting as she had hoped she would be able to. For example, although Maggie remembers that older children work more independently, she reports that she still finds it difficult to know what to do or to say to children when she is helping in the classroom:

> I thought that the first few days I would just be getting to grips with it, and I wanted to show a low profile because my previous experience had shown that the children were disturbed if two adults in the same room were trying to have an equal share of their attention. So I was prepared to take a back seat. And also the class teacher would be trying to get to grips with things and get control. I also thought I could start assessing them. He did introduce me, and included me in saying good morning. But I do have a secondary role really. I do chip in if they're getting noisy, or if he's on the phone I'll help. He's seen what I can do, and as he gets more confidence in me, he'll let me do more things. I'd prefer just to take it steady. But I've started to feel that I need to be a bit more active. On the other hand, I can't

quite see how to do it. The maths system is a scheme. There are three groups in the class divided up on a maths basis, and I was going to look at this particular group . . . But if they're doing maths, then there isn't much teaching. He doesn't do much teaching. A lot of it is one-off and first time for me, that's the trouble . . . I think I'm being useful, but not in such an obvious way as in an infant school. I tend to feel more like a slightly gifted helper here. While the teacher is there, I suppose that's it. I'm a bit demoralized because it's not very lively somehow. Perhaps my expectations aren't very real. A lot of quiet work has to be done . . . I did think I could make my mark there in some form or another . . . but I think I've gone a bit downhill since . . . I don't seem quite so keen.

Maggie experiences several low points and recalls particular times when she feels out of her depth and demoralized. For example, the requirement from college during this time is that she should undertake planning and assessments in geography, which Maggie feels unable to do because she feels uncertain of the curriculum and lacks any clear conceptions of how a geography lesson might be organized:

We were doing erosion and weathering and it was this feeling that many of us express even now, of where do you start? I wouldn't know where to start . . . You tend to think that you ought to know what to do and I didn't.

When she is asked to cover for a teacher who is ill for two days, Maggie reports that she achieves very little of what she has planned, because so much of her energy goes into just managing the children, and she recognizes that the work is not well matched to the children or the circumstances in which she is working. For example, she tries to undertake some practical maths activities instead of simply relying upon the maths scheme, partly because Maggie has gained the impression from college that good teachers don't need to use schemes, and her experiences in school have also led her to question their value. However, she finds that the maths games she uses need much more teacher direction and time than she had originally planned for, and as a result, she abandons them:

This is managing the curriculum really, but I'm blowed if I'm going to give in to Scottish Maths. That would be a real sign of failure . . . [because] I think it's pedestrian, tedious, boring, it doesn't actually teach children anything. It is not assessible. I've seen children go through Scottish Maths and they haven't got a clue about certain basic concepts. I've actually tested that at [first year primary school]. They don't know their two-times table and yet on paper they're streaks ahead. So I think it's the way it's used. I don't know what the answer is. Making out worksheets all the time is one answer but very time consuming . . . You can't just say you've done it verbally, you have to prove something . . . I think it's very doubtful that a completed worksheet is proof of anything. On the other hand, I can see it's expected. I ended up giving them colouring that day and did some reading.

Maggie does experience positive times and she particularly enjoys planning and working collaboratively in PE with a female member of staff. Maggie reports that the teacher makes her feel good about herself because she makes her do things which she can achieve, including teaching an impromptu badminton lesson to a group of children when the planned lesson has to be changed at the last minute. Maggie feels that she would 'make a really good mentor because there was no sitting on the sideline'.

Overall, however, Maggie reckons she is 'back to square one', unable to apply her previous learning in the new, and very different, school context:

> Maybe it's just life or just always hard to start learning again, to go back to square one. It's just that what you know about infants isn't necessarily relevant to top juniors . . . someone could warn you that you were going to be more of an observer than a spare limb-type role.

When Maggie returns to her host school for the second half of term, she works with the Year 1 class she is going to teach the following term. Once a week she takes charge of the class for a full day, so that she can get used to organizing and managing the whole class. During this term, in common with other articled teachers, Maggie is mainly concerned about her spring teaching practice, for which she has several hopes and anxieties:

> I'm looking forward to it like mad already and I'm going to enjoy it. I'm trying to learn to pace myself because I can see me going like a bull in a china shop. I'm going to do three and a half days, Monday to half-day Thursday teaching, half-day Thursday afternoon mentoring and preparation and Friday get them organized. I'm looking forward to it really. I think it will be easier than having done the one day. You do one day and then you worry about leaving a load of stuff for the teacher to finish off. It will be me and I'll be able to roll it on. I won't have to dredge up new things every day. That wouldn't be appropriate, so I'll get some continuation and a proper feeling for the way the children are . . .

> One thing that worries me is that teachers seem to get to grips with things much quicker than I do. Last term [summer, Year 1] I did maths and it took me a long time to sort things out . . . I was trying to work it out for myself. I think now I'll take the starting point of the class teacher, not spending all my time deciding whether she was right or not. I'll just start from where she left off. That's why it's been good to see this Year 6 teacher. Otherwise you don't know where to start really. I don't worry about controlling them. I do have minor worries, I've got to do an assembly and there are some things I feel happier with than others. Some things I feel happier about having a go at when I don't have an audience. But that's daft . . .

> I'm a bit worried about it, but not worried about being able to do it actually. I'm worried about whether I can cope with all my outside things,

like family. Well, I will cope with them but whether it's going to be very pleasant for them remains to be seen. That's the focus of my main worries really. Sorting out the balance between family and work and college . . .

I'm concerned about keeping it all going and having enough energy. The assessing and managing to get enough time to do that and hear them read. I think I can sort out the organization now, but getting these quiet moments to do these other things is the worrying thing, because I haven't really got to grips with that.

Planning and Organization

When Maggie takes over the Year 1 class, she decides to use a whole class approach to start sessions before sending the children off to work in groups. She rationalizes this in terms of it enabling her to give the main explanation once so that all the children can understand what is expected, and the adult helpers can see what the children are being asked to do, what aspects Maggie wants to emphasize and how questions might be framed, so that they would be able to help any children in difficulty. This format of whole class teaching followed by group work is seen as the way to 'manage time and them' and Maggie continues to use this for the rest of her time in school, although she does make adjustments in the light of experience.

Maggie realizes that much of her lesson planning and classroom organization is based on the assumption of having two helpers, one of whom is the class teacher. She recognizes that in future teaching situations she might well have to plan different types of activities, and organize the class differently, and that 'open-ended tasks' which allow children to explore and guide their own learning, might be more difficult to manage if she was working alone.

Although Maggie has clear ideas of how she sees her class functioning, there are a number of occasions when her plans do not work out as expected. Maggie seems frequently to be surprised by the range of factors [the moods of the children and the teacher, the peer groups, the organization of the day, etc.] that influence how children respond to activities. While taking responsibility for teaching the whole class, Maggie often gives the impression of being weary and stressed, struggling with the demands of classroom organization.

Behaviour Management and Relationships with Children

Throughout the first year, Maggie often talked about the importance of behaviour management and her developing range of positive strategies. She is particularly drawn to these because the teachers she admires, and wishes to emulate, manage in this way. Such strategies are also seen as connecting to her ideas on the role of education. In the second year, Maggie continues to emphasize her commitment to these beliefs:

I feel education is here for them to use, and they need to know that it's something worth having, and they won't think it's worth having if they're not enjoying school . . . I hope they'll get enough education to take charge of their own lives, not being manipulated in any way on a macro or minor scale. That they'll be able to stand up for themselves and know that there are choices to be made . . . I want them to enjoy coming to school, to get the knowledge and skills they'll need in their lives to be able to get on to higher things and use society, and get from it what's useful for them, and to contribute to it.

However, when she is responsible for the whole class, having to cope with the day-to-day management greatly affects what she actually does. For example, during an early visit to her classroom in the spring term, Maggie's day had started badly at home and she realized that this was having an effect on her in the classroom. Additionally the children were taking a lot longer than she expected to settle into the routines she was trying to establish:

This morning I wasn't over-pleased because I'm not feeling well and the family are driving me mad. I think that put me in a poor state of mind and I'm a bit upset to think that perhaps I wasn't as professional as I should have been really. I don't know whether it showed or not. Whether the children would have picked up on that. But I was grumpy to start with . . . I seem to be still tackling nitty-gritty things like getting them to line up properly, move about the school properly and sort themselves out in the classroom so that they're not always asking me over every little thing. Getting them to be independent, I suppose. I think it's a long, slow job and maybe they're progressing, but it's certainly hard work and an uphill struggle.

When the children start to play her up during the early morning circle 'news' time, she decides to change it in order to help her to cope, even though this goes against the school policy and her beliefs that the children need lots of opportunities to talk and share with others in order to develop self-confidence. When Maggie talks about her decision, it seems that she is unable to remain patient, because the children are preventing her from carrying out the teaching as she would wish:

I feel this initial sharing time is a valuable time, but two things have happened there. This morning for instance three children claimed to have fallen out of bed, or rather four did. The first was certainly genuine and the others were highly unlikely. So I find that kind of thing irritating. If one responds with a lot of interest about someone falling out of bed and they're all craving your interest and needing you, then perhaps you're going to get a reiteration of that kind of story. I suppose that's what it is. Does that mean you act very levelly and moderately to everything and never show any surprise or pleasure? That seems to be so much like social control that it doesn't seem reasonable. I guess it's just a hazard and I'll have to disregard the ones I think are making it up and not rewarding them with the attention they're seeking, beyond token attention. Also I'm getting slightly bored with it myself. This isn't necessarily something to be taken into account as far as they're concerned because it doesn't mean it's not valid from their point of view. My strategy this week has been to do talking time on one day a week. We have a talk table (which is an idea I got from my mentor when I told her about my problems) and they can put things on it of interest to them. What is the purpose of talk time? Partly it's to increase self-esteem. One loses that aspect if you're not talking in a circle. But if they want to share things with their friends on a smaller scale then they've still got an option to do that. If they still want to bring in a beloved toy or something from home, then they still have the option to do that . . . I've been actively discouraging people bringing things in and I've asked them not to bring things in except for particular topic things . . . Otherwise you get endless little plastic bits and bobs. It seems to be a bit of an insoluble problem, but hopefully their needs will diminish as they grow in confidence.

Maggie recognizes that, at this time, she cannot be the kind of teacher she wants to and that she will have to do the best she can as she tries to balance her own and the children's needs, 'I'm not going to be wonder teacher with everyone hanging on my every word. Trying to get them to toe the line without squashing them completely is my aim', and she worries that when she is 'ratty' or in a bad mood she is not being 'professional'.

When she talks about what has happened during particular incidences in the classroom, she explains why certain constraints or individuals sometimes make it impossible for her to adopt the positive strategies that she would like:

I moved one child out of the circle today. I tried for ages to be positive with her. But there are two or three today who are hyper. Hayley's attention was poor and she was bobbing about. She's a one man show for the person who's next to her. But I wanted them to do some collective listening and attending and their attention skills are minimal. So I decided to put her out. She was unhappy about it, but tough . . . but it made her realize I wasn't having it . . . I'd had enough. I tried not to shout and there was a lot of noise anyway. It was partly unavoidable because we'd spent ages talking as there was a lot to talk about and I wanted to get it finished off satisfactorily. I feel sometimes you carry on talking and you think you should have stopped 5 minutes ago. You need to finish in a satisfactory manner and that [excluding Hayley] was part of it. It just came to me that that's what I would do. I've been reading about exclusion and I thought I'd try it . . . I felt angry I suppose, but whatever needed to be said to get through to her, I couldn't find. I'm not going to find it for them all, all the time. It's short-term action, not a long-term move. It's the most negative thing I did all morning. But it's tough.

During the final term, Maggie undertakes small amounts of teaching in a number of classes, because the main focus for the term is the dissertation. It seems that under less pressure, she has more control over her teaching and is positive, but firm in her management. For example, towards the end of the year, when a teacher is ill, Maggie takes her class for the morning, and then organizes the class into groups in preparation for the afternoon's activities when they are to be split between three other classes. The morning goes well, and Maggie is clearly pleased with her management which she attributes to the development of her teaching skills:

> It's a Year 1 class of only nineteen children, but immensely difficult and already I'm getting to grips with them . . . I've acquired confidence in my ability to judge children, sum them up. I've acquired a lot of skills in categorizing where they are in their current stage of skills and knowledge and what sort of personality they have, so it's a combination of ability to judge personality and picking up on the way they are in the room, body language, behaviour and also in their work, although that hasn't been a factor today.

Maggie compares herself with experienced teachers, recognizing that she still has to refine her 'skills' because, 'Some teachers have got more presence, and their room is quiet, and I haven't quite got that yet, or maybe I haven't been long enough in the same place to induce that. I can get children quiet, but I feel I couldn't honestly say at this stage that a quiet environment is always the product of my being in the room.' She identifies how they are able to achieve this:

> [Through the] skilful use of their voice, consistent firmness, they're giving the right signals to the children. I think I have a bit to learn on the signals to give to make it clear that I'm not messing about. Also they lay down the ground rules and they make those clear at the start. I don't think I do that . . . Some days you start off all right and they're very quiet and then they start pushing you, so it takes a few days for you to know them and them to know you.

Children's Learning and the Teacher's Role

Maggie's very early views of children's learning focus heavily upon experience, often for its own sake. For example, history is seen as an active subject, involving visits and doing things, and gaining wide experience. In a science lesson, her explanation of why a child doesn't realize that water expands when it freezes is because he hasn't had 'enough experience'. She resolves to bring in some ice so that he can feel it, accepting that this would not demonstrate expansion, but at least it would be 'hands-on experience'. A lighted candle in a darkened classroom is similarly seen to offer a 'wonderful experience' from which children would learn about light.

When Maggie is asked to talk about how children learn, during the first year, she is often vague and at times admits that she doesn't know:

> I'm not sure really. I'm feeling a bit confused. Perhaps it's because it was a bit exhausting today. I don't know. I'd like to read some more theory and know more about the theories that are available. There are certain concepts I've been reading and active learning came up again today.

Generally Maggie stresses the belief that children should be allowed to discover for themselves and one of her roles is seen as providing relevant experiences for children which she feels she is able to achieve when she is working with groups of children. Visiting the primary school in Year 1, where she observes children engaged in open-ended tasks, causes her to examine her own practice. When she then works with groups in her own school, she deliberately attempts to stand back and guide children less, something which she finds very hard to do initially because she does not really know what she wants the children to learn. In time she feels that she is helped by her increasing experience and familiarity with various activities:

> I think really I appreciated that I didn't need to be talking all the time for the children to be learning. I could perhaps learn more about what they were learning just listening to them. I think, probably due to lack of experience, I think I've got to keep telling them the same thing, but they have to be allowed to have the time. I've taken that on board more, probably because I'm more at ease. Over-talking was my way of internalizing for myself really. But as I need space and time to learn things, so do they.

In Year 2, as Maggie takes more responsibility for larger groups of children, she begins to focus more upon the management of children's learning. She comes to the conclusion that effective teaching is a combination of teacher instruction and demonstration, followed by the opportunity for children to explore further by themselves through a well-constructed activity. Once responsible for the whole class on a day-to-day basis, Maggie accepts that the quality of the children's experiences is significantly altered by the pressures of attempting to manage the whole class but feels that there is nothing she can really do about this. She relies heavily on class demonstrations, worksheets and 'closed' tasks, which, at times, are not well matched to the attainments of the children. Maggie feels that she is caught up by the pressures of trying to manage the children, transact a very full curriculum and provide evidence of the children's understanding, whilst attempting to achieve meaningful learning experiences. Often, in the classroom, Maggie does not see herself as taking a teaching role, which she associates with introducing a new concept to children, rather she describes herself as 'a leader, manager, organizer'.

Professional Relationships and Support Networks

Although Maggie was initially very concerned about how she would cope within the school, her fears were soon allayed. Within the host school, she feels comfortable and supported, and at ease with the general ethos of the school:

> ... it's committed to involvement with the whole family, and encouraging parents that they have an important part to play in their children's education, and it's also a caring environment. That's positively on the agenda. It's not an incidental. It's a fundamental part of the school's attitude to families whose children are here. That fits in entirely with my own philosophy and it's very important because a caring ethos doesn't limit itself to the children. It means that everyone in the school cares for everyone and it starts with the head and trickles down. It's exactly my philosophy, so I felt very comfortable and the school itself has been a source of support and encouragement for me, apart from my professional involvement, and it's the same to anyone here. Various members of staff have had difficulties of one sort or another and the school has been equally supportive for the most part and cares about all members of staff, and all the members of staff seem to care for each other ... visitors from another school came here and it was reported to me that they were amazed at the generosity of the head in sharing knowledge in the specific area that they had come for, and I think that reflects on the school. If you're somewhere where everyone keeps all their knowledge and resources to themselves, it leads to a very hostile atmosphere where people aren't cooperating and that's not the case here. Anyone will share anything with you, and I'm constantly overwhelmed by the generosity of all the staff here.

Maggie is particularly satisfied that, over time, she has managed to win over the member of staff who seemed rather off-hand with her, reporting that she achieved this by 'treading carefully', 'being tactful' and 'being honest and open' when she lacked confidence in herself.

Throughout the two years, Maggie retains her respect and admiration for her mentor, claiming that Sarah has provided her with the right help and support as her needs have changed over time. For example, late in the first year Maggie feels that she now knows what she needs to learn, and can formulate her own ideas about teaching, what she needs is someone to 'bounce ideas off':

> She's [Sarah] already become more of a sounding board. I tell her things and she agrees or doesn't. But we've always had quite a good relationship anyway. I suppose she was steering me heavily in the early days but she's backed off such a lot. I think I sit and talk to her and in talking I clear my mind ... I get quite worked up about things and she'll diffuse it. She puts things in perspective and when everything piles up she draws your mind to prioritizing, all of which I could do by myself, but it's good to have someone there to remind you.

In time, Maggie feels that she develops the ability 'to break something down and focus on certain areas' and so is able to direct her own learning even more. Also, whilst Maggie had often used mentor time to reflect upon her teaching, frequently requiring Sarah's help to do so, in the second year she more often claims to be able to reflect on her own, particularly when she is planning.

Maggie also values her good relationships with the welfare (classroom) assistants with whom she has worked:

> I do some reflection with the welfare assistants too, because I wanted to get to know them, to find out how they were thinking about things, and that also told me something about the quality of their input with the children, and I feel when you're working in a classroom with people like that they need to feel part of a team and you should value what they do, which I did. So I would share things with them.

Developing Understandings of the Curriculum

Maggie's ideas about curriculum areas reflect her views about teaching generally. Knowledge in areas such as maths and science are seen as capable of being broken down into parts, and over the two years Maggie feels that she is acquiring more and more parts, and an appreciation of how they fit together. At the beginning of the second year, Maggie reviews where her understandings have come from. She identifies that college has provided guiding principles and a focus, along with some ideas of what to do, but for the most part, her understanding of the curriculum has developed from books, other teachers and her own experience in the classroom.

Maggie often talks about adjusting ideas, or even starting activities, without a firm plan in her mind, expecting that she will be able to decide as she 'goes along', judging the responses of the children. Maggie associates such intuitive decision-making with the skill of teaching:

> As more time goes on, and I'm not doing new things, I think I get more confident. If I don't know now what to do I'll be able to work it out, so I feel more confident generally . . . It strikes me I think I'm very slow in some ways at getting things internally fixed, in learning them, and I need to have a go at other things. Some things are instantaneous, and others I need to go over and work out every way. It mirrors in a way the things that are in the maths and science. In maths, you tackle something like subtraction and there are loads of different ways of doing it. It's like needing to get to grips with all of them. I need to think about it and discuss it and try it. Often I'm making judgments as I'm teaching it and changing my mind. The reaction of the children too. That directs what you say when you're actually teaching.

However, observations of Maggie over the two years reveal that she is often unsure about the curriculum and is sometimes swamped by ideas from her reading which she has difficulty relating to her own teaching. She frequently gives rather confused explanations for what she is hoping to teach. Although she regards the curriculum in terms of a large number of parts which she herself has to master and be able to assemble, she readily acknowledges that her understanding is 'a bit gappy', particularly in the areas of music and art. This does not seem to concern her, however. Throughout the course, Maggie seems to have been more concerned with the organization and management of activities rather than their content. As she explains, when talking about her aims in teaching:

> What I would be most pleased with is an atmosphere in a classroom, the way the children are to each other, and I think that leads to a learning environment really.

Conclusion

At the end of the two years, Maggie secures a post in another village school. This gives her confidence a tremendous boost and she faces the future with an image of herself as the kind of teacher she has wanted to become, 'lively, stimulating, interesting. I think most children relate well to me and they feel I'm positive, which is what I want to be'.

Her views of education, while expanded, are similar to those expressed at the beginning of the course. The school in which she has undertaken most of her teaching has, she feels, very much reflected her own beliefs about education. This, she argues, has, in turn, helped her to understand her own guiding role as a teacher:

> You maintain a secure base and environment where all this can take place. You help them evolve ground rules for their own and other people's behaviour within the framework that's safe and secure . . . and you can then proceed to help them develop their skills and knowledge by providing them with the material on which to practise and explore.

Although Maggie acknowledges that some of her curriculum knowledge is weak and that she still has many teaching strategies to acquire and perfect, she completes the course with clear views of the kind of classroom environment that she seeks to establish and with a confidence that she can achieve this.

Chapter 8

Student Teacher Development

Chapters 4 to 7 presented an overview of the experiences of four of the twenty student teachers studied in the project. These overviews, or case histories, provide an account of the students' progress over the two years, offering some insight into the factors that motivated the students to come onto the course, highlighting what they extracted from their experiences in college and in school, and illustrating how they grappled with the everyday difficulties of learning to teach. By looking across the case histories of all of the students, it is possible to identify a number of common themes or aspects of learning to teach which map out the development of the student teachers or which provide useful markers on which to compare and contrast their experiences. Mostly these relate to the questions that either initiated the study — concerning for instance the nature of the students' understanding of subject matter — or that have emerged through the ongoing analysis of transcripts and become the foci of subsequent discussions with students. An example of the latter is the students' emphasis on 'feeling like a teacher' which, after further inquiry, directed the researchers' attention to the processes of assimilating and developing a teacher identity and the associated social and personal pressures which students reported.

Chapter 8 draws upon this data to give an account of the student teachers' development around these specific themes. It draws upon the transcript data for the students described in Chapters 4 to 7, but also upon that of the other sixteen students. After examining each of the themes, the chapter uses this analysis to suggest a typology of learning to teach, indicating the different types of learning process in which student teachers are engaged. Interviews with mentors are also drawn upon in a discussion of the role of the mentor in supporting student teachers' development.

Aspects of Student Teacher Development

Student Teachers' Initial Conceptions of Teaching and Learning

One of the first aims of the study was to assess the conceptions of teaching and learning which the students held on entering their course and to assess the impact of these conceptions on their later experience. Generally, the student teachers started their courses with clear models in mind both of teaching and of themselves as teachers. These models, or images, conveyed a mental picture of how teachers act and how they relate to children. They frequently originated from the students' own experiences as pupils at school and were commonly modelled on one or two particular teachers who stood out in their memories. Often these teachers were regarded as being particularly charismatic and inspirational, and were good communicators who enthused children. Tamsin, for instance, describes two teachers who stand out in her memory of her schooling and who provided the basis for her ideas about good teaching:

> I can remember an English teacher who was a big, bold character. She was physically big with a big voice, and she was quite influential because I did an A-level in English. And a Latin teacher, who was also one of the old traditionals, a great enthusiast for her subject . . . I think it's to do with a balance the whole time, the juggling between having a laugh with the children and being their friend if you like, but not being too close to them, and being able to tick them off where necessary and shout at them if necessary and keep them occupied. One of the worst things a teacher can do is to be boring. You must interest them and keep them interested. So I think you should aim towards stimulating and interesting them all the time and also I don't think it's necessary to be an ogre and be too hard. You must be able to get their respect in other ways. Get them to listen to you by being a softer, more gentle person as well.

The quality of the relationships between teachers and pupils was often particularly memorable and some student teachers even reported that their model teachers were the only teachers they had come across who actually related to them as individuals and expressed concern for their welfare. Aisling, an articled teacher, explained:

> One of my sociology lecturers at college . . . was a primary teacher before she went into lecturing and she's definitely influenced me. She taught me sociology for three years. She just had time for all of us. At college you don't get it very often in a lecturer. She was the only one at college who took an interest in what we were doing and whether we could do better. Obviously there are so many students many of them don't have the time.

Rebecca, commenting on her best teachers, similarly claims:

> They had an understanding of you as an individual and also your age group and they were really interested in what they were doing and had a way of getting you interested because they managed to get their point over in a really interesting and motivating way. They'd get you to think and really get involved.

Having one or both parents who are teachers also introduced students to the culture of teaching and frequently played an important role in clarifying their expectations for the teaching role and the amount of time and dedication that might be required to fulfil it. Other life experiences, however, were also reported to be influential in shaping some students' images of teaching. Experience as a Sunday School teacher, and in the Boys' Brigade as in Adam's case, both provided opportunities to relate to young people in a teaching context, and provided some student teachers with rewarding experiences that led them to think of themselves as potential school teachers. Some mature students also drew upon other work experience (particularly managerial experience or experience, such as nursing, that involved working with people) as a source of images of a teaching role and such experience had led them to develop clearer notions of their own abilities and of themselves as teachers. Maggie's experiences as a care assistant and a playgroup leader, for example, helped her to reconcile her conception of her own abilities in working with others with the image that she had of teaching. Stephanie's experience as manager of a high street clothes' shop provided the basis for her views of herself as a teacher who could organize clearly focused tasks, maintain cooperation within a group, and motivate young children and sustain their interest in learning.

Some students expressed their images in metaphorical terms. Jeremy, in common with several student teachers, likened learning to teach to learning to drive a car in which one gradually builds up confidence in different aspects of the task and eventually one is free from thinking about the immediate actions involved and able to consider more distant goals. This metaphor persisted throughout the PGCE course and, in the middle of the second term, he reflected back on his progress to date:

> I was so busy surviving that I tensed up and didn't really step back mentally to see what they're learning. So that ability is coming and it's fundamental. I may be doing what I think is a fantastic job of teaching, but unless the children are learning there's no point in doing it.

> At the beginning, I was gripping the steering wheel so tightly that I wasn't actually driving. But you have to have enough confidence and there's no shortcut to that. You have to say I know where I'm travelling and I can now learn to steer it properly and react to things. I knew I wanted to get to that.

These images were often associated with strong emotion and they appeared to provide part of the motivation for entering teacher education — implementing their teaching image was partly seen as a matter of self-expression or self-fulfilment. The students started out with a conception of teaching, a knowledge of themselves and a commitment to becoming a teacher that was associated with expectations of positive intrinsic rewards.

Gary, for example, is a mature student who has worked for several years as an engineer. He reports always enjoying working with his hands and making things, and attributes his initial choice of occupation to many satisfying childhood experiences working alongside his grandfather who was a blacksmith. Promotion at work, however, had taken him more into sales than what Gary perceived as 'doing engineering' and he now sought to regain job satisfaction by becoming a teacher, an occupation which he believes is similar to engineering in that it requires a similar creative, problem-solving process:

> The way they put their mind to a problem, way back when they had to work from basic principles . . . I think I'm always striving for that . . . I love solving problems on basic principles . . . Teaching is working with basic principles again. A blank sheet of paper or, in this case, a group of children. They're not a blank sheet of paper obviously, but at the end of the scholastic year you can see what you've achieved by bringing those children from position x to position y.

Ideas about teaching were often associated with a sense of social justice. The students felt strongly about all children being given an equal chance in life, and the importance of teachers catering for children's individual differences. Frequently the students came from a background themselves in which they had witnessed, if not experienced, children losing out and becoming a poorly educated underclass. Maggie was not the only student to talk in strong emotive terms about her past experiences of the 11-plus examination and streaming, or of the importance of establishing a school and classroom community in which every child is valued. Interestingly, even before the start of the course, the students expressed strong views about the importance of teachers accepting and supporting children, from whatever background they came, and the need for teachers to 'get down to the children's level'. Although notions of 'child-centredness' and 'progressivism' have often been blamed on 'trendy teacher education colleges', the students in this sample had quite strong commitments to such ideals even before their training started.

A few of the student teachers did start the course with a mismatch in mind between themselves and how they conceptualized teachers and teaching. The view they had of the typical teacher conflicted with how they viewed themselves, and occasionally resulted in some discomfort in the thought of having to fit an occupational stereotype. Jess, for instance, a PGCE student, summed up her image of the teacher as: 'They talk very slowly, and they are very sincere, and they have that patronizing intonation, and generally they go to Tenerife for their holidays!' Though intended partly in jest, her comments sum up a stereotype of the primary teacher as conservative and overly serious, a stereotype which, for this student, acted as a disincentive to becoming one. In her first year, she did on several occasions question whether she was really the 'right sort of person' to become a primary teacher. The image of herself as a teacher remains a source of discomfort throughout the two years. She regards herself as being different to the teachers she sees around her, and is initially concerned that she will have to change to be a different kind of person in order to feel comfortable in a teaching role. Towards the end of the year, however, she realizes that she is being effective as a teacher despite her perceived differences:

> I'm the only one who hasn't got a house and a mortgage, isn't going out with someone, isn't planning to settle down, would like to travel for two years, so I don't feel I fit in with the image of teaching so to speak. I've always had in my mind that perhaps I'm not a professional, but now I've

come to the conclusion that as long as I can do the job satisfactorily I
don't have to be that image. But I've always been worried about it.

At the end of the course, Jess leaves to work as a teacher in a Third World country,
a role to which she can more readily accommodate her own image of herself as a
person and as a teacher.

In contrast to the conceptions that the student teachers had about teaching
and themselves as teachers, their ideas, views, and speculations about children's
learning were usually much more difficult to elicit. Typically, learning seemed
to be perceived as unproblematic, at least early on in the course. Student teachers
generally believed that children learned through activity. If teachers created the
appropriate environment, presented interesting activities and children were involved,
then the children, it was believed, would automatically learn. This was a fairly per-
sistent belief. Well into the course, some students' ideas about children's learning
remained at this general level, even when students were asked to comment upon
particular children or particular lessons that they had taught. For other students, however, there did seem to be a gradual change in the ways in which they spoke about
children's learning. Early in the course, they tended to equate learning with engagement, enthusiasm and 'children having fun'; as long as children were involved
in an activity they could be assumed to be learning. Stephanie, for example, when
asked to talk about examples of children learning in her classroom, comments on
her equation of attention with learning:

> . . . there are occasions when they're all sitting there and are listening and
> are interested in what's going on. I think when you can see that picture on
> their face and they're not fiddling with pencils and things, I think that's
> a pretty good example of the children learning something.

It was also common for students to stress the emotional needs of children in
learning: the need for security, and for a warm, sympathetic, encouraging environment in which to work. Emphasis on environment and relationships was frequently
in evidence in students' talk of teaching and learning, particularly amongst those
who intended to teach the younger age range. Tamsin, for example, stressed young
children's need for security:

> They need reassurance and need to feel secure. It's a shock after the cosy,
> womb-like atmosphere at home to go to the coldness of the school, which
> has to be made into another secure environment they can feel happy in.

Some students' ideas of learning, later became associated with strategies that the
teacher might adopt to influence children's interest and motivation. Nancy, for
instance, explains:

> The secret is to get onto their level and see how they see things, what they
> think the world is all about and what they see the point is in doing fractions,
> for instance.

Similarly, Julie describes her strategies for promoting learning as:

> By having interesting resources around and by showing enthusiasm and
> interest in the subject area myself, and to bring the children in with their
> own existing knowledge as soon as you can, to work on what they already
> know and draw out of them ideas and information about the subject you're
> doing, so that you perhaps give them a feeling of enjoyment that they can
> take part and show the class what they know and bring things in from home
> if they have appropriate books or toys. Just allow them the opportunity to
> identify with what you're doing.

In the case of a few students, they were able to talk about learning in much more
specific terms, identifying the difficulties experienced by particular children, or
becoming aware of the learning involved in specific areas of the curriculum and
recognizing appropriate teaching strategies that they might adopt. Jeremy, reflecting on a mathematics lesson that he had just taught, explained the difficulties that
one child had with subtraction and how he attempted to help her, drawing upon
strategies that he had learned about in the college curriculum course and which he
had used successfully on a previous occasion:

> I was able to look at several children, many of whom were clearly under-
> standing it fine and the work could be marked and they could carry on
> and that's what I did. But some — and there was one particular girl who
> clearly wasn't understanding what she was doing fully, so her answers
> were sometimes right and sometimes wrong. It was chance really. I picked
> that up straightaway. So having got the class working quite steadily on that
> and establishing the fact they were working on the scheme, I was able to
> do some individual work and get alongside her problems on subtraction,
> a basic arithmetic operation. Addition was all right. With two digit num-
> bers though she was clearly having trouble with subtraction ... I brought
> her right back to the concrete experience again and used the Dienes equip-
> ment ... It did accord with what we did at college in the maths ses-
> sions that were excellent. To start with a concrete experience and then
> talk about what we were doing with the child, and make them think about
> that before actually going to the abstract problem in the book and just
> taking the numbers and trying to subtract them. So I got her to actually get
> the blocks out, set the thing up, make the difference apparent, taking a
> subset out and then seeing what she had left. I did that with single digits
> initially and then we went on to parallel the problems in the book. Set them
> up with the blocks and do the two digit numbers and make the difference.
> Obviously, because of the class needs generally, I couldn't go on for a
> very long time but I did it long enough to get her at least nearly there. She
> was making a lot of progress. I said she should go back again and again,
> not to be afraid to get the equipment out, work through it and see what
> she actually had before worrying about just dealing with the numbers

and that's what she was doing. I'd like to have been able to follow that up to see what those answers were, just as I did on TP when I had a much longer period. I had several weeks in the class and could go back to the little girl who was doing it and I could see her progress, which was very real. She was doing it right and knew what she was doing. She'd cracked it.

In another example, Tamsin talks about a dance lesson she is about to take with her Year 1 class, in which she demonstrates an awareness of how the children's learning in dance might relate to their work in art, mathematics and geography in the class topic on shape and space:

We [will] all find a space and start off with a warm up. Today the object is actually using space, and direction is a lesser theme . . . So we'll start off with a warm up and they have to use all the space in the room, to make their way around in a straight way, changing direction as they go all the time. Then they have to change it to a wiggly fashion, changing direction as they go, then to a graceful sort of sweeping fashion and then hopefully by then we'll have used all their body parts and have got them warmed up. Then we'll move on to more specific activities and they have to travel in a big square, and each time they move to a new side they have to change their action, and then they have to use galloping to go forwards, sideways and backwards and I'll indicate when I want them to change because otherwise they'll be everywhere and all over each other. Then to further develop that they have to travel backwards, sometimes on their front and sometimes on their back, but whichever way they interpret it. Then they have to find two different ways of using the space to go sideways and backwards. They can do that however they like or however they interpret it, as long as they follow my instructions. Then they have to use their hands and feet to travel in a wide shape and then in a narrow shape and then they have to travel around the room using all the space and making themselves as wide as possible and then as small as possible — differentiation — since space is not just about using all of it, but using small amounts as well. Then I'll get them to do it again all together and they'll have to make themselves wide and think about the space they're using and their arms and everything . . . I think that's something that infants have trouble with for a start. They're notorious if you ask them to draw a picture for example for doing a little stick man in the corner instead of using the whole space. So it's a way into that and making them realize about their own body space, what they have to use for their own body space. They have trouble with each other, colliding with each other and things like that. It's something that I'll spend time talking to them about, and I'll ask them what you should make sure you do or not do so that they're aware of their own bodies. Some of the little ones or less able children are still quite uncoordinated. So it creates that awareness and it makes it something that they really think about. Obviously in terms of direction that gives them a lead in to geographical things so that they start to think about different pathways where things go. In a further lesson I would probably take that further and get them to invent perhaps their own pathways and even draw one and get a friend to follow it or give instructions to a friend to get to a certain point.

A more situationally specific view of teaching and learning is dependent on a relatively sophisticated knowledge base. It requires student teachers to have a knowledge of what the curriculum includes, some ideas about how it is sequenced, a knowledge of the activities and strategies that are associated with particular components of the curriculum, an understanding of which activities are appropriate for a particular lesson and for particular children and contexts, how long children take in completing different activities, the difficulties that children might experience and the various alternatives that might be open to the teacher to attempt to help children solve them. This detailed and extensive knowledge base could only emerge from the synthesis of a wide variety of factual knowledge and also experience in the classroom. To be able to talk in any informed way about the particular difficulties a child may have with reading or a specific mathematics topic, and to be able to suggest how the child is learning, and the activities and strategies that might support his/her learning requires substantial detailed knowledge and vast experience of how things work and fail to work in classrooms. It is perhaps not surprising that examples such as those above occurred only in the second year, and that even towards the end of the two-year period it was still quite infrequent for the student teachers to reveal any insightful accounts of children's learning. Progress towards being able to think about children's learning in more detail was generally a slow process. In some cases, children's learning and the teaching strategies used to support it in different areas of the curriculum remained quite mysterious. As Kate, a PGCE student, explained, when asked, after a story writing session, how she would aim to develop children's writing skills:

> I really don't know. It's one of the things I pick my brains about, night after night. I hate to say it, but I keep saying to my mentor that only having done six week practices here and there, I've never seen progression in writing and, with all due respect to the college, I've never been taught how to do it. So I really get so frustrated about it. I just try whatever I can, but I don't know if I am doing it right. No one has ever said, so it's trial and error really.

Understanding Subject Matter

Studies of secondary teachers by Shulman and others at Stanford University (Shulman, 1986; Wilson, Shulman and Richert, 1987) suggest that a significant part of learning to teach concerns relearning the subject matter for the purposes of teaching, and developing a repertoire of pedagogical content knowledge (examples, analogies, explanations, etc.) that enables teachers to facilitate the learning of the subject by others. In this study, however, interviews with student teachers about their planning, and specifically about their understanding of the mathematics, science and language curriculum and how these are taught, revealed little evidence of such processes. In fact, the students' understanding of some of the subjects they taught appeared to be quite shallow and students themselves often reported feeling quite insecure in their subject knowledge, particularly in maths and science. Given the wide range of subjects that primary teachers are required to teach, this is perhaps to be expected. However, even in subjects where the students held a degree, they would sometimes indicate a passion and enjoyment for their subject that they would like to communicate to children, but rarely did they have an overall conception of the nature and function of that subject within the primary school curriculum and the subject methodology associated with it. Julie, for example, whose degree was in computing and was specializing in mathematics and IT, was asked, at the end of her PGCE course, to describe the role of mathematics and IT in the primary school curriculum, and seemed unable to go beyond a general statement:

> I think they should be fun and very practical and allow the children plenty of opportunity to have hands-on experience of things and learn through doing and playing as much as through being tied to a particular book and just going through sum after sum.

Tricia, who has a history degree, is initially quite enthusiastic about approaching a topic on the Romans with her class of 8-year-olds and believes that her history background will be useful:

> We're actually doing the Romans at the moment in my articled teaching and I did a special paper on Roman Britain for my degree. So in terms of actual knowledge and facts I have that to reflect on . . . It's nice to have had that knowledge . . . it is useful.

Later in the same term, however, she finds that her knowledge of history has not itself been sufficient to develop children's interest and learning, and she starts to doubt the value of the subject within the primary curriculum:

> I'm beginning to question the history altogether really and question its value. I did find the Roman topic very dull and maybe it was the kids and the way it was approached. It didn't seem to come alive at all and I thought 'Does it matter?' I know it's all culture and it's the basis for modern living . . . but I did find it very dry and thought 'How is this going to really achieve a happy child and [help them] get to grips with the problems of modern life?'

Rather than formulating any deep understanding of the subject and its pedagogy, students appeared instead to develop a general orientation to the subject and to learn associated activity structures. For example, mathematics would commonly be thought of in terms of children working individually on sequenced activities and investigations, and the teacher maintaining and monitoring steady progress through the mathematics scheme. Science tended to be associated with the teacher introducing a topic and the children working in small groups, finding out for themselves, with a range of materials and questions for them to explore. These general orientations and activity structures provided a framework for lesson planning and teaching.

Aisling, for example, regards science as involving practical activities where the children have 'hands-on experience'. She works with the class teacher on a series of science activities concerning floating and sinking, but when she is left to plan activities for a subsequent topic on 'living things', she finds it difficult to construct what she regards as a proper science lesson. Instead, she falls back on using a worksheet in which the children have to identify animals and draw a picture of their favourite animal, an activity that she associates more with the language area of the curriculum.

Similarly, Stephanie has acquired a clear conception of writing lessons, derived from a mixture of some college demonstrations and her observations in schools. For Stephanie, writing lessons require a strong input session, followed by support for the children to redraft and edit their work. This conception is evident in her description of a poetry lesson that she is about to take:

> . . . they're going to write a poem and . . . the first part of the session will actually be me explaining what they're going to do and how they're going to do it, and I've written a poem. I shall go through with them how I wrote that and how I redrafted it to improve it. I'm going to read a few poems that other children have written on similar lines and show them the processes I want them to go through — that is, think about it and then go on to write it and redraft it and edit it and then write it up in best . . . I want at this stage to give them quite a bit of structure to help them so they won't flounder too much and they could have a go and get some satisfaction from it.

While there were instances where students thought about the purposes of particular lessons and sequences of lessons, and where they tried to see the activities from the point of view of the children in order to think through how best to explain and present particular activities, much of the decision-making about topics, sequencing, long-term aims and teaching techniques were left to the textbook, the school's schemes of work, and to existing teaching practices within the school. The student teachers' attention seemed to be focused from an early stage on distinguishing between different types of classroom activity, associating particular types with different subject areas of the curriculum, and learning the required organizational and management skills to set up and run these activities. For the student teacher, what seemed to be important was getting a general feel for what a mathematics session or a language session, for example, looked like. Part of Maggie's difficulties in moving between Year 1 and Year 6, for example, seemed to be attributable to the very different activity structures that were commonly found in the two schools and the time this took to adapt to them.

This may reflect a difference between novice and experienced teachers. Perhaps the novice teachers, in their efforts to survive in the classroom, must necessarily focus on mastering the management of various types of classroom activity, and once this has been achieved greater attention might be given to the purposes of the teaching and ways of promoting children's understanding. Alternatively, there may be a difference in the ways in which primary teachers and secondary teachers view teaching or a difference in the contexts in which they operate which influences their teaching approaches. For example, secondary teachers may think of their task more in terms of directing the children's mastery of a specific curriculum area, whereas the primary teacher may tend to think more in terms of directing activities from which individual children learn different things in different ways. It may also be the case that the primary teacher, faced with teaching in several subject areas, and faced with severe time and resource constraints, may have great difficulty in doing anything other than thinking at the level of managing activities. It could also, of course, be a mistake to presume that a greater subject focus on the part of primary teachers will necessarily lead to greater achievement on the part of children; an activity focus might in fact be more engaging and effective with young children. Further research is clearly needed in this area in order to identify the extent to which experienced, effective primary teachers engage in similar processes, to assess the relative effects of the 'subject' as opposed to 'activity' focus in primary teachers' planning and teaching, and to identify how teachers might be helped to move from one focus to the other supposing that this is desirable.

Conceptions of Learning to Teach

Students varied considerably in the complexity with which they viewed the processes of learning to teach. A few students did start out with quite complex views. Nina, for instance, viewed it in terms of three aspects that needed to be developed and integrated: *the personal*, concerning the development of abilities to relate to children and others in order to maintain an appropriate working environment; *the professional*, concerning practical teaching skills; and *the academic*, relating to a thorough understanding of the subjects of the primary school curriculum. Most common, however, was a fairly technicist view that learning to teach involved acquiring specific knowledge and skills that would be acquired and developed through modelling themselves on other teachers and through trial and error experience in the classroom. Gerry, for instance, at the end of the second term of the PGCE course, describes how he has so far learned about teaching:

> By observing other teachers and from my own mistakes teaching myself. It's not to say that you don't get something from the theory at college, but the bulk comes from school . . . Basically, it's applying what I've already known from life and from observing the teachers that I've been with and being with a group of twenty to thirty children.

Over half the students, however, also saw a strong personal dimension in learning to teach. Teaching was viewed, to some extent, as an individualistic activity in which aspects of the teacher's own personality are involved. Stephanie, for example, towards the end of the articled teacher course, demonstrates how her own individual characteristics, particularly her insistence on neatness and order, have influenced the kind of teacher she has become, and how many of her ideals for herself as a teacher have still to be realized:

> I'd like to think I'm quite a caring teacher and interested in the children themselves. Having said that, I think I am probably quite firm. I'm quite pernickety about things . . . There are little things that bug me and I will try with my class to try and get them ironed out to start with and get a routine into the class. I like to think we can have fun sometimes. I think I'm sometimes a little serious and try to get too much done . . . I find it very difficult to deal with behavioural problems with children. I don't think my sense of humour comes out as much as I would like. At times I can be very serious, but I think that's because I'm still trying to find my way and decide what I'm happy with.

This emphasis on the personal dimension of teaching seemed to grow over the two-year period and several students would talk of 'finding themselves as a teacher' or discovering a lot about themselves in the process of teaching, or perceiving an aspect of teaching that is concerned with personal expression. Jess, a PGCE student, towards the end of the course, comments:

> I've seen teachers who are really calm in their personality, and the children are really calm and I always wanted to be like that, but I've concluded that that's not me. So you can't cover up your personality. You do sometimes have to be stern and things like that, but your underlying personality always comes through . . . I feel relaxed and feel I can be me, so I am. I'm probably an exaggerated version of me because you have to project yourself, but up to half term I was always thinking perhaps I wasn't coming across the way I should be. Perhaps now that I know the children better I do feel as though I can be me and my personality, and teach without having to change it too much.

They also became aware that there were undesirable aspects of their personality, such as their 'impatience' or 'intolerance' of certain behaviour, which they were uncomfortable with in their practice. Because of this close link between personality and teaching, several students seemed to associate becoming a teacher with personal change, becoming a different kind of person, a process of identity transformation, a feature which is highlighted in the previous case studies.

The importance of being able to establish relationships with children was also commonly stressed by students from the beginning. Being able to relate to children, and being able to develop a supportive community within the classroom, in which children respect one another, was generally highly valued. To a large extent this was again viewed as a matter of personality as well as learning to act like a teacher, though most student teachers also thought they could learn some useful skills in this area from experienced teachers who were particularly effective in developing 'the right atmosphere'.

There is evidence that there was a gradual shift over the two-year period, in the case of a few students, towards more complex, holistic views of professional development, in which students began to recognize teaching to be a complex activity which could be mastered in a variety of ways and which involved some essential development of the person. Maggie, for instance, although she started out with a view of learning to teach which seemed to focus substantially on the accumulation of technical skills, at the end of the course refers to teaching as being like a complex jigsaw in which different ideas and strategies are picked from different places, and judged in relation to the way one wants to teach and in relation to particular principles for teaching or ideas of what is acceptable within the school or what is appropriate for the particular children being taught. She begins to look upon learning to teach as involving a constant process of comparison, adjustment and change.

Teaching Knowledge and Knowledge Growth

In interviews throughout the two years of the study, student teachers were regularly asked to talk about what they were learning from both college and school experience. Their answers most often focused on ideas for lessons and teaching strategies. Even in the case of college lectures, which focused on teaching principles and their theoretical underpinning, students tended to judge their value in terms of ideas and strategies that could be directly implemented in the classroom. Students also acquired repertoires of knowledge about children, activities and school procedures. When asked to talk about how she is learning to teach, Nancy, for example, explains how both school and college are sources of 'information' useful for teaching:

> The teachers I think are like something you look at and either you like the way it is done or you don't. You can use it as a role model I suppose. I don't always agree with the way they do it, but I'm learning because I can then go off and try what I want to have a go at, and if that doesn't work then fine. I suppose the school is like giving another opinion. It's like lots of different opinions I suppose and you're sifting through and finding out which one works for you. I find it very interesting going to college and then trying to do things. You can't do it the next week necessarily, but it's all information that the teachers wouldn't be able to sit down and explain to you.

A major aspect of student teachers' development over the two years was in being able to 'situate' their knowledge about teaching. Student teachers talked much more readily at the end of the study, for example, about how a particular class might respond to a particular idea, activity or way of working. Even though the students might have a more elaborate perception of their situation, however, they frequently still lacked knowledge of appropriate strategies to cope effectively with it. Kate, for instance, in the second year of her articled teacher course, is aware of the difficulties of introducing group work to her Year 1 class because of the children's constant need for approval and attention, but has difficulty finding appropriate solutions:

> Today, I just drew pictures on the board of the things they had to do and went through it all. I said they could do them in any order as long as they all got done, but they don't seem to take it in. They'll come back after the first one and ask what to do next. They need to be pushed all the way.

Julie demonstrates how getting to know the children well helps when deciding how to group them:

> I've moved a few of the children since Christmas so that the tables and activities going on are more fluid in a way. They're not grouped so much according to ability. Sometimes they stay together and other times, if there's a situation where I feel they'll benefit from working with a partner, they'll move from their own to another table and work with a different child for a while. I've actually put Mike on a table where I felt perhaps personalities would help him in his work, more calm and less fractious an environment to work in. Where he was before it was working quite well, but there were one or two personalities where I felt maybe it would benefit for Mark to move to another table. He's at a similar level to the children on the new table he's working at, but I feel from the personality point of view it's a good move for him when he's had a chance to settle down. The same with Barry. I've moved him to a group where the children in general are of much higher ability, but I'm hoping that they'll be able to squash him into applying himself more to his own work and give him the idea that he can actually move, and hopefully if he works like those children he can see that he can come on.

From their specific knowledge, they were also able to abstract ideas about typical behaviour or typical activities. Typifications were important for students in planning and predicting children's responses. Typifications enabled students to estimate how children might respond to particular ideas and activities, how long they might take on certain tasks, and what might make them interested, bored, or over-excited. Students clearly constructed and adjusted their typifications of children as a result of their classroom experience over the two years. Near the end of her second year as an articled teacher, Nancy comments on why she has chosen to start off a new topic on 'water' by reading a story to the children, justifying this in terms of how children typically respond:

> I've found that when you use a book to start it [a topic] off it allows children to point things out and use them . . . A lot of the times I found at

W. when I used a book as a stimulus they instantly think of the things they want to do, without necessarily knowing that's what they're doing. They point to things they like and are interested in. If you started off with the book, you could work it so that they could provide you with the flow if you like. You would have to structure around that though. Then they'd be doing what they wanted to do and would be more interested . . . It makes it more a part of them somehow telling a story and going through a book with them. They're more in control and can see more why you're doing things.

Learning about teaching was stimulated in a number of ways. Sometimes it resulted from observation of the children, particularly when their behaviour or performance contrasted sharply with the student's expectations. For instance, Nina was surprised to find that although her class of 6-year-old children could readily talk to her about their ideas for a story, the children were much more restricted in their written communication. Although she is a language specialist, it had never come to her attention before that the two different means of communication demanded quite different skills, and that young children might be able to communicate orally quite competently but have great difficulty communicating the same ideas in writing. Sometimes, learning would also result from trial and error practice. Nancy, for example, recognized that she was interacting mostly with those children who sought her attention and as a result several children were being overlooked; this made her aware of the need to develop more proactive strategies for involving children in activities and monitoring their performance.

Interestingly, the college encouraged students on both courses to maintain a reflective diary — a log of events and experiences which was to be regularly written up throughout the course and used as an aid for reflecting back upon practice and analysing, and learning about, one's own teaching. In both courses, the students generally found the diary to be useful in the very first term. Although they approached the task of maintaining their diary in different ways, some noting down significant events, others their own reactions and feelings, or a narrative account of their experience, they commonly reported that the writing itself was a useful means of focusing attention on particular aspects of their experience; it also acted as an aid to their memory when they reflected back on particular problems. A few students found a diary difficult to maintain, and some reported the 'cringe factor' experienced when reading it afterwards — there were some experiences students would rather not be reminded of! However, the advantages of keeping a diary tended quite quickly to be outweighed by the disadvantage of the amount of time needed to maintain it. By the second term, most students had ceased to write regularly in their diaries, and reported no longer finding it as helpful as they did in the early stages of the course. Bearing in mind that students at the beginning of the course often had difficulty interpreting and making sense of classroom practice, it could be that the diary helped them to interpret classroom life and identify significant events within it by focusing their attention and providing a written record that they could later return to. By the second term, the students had developed ways of perceiving and making sense of classrooms. They more commonly reported noting the significance of many of the non-verbal aspects of teachers' behaviour, for instance the tone of voice, the timing of commands, the relevance of eye-contact. They had often acquired a confidence in their own interpretations which perhaps also made the diary a largely redundant aid.

One further stimulus for learning which several students reported was their own feelings. Often, particularly in the early stages of teaching, they were aware of feeling uncomfortable about a particular teacher's practice, or about an activity they had observed or perhaps taught themselves. These feelings of awkwardness were often prompted by a clash of values or an unexpected event, and often resulted in the students mentally reliving the event, puzzling over their own feelings and seeking a rational explanation. Beth, for example, explains how being with a teacher whose ideas about education clash strongly with her own makes her more critical of what happens in the classroom, this encourages her to seek explanations for what she observes as well as justifications for her own preferred approaches.

Similarly, Nancy is working in a school where planning and organization are highly structured. She initially regards this as 'very professional' and is somewhat in awe of the staff because 'the language they use and the way they're thinking is really very impressive'. But she feels uncomfortable working within this school. She initially puts this down to her own inadequacies in planning but, after experience in another school, begins to rationalize her feelings of frustration in terms of the school's rigid system of planning preventing her from being the kind of teacher she wants to be and also placing constraints on the children's learning:

> Overall it's a very academic school and strong at getting results. But when you do that you're biased in one way, and you miss out on all the other things . . . If you have a structure as rigid as that, it's very difficult. There's a time when a child needs to play, sit and fiddle and learn something for themselves. Having a think about things or whatever, just letting them do that. It struck me that there was a lot missing but it's very difficult . . . I do get the impression that what I'm doing there isn't considered to be a 'real' thing.

When asked to report recent learning experiences that had been significant to them, students gave a range of responses. On some occasions, they would report having 'reached' a child who was experiencing difficulties, though they might be unable to identify what their particular strategy was or why it was successful. They would comment about individual children or ideas for activities, or would report experiences of having managed a particular activity, or having established a classroom routine. Julie, for instance, when asked, towards the end of her PGCE course, to talk about any recent learning experiences, comments:

> It's getting them into little routines. One day I just hope we won't need 10 minutes nagging to settle them down. Some days it's like that and others, like Monday morning, I stood at the classroom door and said as

they came in, 'Come in quietly, take your coats off and sit down and then I'll explain what we're going to do,' and they were like little lambs. But other days they can be so different. When they come in they're so busy talking to their friends that they don't take any notice. But then I've got to try and bring them all together again and settle them down. A lot of it is still trial and error, finding out what works and what doesn't. I can't explain why one day it does work, standing in the door, and another day when you use the same tactic it doesn't work. But that's the nature of the children we've got. The rest of the staff say that Mondays are particularly bad because they get the impression that the children are allowed to run wild all weekend and get their own way.

The difficulty that some student teachers had in recalling significant learning experiences, and the apparent triviality of some of the events that were recounted, tended to give the impression that little learning was actually occurring. Later conversation, however, would sometimes suggest an alternative explanation, namely that many significant learning experiences were more long-term, involving the piecing together of several experiences, observations and beliefs to arrive at a way of perceiving or thinking about teaching, learning or their own practice. Although there were many individual incidents from which student teachers did acquire useful knowledge, especially about children's interests and capabilities and how children responded to particular situations, many of the significant advances in student teachers' learning required a longer term synthesis. Sometimes this involved linkages between matters that had been discussed or demonstrated in college and events that had been observed in schools. In other cases it arose from a mixture of experience, knowledge, beliefs and values which in the process of reflection became slotted together to provide a seemingly appropriate and insightful interpretation of practice. For example, in the third term, Diane planned and taught a practical science lesson, managing various practical group activities simultaneously. Although the activities had been hastily assembled, Diane was afterwards pleased with her effectiveness in managing the groups and in keeping a potentially chaotic lesson under control. She had previously been rather sceptical of the value of such lessons, though on reflecting back on what children had done and the questions they asked, she began to think about the connections to her lectures at college in the first term on independent learning, making the link between teaching principles and her actual practice.

After the first term, by which time both groups of students had acquired a great deal of new information about children, the curriculum, teaching strategies and the school, much of the student teachers' classroom behaviour had already become routinized. New learning was much less frequent, but what learning occurred was often as a result of living and re-living various experiences, connecting together different experiences, knowledge, values and beliefs, thinking about the matches and mismatches of these and generating new insights. The students' learning was often the result of these long-term struggles to make sense of their diverse experience and knowledge, and whilst one event might sometimes help to piece the mental jigsaw together, the event alone was not what the students learned from.

The living and reliving of events often led to the addition of new knowledge and different understandings, and events could sometimes take on a different significance over time. Beth, for instance, had quite a traumatic experience early in the articled teacher course when her mentor left her in charge of the children and she felt unable to cope. For several months afterwards she felt troubled by this experience and felt as though her confidence had been shattered. By the end of the course, however, she began to see it as part of her own development as a teacher; a rite of passage.

Similarly, Adam struggles to emulate his supervising teacher's non-confrontational approach to behaviour management, and eventually 'explodes'. Reflection on his outburst, and on his own and his supervising teacher's teaching, however, enables him to think further about his own personality and the style of teaching that he is able to adopt.

Effects of Different Training Programmes

Given the wide range of student experience within each programme and the small sample studied, it would be inappropriate to make generalizations about the differential effects of the school-based articled teacher training course and the PGCE course. However, there were some consistent differences between the two samples that are worth noting because of the questions they raise about their impact on the students' professional development.

First, from the interviews with the students it is clear that, throughout the course, the articled teachers identified themselves more readily with the school than with the higher education institution. They more commonly viewed themselves as part of the school, they felt a stronger attachment to the staff and pupils, and more often cited experienced teachers in school as the main source of their learning. PGCE students also sought a sense of belonging in schools, but, with the much briefer periods of school attachment, found it more difficult to establish the relationships that the articled teachers experienced. Also, when they noted any dissonance between the practice observed in schools and that advocated in college, the PGCE students would more readily distance themselves from the school practice and identify with the college view. Diane, for instance, like many of the articled teachers, found it easy to slot into the school community:

> I feel as though I fit in . . . I don't feel like an outsider, but one of the staff really.

As did Tamsin:

> As soon as I started in that school I just felt I fitted in and was in the right place and I haven't felt that way before. I felt enthusiastic all the time about the different things we're doing and the children and the way they are . . .

Julie, on the other hand, a PGCE student, experiences some tension on her final teaching practice when she is teaching a difficult Year 3 class, which she feels would benefit greatly from play activities to develop their language. She feels she can justify this approach on the basis of the ideas and rationales that have been discussed in college but she knows that the deputy head and the teachers in the school expect a much more formal teaching approach, and she is unsure of how to handle the conflict.

> . . . as a new person I feel slightly in a difficult position . . . I did suggest it in a jokey kind of way and it wasn't that well received. It's having the clout to do something about it really. And I think I'd like advice on that, how much autonomy can I push for and how much is it realistic to expect. Should I rise above what is expected in the school and really come down with what I feel the children need?

Second, articled teachers were more aware of the potential contribution of school-based mentors and, sometimes through experience with different mentors during the course, came to know what mentors could usefully provide to aid their professional development. In general, the articled teachers developed much closer relationships with their mentors and were more willing to approach their mentors for support and to share ideas and concerns. The PGCE students, on the other hand, were more likely to confide in a peer group and to seek support from their student colleagues, an option that was also valued by the articled teachers, although the opportunities for peer group support were greatly restricted for them by the structure of the course, particularly in the last two terms.

Third, it was the PGCE students who attached more importance to planning and preparation and also to classroom management. The PGCE students' teaching practice files were generally more detailed and more thoroughly worked out. PGCE students also gave more thought to classroom organization and management, and these matters were also recorded in their teaching files. The articled teachers possibly had a more gentle induction into teaching, they assumed responsibility for the class more gradually and these aspects of the teachers' work were probably developed over a longer period of time. These aspects of teaching may also have been less emphasized by school-based mentors than by the PGCE college tutors who tended to see them as crucial areas for the novice teacher to attend to.

Fourth, articled teachers appeared to attach much more emphasis to fitting in to the class teachers' ways of working. Being attached to one classroom for the major part of the course, the articled teachers also tended to view their role as one of substitute teacher maintaining the status quo. Mentors also frequently regarded their relationship with the student teacher as a long-term one in which the student was to learn from the experienced teacher's practice. The PGCE students, however, were more likely to view classroom practice as an opportunity to experiment, to try out different activities and to introduce new ideas, particularly once they had established some confidence in their own teaching. This view was also shared by several teachers and tutors who would encourage experimentation. In the case of the PGCE students, the period attached to one class was generally only a matter of a few weeks, culminating in the final practice of seven and a half weeks; teachers probably did not view the students' presence in terms of a long-term working relationship.

It would be difficult to draw any conclusions from these trends about the effectiveness of school-based teacher education, since school-based courses themselves vary widely, and the articled teacher scheme was a particularly well-resourced example. Nevertheless, these trends do raise a number of questions about the possible effects of particular aspects of the design of teacher training courses — for instance, in whether opportunities for peer interaction are allowed to occur, or whether a particular view of learning to teach (such as modelling) is encouraged, or whether students have the appropriate experience to appreciate the contribution that mentors can make to their professional development. A more detailed consideration of the effects of various aspects of course design on the experience of student teachers would obviously be of value in informing the design of initial training courses in general.

Factors Influencing Teachers' Practice

Another area on which discussions with student teachers during interviews regularly focused, concerned the influences and constraints on their practice that students experienced. Occasionally, these would be volunteered by students expressing concern about particular limitations on what they found they were able to do. Also, when students spoke about their practice in interviews, they were frequently asked about how their approach to a particular lesson or their way of dealing with a particular incident had come about, and this would often lead into a discussion of particular influences and constraints. It was found that the factors mentioned by student teachers could usually be classified into one of three possible groups: the socio-cultural, the personal and the technical.

Socio-cultural factors concerned taken-for-granted practices within the school, and the expectations of teachers, children, headteachers, college tutors or parents. Particular ways of planning, ways of organizing the curriculum, or techniques of classroom organization and management, such as group teaching or following an integrated day, were sometimes established within a school, and there were clear expectations that student teachers should conform to these. Individual teachers would also sometimes have particular ways of organizing the class or particular signals (that indicated to the children the need for silence, or to stop what they were doing or to move to a particular part of the room) that had become accepted by the class and to which they were responsive. These practices would often constrain what students themselves did, not necessarily because teachers and headteachers expected them to follow this example, but because the system was there and running, and it was much easier to be effective by fitting into the class's normal procedures than to try to establish a parallel system of working. The children themselves often became a constraint in this respect in that they had become accustomed to the class teacher's way of working, they had developed certain expectations for the teacher and, through patterns of cooperation and non-cooperation, would communicate these to the new student. Tricia, for example, an articled teacher, describes how the nature of the children themselves in the two schools in which she has taught provide different contexts for teaching:

> The whole problem at N., as I see it, was one of discipline. In order to tell the children anything as a whole class I had first to get their attention and get them to be quiet and listen. Whereas at B. if you get them to be quiet and listen they will stop and listen and you can speak. At N. they would stop and listen for a few seconds and then someone would interrupt. You could ask them not to again and again, but there were one or two who would constantly call out without putting their hands up. So it was a battle to actually teach because you're constantly trying to get an audience who will listen to you.

Nancy illustrates how the student teacher is faced with everyday practices that the children expect to be continued:

> So many times I've had children say to me, 'Mrs McDonald doesn't do it like that. We do it like this.' And after a while, you just think 'Sod Mrs McDonald.' You say to them, 'I don't care how she does it, you're doing it how I want today.' But the pressure is there, from the children even, to do it in the way everyone else does it. What's even worse is that they'll even go and say 'But Mrs McDonald, we've been doing it like this with you and Miss Morton wants us to do it like this!'

In interaction with teachers, children, parents and headteachers, there were often cues which the student teachers noted that indicated approval or disapproval either of particular actions or of the student's overall competence as a teacher. For some students, these cues were important signals that helped the student to judge their own progress. For example, Maggie commented about how reassured she felt when parents came to collect their children at the end of the day and they would talk to her as if she was the class teacher.

In some schools, students felt under strong pressures to conform. For example, the noise emanating from a classroom would commonly be interpreted as an indicator of the teacher's competence, and student teachers would realize the importance of keeping noise levels down. Adam recalls one incident when a pupil in his class is told off by the headteacher in morning assembly for a minor misbehaviour, but Adam finds himself in a bad mood for the rest of the day because he feels accountable for this misbehaviour and believes the reprimand is in an indirect way attributable to him.

Personal factors related to the images the student teachers had of themselves as teachers, their own past experiences of schooling and their beliefs about good teaching. Frequently, the kind of teacher students saw themselves becoming or the types of behaviour that they saw themselves as capable of, would act as a powerful influence on their teaching. For example, several of the students when working alongside fairly authoritarian teachers reported feeling uncomfortable with the teacher–pupil relationship; their own notions of how they saw themselves relating to children were in conflict. Julie, for instance, finds herself reluctantly adapting her teaching style to suit the demands of her supervising teacher, who is also the acting headteacher of the school:

> . . . although I want to show my personality to the children, because of other things, like having discipline and control, it's not always possible for your personality to shine through . . . I think it's something I've come to terms with now. I feel there has to be a professional distance between myself and the children and to do the best for them I can't always be myself. There are times when I have to do something that I might not do if I was being myself. Little things, like PE kit, I found difficult. The ruling was that if they didn't have the correct gear they couldn't do PE. If we were going outside and they had trainers on and they were dressed in reasonable clothes to have freedom of movement, my personal inclination would have been that they could still join in. But the school ruling was that they required the correct kit. It's how far you take these things a lot of the time and your reasons for it, justifying it.

Technical factors were the textbook ideas and strategies that student teachers were exposed to and came to adopt in their own practice, and the physical and resource constraints that existed within the school. Both courses encompassed a technology of teaching. Method courses espoused particular ways of teaching a subject, curriculum resources were associated with particular patterns of classroom organization, and the physical layout of the classroom itself often placed constraints upon what student teachers could do. Tricia, for example, works with some children on poetry and takes ideas suggested by an advisory teacher during an inset day, where children brainstorm and then use cutting and pasting of their writing in order to draft and redraft. She adopts this approach because the whole staff decided to employ it, but finds it a difficult approach to use to develop 'something of quality'.

> I think the danger with this is that you're going to get a non-quality piece of writing that goes on forever and doesn't make much sense. I'm going to have to make sure I'm in there asking them to cut it down and doing something good rather than having something that flows on forever. I think it's a very hard thing to do.

Student teachers reported many different factors which they believed influenced or constrained the development of their own teaching practice. Identifying and recognizing the potential impact of these factors is important in furthering our understanding of the professional learning process and in designing productive professional development activities and courses.

Mentoring — The Students' Experience

Students reported widely differing experiences with their mentors, who, as discussed later, similarly reported quite different conceptions of their roles and responsibilities. Many of the students recognized the importance of mentors being both supportive and helpful but also constructively critical. Although mentors generally found it easy to be supportive, they found it much more difficult to be constructively critical, or to offer the guidance that many of the students expected. Nancy, for example, expresses disappointment when she has to deal with a classroom incident in which a child loses his temper and throws a chair across the classroom. Nancy recounts how the mentor was in the classroom at the time, but offered no support and left Nancy to deal with the incident on her own. In discussion with the mentor afterwards, Nancy finds that the mentor does not seem at all perturbed by the incident, and feels let down that the only advice that she is offered is: 'You should have told him to shut up!' Tricia also comments on the lack of constructive support, but puts this down to the complexity of teaching and the fact that there often are no ready answers:

> It's hard for the mentors. They can give you hints on what not to do and how best to approach it, but if you have had a bad session, they'll say 'Go home and have a gin,' or something. There's no ready answer . . . Perhaps we're expecting the impossible, but I sometimes feel my mentor doesn't have an answer. She sympathizes and that's great. She says she has days like that as well: 'That particular child is a nuisance isn't he?' sort of thing. Sometimes I'd like it to be a more organized approach — 'That went wrong, so next time do it this way.' But life's not like that.

However, some of the articled teachers towards the end of the course became more proactive in shaping the mentoring relationship, attempting to set specific agendas for discussion with their mentors, for example, and directing mentors to the fields where they required particular feedback. Some of the articled teachers reported being constrained by their mentors in that the students always felt that they were sharing the class teacher's class and weren't allowed the opportunity to experiment and find their own style of teaching. Tamsin, for example, reports feeling highly constrained by the mentor's practice in her first school, and it is only when she spends a period of time in her second school that she feels able to 'move out of the mentor's shadow'.

The relationship between student and mentor was an important feature in determining how effectively the student learned from the experience. Being able to confide in the mentor was felt to be important by several students. Sara, for example, comments on her supervising teacher:

> I feel comfortable with the teacher . . . She's quite supportive and honest about how she feels about teaching . . . So I feel she's on the same side as me because she's prepared to confide in me.

There were several cases where a close, trusting, mutually accepting relationship did not emerge between student and mentor. In such cases, the student might not seek help when needed, was less likely to discuss matters with the mentor, and was more likely to ignore or reject the mentor's advice. Beth, for instance, reported feeling very uncomfortable with her mentor, whom she thought had very fixed views about teaching and tended to be overly critical of what Beth perceived as minor incidents. Beth felt that she was constantly being watched in school and 'couldn't let her guard down'. As a result, she found the emotional support that she needed by turning to her peers and friends. It was through exchanging experiences, ideas and difficulties with others that she kept her own situation in perspective and maintained a clear view of the kind of teaching she wanted to engage in.

The students, particularly early in the course, tended to look upon their mentors as role models, able to demonstrate the skills of teaching. However, in some cases, having a mentor who was an exceptionally able teacher was regarded by the students as intimidating. Jess, in the first term, commented about her supervising teacher:

> She's amazing. I went in and wondered what it was going to be like. But she's just made to be a primary school teacher. She's got the voice. She never shouts. I think there are twenty-four Reception children and she never has to shout at them. She gives off this aura of calmness and it seems to influence the children . . . When the supply teacher was in this week there was bedlam . . . She doesn't have that presence the full-time teacher has . . . I came out of the first day thinking 'How can this woman do it?' . . . she's a real role model of a teacher and it's quite hard to feel confident and competent when you're in with someone like that. It's brilliant to learn, but the way my character is I found it really hard to get my own confidence up being with someone so good.

Other students found they learned from their mentors even when they were not particularly good role models, especially once they were able to evaluate the practices they observed. Sian, for instance, comments:

> . . . to begin with, I thought everything she did was wonderful because I had no other experience. I hadn't observed someone else and I thought it was the way to do it because she seemed in control and to know what she was doing. Whereas now I watch and think 'I wouldn't do it like that' or 'That's a nice idea' or 'I like the way she's done that.' So I feel I'm learning from the way she teaches. She doesn't have to be the ideal teacher because, even if I don't agree with what she's doing, it makes me think how I would do it.

Induction of New Teachers

All of the PGCE students who obtained work in the second year experienced a highly stressful first term in full-time teaching. The most common report was of not being able to 'switch off' and of living with teaching 24 hours a day. All the students reported thinking about their work all the time, spending large numbers of hours in preparation and record keeping, of dreaming about teaching and even, in some cases, having nightmares about it. The demands of fitting into a new school, of developing their own competence further, of getting to know the children, of planning work and being responsible for a class full-time weighed heavily upon the minds of all the students. The first term was largely a battle of seeking enough time and energy to do all the things that they felt needed to be done. Although the students were usually assigned a mentor — often a senior teacher in the school with responsibility for overseeing the induction of new teachers — in many cases, little support was actually received. Contact with the official mentor was infrequent, and it was usually the case that it was left to the new teacher to seek help if and when they felt it was needed, and from whomever they found available or approachable. The close mentoring relationship that some of the students had experienced during initial training was absent. Even where it seemed that teachers were keen to be more active in their mentoring role, there was little time in which to develop it. The new teachers in their first year were left largely to their own devices. By the second term, however, the new teachers had settled into a routine; they knew the children, and had a clear idea of others' expectations of them. The stress eased up, and one or two even reported beginning to enjoy teaching. Jess, looking back on her first term of full-time teaching, comments:

> Every week things changed and I have found that it's got gradually in proportion. You don't feel under pressure so much and that helps because you can think straight if you're not out of your mind with worry about what you haven't remembered. You suddenly realize you have remembered this and you have got that organized or you have got your survival tactics down to a tee. And the time-fillers that originally you feel guilty to use, because you don't think it's constructive or you should be doing something worthwhile all the time. But then you think 'No one else does' and you're not superhuman. It's just as it all comes together more and you can handle it better . . . The main thing when you go and don't know the routines is that everything is new, so every day you're doing something that you're not sure about, and people take it for granted that you know, like dinner money or doing the register. It puts so much strain on you because you're trying to get everything right and you're not familiar with the routine . . . all those little things . . . it's getting it to run smoothly. Once you get to know your children, you know they respect you as their teacher and you know how to handle them, so you're not on edge, wondering if they're doing what they should be doing, whether you're stretching them enough. You feel you can get better control, which helps you and your confidence, and that has a knock-on effect.

Although systematic interviews of the articled teachers were not conducted during their induction into full-time teaching, informal contact was made with several of the articled teachers once they had taken up appointments. Given the much longer period of time they had spent in schools as part of their initial training, and given their much more gradual induction into the demands of teaching, it was expected that their induction into full-time teaching might be much less traumatic. Interestingly, it was not. The students reported the same high levels of stress, and the same problems of too much to do and not enough time to do it. Reports of long working nights and weekends, difficulty in sleeping and 'not being able to switch off' seemed to be as common amongst these teachers as amongst the former PGCE students. The first term of full-time teaching was fraught and anguished, no matter how they trained!

The articled teachers, however, did seem to be more prepared to seek help in the school, whereas the PGCE students overall were more inclined to believe that one ought to keep one's concerns to oneself and that exposing one's concerns to colleagues might be perceived as a sign of incompetence. Those trained through the articled teacher route were more aware of the potential benefits of an open and trusting mentoring relationship. Diane at the end of the articled teacher course, commented on the role of her mentor:

> We discuss things as colleagues and if I ask things we discuss them through and she accepts how I feel about things. We have different ideas and we discuss them without any outcomes. We just evaluate things and I work out the outcome myself. It's more of an experienced colleague really and I go to her for advice, which I either take or not. She's not imposing her views and I now feel I would do things differently to her and she recognizes and accepts that . . . We discuss children and how I've reacted or responded with individual children, particularly the special needs. They're the ones I really needed help with because I've always included them and set them work, but needed reassurance that it was sufficient and I was approaching it in the right way, especially with reading and writing skills, which this one particular group were very poor on. So we've tended to discuss that or emotional problems or parental problems, things like that. Also, we've used it to discuss my planning and if I needed help once I'd planned it all.

Image of Teaching as an Organizing Framework for Student Teachers

Most of the students began their course with an image in mind of themselves as a teacher, and this image for many of the students was repeatedly referred to over the two years during which contact was maintained. Student teachers' images of teaching seemed to have three distinct dimensions — *the moral, the sense-making* and *the existential*. Images had a *moral dimension* in that they were often idealized images of teaching. They represented for the student how teaching ought to be and, as such, held out a desirable generalized model of teaching. Some of the students recognized this, pointing out that although they had a vision in mind of how they would like to be as teachers, this might have to be compromised in reality. Jeremy, for instance, asserts that it is important for teachers to hold on to an ideal, 'to widen [the children's] horizons humanly and towards other people' but acknowledges that there are severe limits on what teachers can actually accomplish: 'I don't think that rationally it is achievable and in the end the individual teachers have to make their contribution, the fullest one they can, where they can.' Rebecca recognizes strengths in herself which contribute to her teaching ability: 'I've got patience. I'm good at organization, good at organizing people, and I like responsibility. And everyone says I communicate well.' At the same time, she recognizes the almost impossible demands of the teacher's work: 'I need to develop the ability to motivate myself even when I'm tired. You have to give 100 per cent from 9 am to 3 pm so to speak, and I'm not one for having lots of energy to expend. When I get tired I do get ratty and I'd hate that to come out with the children and other teachers.'

Images also appeared to serve an important *sense-making function* for student teachers throughout their teacher training experiences. The students' images would appear to predispose them to explore particular strategies and to acquire particular ideas and activities for teaching. Their images provided a yardstick by which to judge whether certain activities are appropriate or fitting for them to use. After observing another teacher's lesson, for example, students would ask themselves whether they could see themselves doing a particular activity, and they would judge others' styles of teaching in relation to their own image. The students' images of themselves as teachers also influenced how they thought about school expectations, and helped some of them to formulate ideas about the kind of school and school ethos that would be most fitting to support their own style of teaching. Jeremy's image of teaching, for example, enables him to identify qualities and strategies of his supervising teacher that might translate to his own practice and he begins to identify characteristics of the school that support his preferred style of teaching.

> His resilience, being able to be bright and positive and business-like at the start of every lesson. That's something I felt I had to develop and copy. I don't try to mimic it absolutely but within my own personality I'll try to match it . . . Most of the things I observe I want to be able to do likewise. Like being interested and cheerful and keeping control in the right way, which is disciplined and professional without going over the top. We're similar personalities and he doesn't raise his voice very much. A lot of this is down to the ethos of the school as well and the fact that the class is used to behaving in a particular way. That style of management might not be adequate to control classes in some schools. But I agree with that ethos. It's very positive and it's a happy school.

For most student teachers, their image of teaching remained fairly unaltered over the course, and it enabled them to make sense of the diverse experiences of training and to synthesize ideas, activities, strategies and expectations into a coherent practice, meaningful to themselves. A few students, however, began the course without any clear image of themselves as teachers. Interestingly, these students seemed to be more stressed and disoriented by their training experiences. This might be explained by their lack of a reference point by which to filter the experiences offered to them in training. Faced with a mental overload of prescriptions, observations and experiences, they seemed to lose direction, lacking an overall image by which to compare and contrast, sift, select or reject them. Sara, for example, is a PGCE student who decides to enter teaching because she believes it to be associated with a strong sense of job satisfaction. However, she lacks a well-formulated image of teaching or of herself as a teacher. When she enters a classroom for the first time since her own schooling, she is confused by the level of noise in a Reception class which she associates with lack of focus and a poor learning environment, yet is amazed by the happiness she sees on the children's faces and senses that the children are learning a great deal. As she enters the course, she cannot say what she expects her training to be like. At the end of the first year, she discusses the difficulties she faces in acclimatizing to the culture of teaching:

> I do see them [teachers] as a separate breed. Partly I think a bit negatively about it because I don't have a job. But so many of the teachers in school are so much older and are mature women with families, with whom I felt I had nothing in common apart from being in their class or school. And I saw them on a different plane. Their whole lifestyle. The really strange thing about being in school is that when you feel a day hasn't gone well and you can take the criticism from a teacher and they'll direct you. But I felt it was my lifestyle that was getting a bashing too. It seemed to be deeper than how I was in class sometimes. It was my whole lifestyle that affects what I am in class. I'm not organized and clear thinking at home. I don't have the same attitude as the teachers in school . . . I'm not prepared to change everything about me to do it . . . I feel that your own personality is stifled. I find it really restrictive and limiting. Although I've enjoyed being myself at relaxed points of the day, they're few and far between. The bits at home in between really restricts what you do and how you behave. There's a huge net over my whole lifestyle. On the Friday it's really nice and I think I'll do work on Saturday and then you don't because everything is happening and it's suddenly Sunday afternoon and you haven't done anything. That's happened over and over again at weekends. Every weekend I'd be up really late on Sunday night wondering what I'd be doing with them on Monday morning. Just the Monday morning. Sometimes I'd be in tears. I'd be a complete mess, no resources ready, no card to make things with, no photocopying and not the right books at home. That was awful and all weekend it was hanging over my head, that guilty feeling so you don't have a good time. I used to hate that. It was one of the worst bits of it.

It's had quite an effect on me, more than other things I've done. It's made me wonder if I really do want to teach and if I'm capable of doing it. It's made me wonder if I'm quite a weak person, too easy going. At college you're fed this idea of being really confident and being clear about objectives, and I never have been. I don't know that I actually want to be. Maybe I should. It affects me on quite a deep, personal level, which is quite disturbing really. The lecturers at college are quite strong people. They're big, punchy women and sometimes I really admire them. Sometimes I think, 'God forbid'. I can't imagine some of them in school. The school I went to for the interview, they were tiptoey mousey women ... they're not confident and demanding women that you find in college. Are they the ones who are teachers, and the ones who are lecturers are the beefy ones?

I am enthusiastic about it and do believe I have some of the qualities that would make me a good teacher. I genuinely like the children and I'm patient and kind to them, but I don't think that's necessarily so important. I don't know that I actually have a place in it because even when I compare myself with people on the course, I don't think I was either eager or committed in the end. I was at the beginning. I really did want to do it and knew I wanted to do it. But then I began to dislike so much of it and I don't know what I now have to offer as a teacher.

Sara continues to feel uneasy with the role of teacher and in the second year she takes up a voluntary post in a special school, where she finds a school ethos that is closer to her own values.

A further dimension of the students' images might be most appropriately termed *the existential*. Student teachers' images reflected a view of themselves as persons as well as teachers. The student's image was often part of the intrinsic motivation for becoming a teacher — their image represented an identity that they could see themselves adopting, and in some cases it seemed that fulfilling this image was an important part of the student's own self-expression and life development. Jeremy, for instance, felt very strongly about the importance of understanding science, his own specialist subject, and appears to view himself almost as a missionary with the task of taking this understanding out into the wider community:

You can teach people the things that really matter ... Science can help philosophically or even spiritually in the right hands because it is dealing with the things we are given.

Similarly, Maggie strongly values education from the beginning, she views it as an empowering process, and becoming a teacher is becoming part of 'the most important thing in the world'. Diane also comments on an underlying mission that several student teachers were committed to:

I just want to be remembered and that in twenty years' time someone will be sitting saying, 'The reason I'm doing this is because this one teacher motivated me.' They don't have to remember my name but I'd like to think I've passed something of my enthusiasm on.

It was also important for several of the students to feel as though they *were* teachers. Being a teacher and feeling like a teacher, being at ease in a teaching role which they valued, was important to the students. This seemed to represent a sense of personal achievement or self-actualization. In the early stages of teaching, it was often attained when children obeyed simple commands or requests, confirming their recognition of the student as a teacher. Later in the course, students would cite examples of where they had been spoken to as a teacher by other adults — parents, other teachers, teaching assistants. This similarly boosted their confidence and reaffirmed their role as a teacher. Later still, however, feeling like a teacher became associated with a sense that a number of teaching outcomes could be attributed to them — a good classroom ethos, activities that are well planned, organized and managed; children moving about the classroom in a purposeful way. At the end of the two years, students were particularly satisfied by incidences where they were able to think on their feet, respond to children immediately, or point to incidences of children learning. Feelings of success also arose from a sense of implementing the image that the student held for him/herself as a personal goal. Feeling like a teacher and being comfortable in that role seemed to have an empowering effect upon students — it often seemed to accompany a feeling of being in charge of themselves and their job, rather than being an outside observer or simply responding to external directives and constraints. Stephanie, for example, towards the end of her articled teacher course, comments on the intrinsic satisfaction of being able to influence children's ways of working:

I did enjoy my time when I had the class for a term because it was the first occasion when you can follow work through from start to finish and it didn't matter if you didn't get it done in the two-hour session. I was quite pleased with some of the English work they did and the fact that over the twelve weeks they did get into a routine of checking their work and redrafting, and I felt quite pleased at the end of it that that was starting to be a natural routine for them. They knew what I meant and they could go away and do it and talk to their partners about it. That was quite nice.

Similarly, Adam took great satisfaction from having identified ladybird chrysalises in his garden and bringing them into school for the children to see. For him, this signified a change in himself — a transition to being able to think like a teacher.

The notion of an 'image of teaching' and how this is developed may be more complex than originally conceptualized. It appears to serve a number of different functions in directing the learning of student teachers; these require further exploration if we are to understand their full significance in teachers' career-long professional development.

Relationships

Student teachers often spoke about the importance of relationships in teaching. Often relationships — in the sense of the ways in which teachers and pupils relate to one another — were a central part of the students' images. Students would have an ideal in mind of the ways in which they felt they should interact with children, and also ideas of how they should relate to other individuals with whom they came into regular contact, particularly other teachers and parents. It was relationships with children, however, that tended to dominate students' thinking. Whether they were pleased or not with the relationships they had established in the classroom was a matter of great importance to the students. It was often the means by which they judged the success of their teaching. Nancy, for example, feels she has 'really got to grips' with the 'ethos of the classroom', and reckons that developing good relationships and an appropriate atmosphere for learning are important parts of the teacher's work:

> Those [good relationships] are real high points for me, more so than the learning. I really feel if they can't sit in the classroom and get on . . . you can stand there and throw all this stuff at them, but if they are not together up here then they can't cope with it anyway, so it's pointless. They need *to be able to learn* if you like. If they have problems at home and are thinking about other things or just don't know how to concentrate, then those are the things you need to work out before you can do all the other stuff.

Students frequently mentioned the importance of developing the 'right atmosphere' or 'working environment' in a classroom, and such terms often seemed to refer to the quality of the teacher–pupil relationships. The nature of the relationships that student teachers sought varied somewhat, though aspects that were commonly referred to included mutual respect, sincerity and trust.

Some students frequently analysed the quality of the relationships they established with the children, reflecting on whether a lesson 'felt right' or whether their relationships in class were working well. When they weren't, some students were quite analytical both of the children's behaviour and situation and of their own personality and attitudes.

When Adam analyses his failure to emulate his supervising teacher's non-confrontational approach, he recognizes that his own personality is quite different and he does not have the same relationship with the children. In time, he appreciates that he is not yet able to employ some of the teacher's subtle skills in avoiding confrontation, such as using humour to diffuse a difficult situation.

Stages of Development

Several researchers have suggested that student teachers progress through a number of different stages in the process of becoming a teacher. In looking at the kinds of concerns that student teachers report, Fuller and Bown (1975) suggest that they progress through four different stages, starting with no concerns at all and passing through stages of survival concerns, teaching concerns and eventually pupil learning concerns. Berliner (1988), in a study of the ways in which teachers with different levels of experience interpret classroom incidents and videotapes of classroom life, adopts a cognitive performance model of teaching which identifies five stages of development, beginning with the novice who has difficulty identifying classroom situations to the expert whose performance is fluid and responsive as the teacher's perceptions and actions appear to be remarkably well coordinated. Studies of student teachers on field placements (e.g., Calderhead, 1987; Furlong and Maynard, 1995) have identified stages of development that students appear to progress through which are characterized by their approaches to learning. Early in field placements, students are on a steep learning curve; they absorb a great deal of information, are keen to learn from practice and quickly establish routines to cope with the situations they face. Later, however, the learning seems to reach a plateau, the students' efforts are directed towards maintaining the classroom routines and gaining their own certification. Once over any examination process, however, students can afford to be more experimental and to try to identify and refine their own teaching style.

While all of these stages can be identified within the transcripts of the interviews with the student teachers, it is also the case that to think in terms of stages of development oversimplifies the data. While some students did progress through distinct stages, others did not. At times, the stages are not as distinct as one might imagine. And, of course, some students even at the beginning of the course seemed to have quite advanced ways of thinking about teaching and did not report the usual student teacher concerns.

Stage models are useful heuristics in highlighting the complexity of teaching and the possible routes of professional development, but the diversity of routes in becoming a teacher is wide, the people and the situations involved are different, and attempts to reduce learning to teach to a few stages inevitably remain broad generalizations.

Types of Professional Learning

As has been suggested elsewhere (Calderhead, 1991), one of the reasons why learning how to teach is difficult and challenging for many student teachers is that it requires learning processes that are different from those that students have typically engaged in during their other experiences in higher education. The kinds of tasks they face in becoming a teacher and the demands that are placed upon them introduce them to new types of learning.

In examining the reported learning experiences of the twenty student teachers in this study, five different types of learning experience could be inferred. First of all, there is *knowledge accumulation*, the learning of information vital to the task of teaching. Student teachers are bombarded with enormous amounts of information — about schools, about children, about the curriculum, about procedures and strategies. Much of this is simply factual information that students need to have readily available, and is learned (or not) from college lectures, books, school documents, and conversations with teachers and tutors.

Second, there is *performance learning.* Part of the task of teaching is to perform, to act as a teacher in the classroom, and learning to perform is quite a different experience from learning about Key Stage assessment or the National Curriculum requirements. Performance learning requires a detailed awareness of self and others and an ability to cue in to the various actions, movements, tones of voice, speech and gestures that are used to communicate in the classroom. Teachers are often the focus of attention in the classroom and what they communicate non-verbally as well as verbally can be influential in shaping the relationships and the routines of the classroom, as the student teachers discover. Performance skills are therefore an essential part of teaching, but are dependent on learning processes that many student teachers have not previously been introduced to in any systematic way.

Third, learning to teach involves a lot of *practical problem-solving.* Planning lessons, thinking about how to cope with a particular form of classroom organization, or arranging the day's activities all involve juggling various interests, opportunities and constraints in order to broadly achieve one's goals. Practical problem-solving was a time-consuming activity for many of the student teachers, particularly early in the course, because, as Schön (1983) explains, practical problems are often *messy* and offer different ways of being perceived as well as diverse routes to solving them. Practical problem-solving involved bringing together various areas of knowledge and experience, looking for patterns and explanations, and mentally rehearsing various strategies in attempts to define and solve problems.

Fourth, there is *learning about relationships.* In the view of the student teachers, negotiating and maintaining relationships in the classroom, and also to some extent outside the classroom with other teachers and parents, was a significant part of the teacher's work. This may have some aspects in common with performance learning, but when students are engaged in developing this aspect of their work as teachers, they also appear to acquire a sensitivity to themselves and others that is peculiar to the processes of establishing relationships. Students often perceived the development of relationships as involving themselves as people much more than performance skills. To relate well to children, it was often suggested one had genuinely to like the children, to want to work with them and to be able to communicate that genuineness. Some students also suggested that there was some degree of vulnerability associated with developing a good relationship with the children, because one had to some extent to expose one's own personality and to let the children know who you are as a person. Many of the student teachers found the development of classroom relationships to be difficult. They were sometimes unable to appreciate how the good examples of teacher–pupil relationships that they observed had been built up over the year, and took a long time to recognize the complex interplay of factors that made such relationships possible.

Fifth, there are *processes of assimilation* in learning to teach. Teachers are constantly drawing upon a diverse range of strategies, beliefs, values and information in their everyday work, and there is considerable scope for dissonance, even in the case of experienced teachers. This may be a source of anxiety but it is also a source of learning. In the case of student teachers, the dissonance is often high. The images they have of themselves as teachers don't match the kind of teacher they can see themselves becoming. Student teachers find themselves juggling different images of themselves and teachers, searching for rationales and justifications in an attempt to develop a more coherent and comfortable understanding of teaching and of themselves as teachers.

Further research is clearly needed to elaborate on these processes and to identify how student teachers might be better supported in developing the various aspects of professional learning that are involved in becoming a teacher.

Mentoring — The Mentor's Perspective

Towards the end of the first year of the study, nine of the mentors in the articled teacher scheme agreed to be interviewed about their perceptions of the course in which they were involved and about their ideas concerning the role of the school-based mentor. The schools in the articled teacher scheme had been specially chosen by the local education authority and the college, and were judged to be offering supportive environments in which to learn to teach. The mentors were generally selected by the headteachers within these schools. Mentors were provided with some college training for their role, which focused both on the structure of the whole course and how the mentor's role featured within it, and on strategies that mentors might use in supporting the professional development of their students. These mentors were therefore probably better prepared for their role than the supervising teachers who worked with the PGCE students.

Although mentors differed slightly in their views about the course, with different emphases on what they perceived to be the main purposes of teacher education, two dimensions of learning to teach were commonly emphasized. Most saw learning to teach as largely a practical matter: students learned by being in the classroom, observing and trying things out for themselves. As one mentor put it:

> There's no better way to learn than being in the classroom with the children. That's how I feel. It's quite easy for people to lecture about a particular thing but it's something else to actually be in the classroom with the children and teachers and do it.

The other aspect of learning to teach that was frequently emphasized was a personal dimension. Teachers commonly believed that teaching was a matter of personality and coming to terms with one's own style of teaching:

> I'd like them to be able to find their way through the pathways and do it their way, so that they develop in their own individual way.

Two of the mentors spoke about the division between theory and practice, where the 'theory' input was expected from the college, and the role of the mentor was to help the students understand the theory and to put it into practice; the tasks which the college set for the students to carry out in schools were seen as important means by which this translation was made. Several of the mentors, however, viewed the college course as overly theoretical and insufficiently focused on the practical task of teaching. As one mentor commented:

> There's an awful lot of 'This is what teaching is all about, you put in and put up your displays, and it's all lovely and you get very carried away with it', but when you get down to it, you have the child who *will* throw the paint around and the one who *will* sit under the table. But they don't tell you so much about that part of it, which can throw all your plans out totally. So there's an awful lot more the college could do about the reality of teaching I think.

Mentors often confessed to being unclear about what the mentor's role actually involved, but the most frequently mentioned aspect was that of 'guide', closely followed by that of 'friend'. Having a good, supportive relationship with the student was seen as important, and this was viewed, at least in part, as down to the mentor's personality:

> I don't even know what mentors do. I just have to be the sort of person I am and hope it works.

Other terms used to define their mentoring role included 'good listener', 'facilitator', 'supporter', 'good model' and 'organizer'. A typical comment was:

> I think my main role has been listening. Helping her evaluate her own performance and helping her evaluate my performance and that of the school and helping her get things straight really. Just by letting her talk she often comes to her own conclusions. Really my main function is just to listen and guide . . . She took the class on one afternoon last week and she was extremely worried about the behaviour of the class. She felt that she wasn't in control as much as she would like to be and we talked about it. She watched me deal with similar incidents during the rest of the week and then we talked about it again and she felt a lot better and realized she was in fact dealing with it in a very practical and suitable way and she felt a lot better about it.

Another mentor commented on her role as:

> Being a very active listener I think would be my main priority. Just to be there when they want to talk to you, and to listen more than talk to the person. So that they can pour their worries out or if they have problems you have to be there. That's the most important factor.

Only one mentor commented on the importance of challenging the student — in the sense of providing alternative ways of thinking about what they are doing.

The strategies that the mentors reported using to support students included: structuring the students' observation; offering advice in the planning and preparation of activities; providing feedback on lessons; discussing problems; working collaboratively with the student; liaising with the college; and simply listening to the student and lending a 'sympathetic ear'. All of the mentors reported strategies for listening to, and reassuring, students; collaborative work with the student, such as jointly planning, teaching and evaluating lessons, were more rarely mentioned. Some of the mentors commented on how uncomfortable and claustrophobic the mentor–student relationship could become if they were both working closely together all the time. Beth's mentor explained why she found it more useful for Beth to observe and work with other teachers within the school:

> She's not with me all the time seeing me in my role and me seeing her in her role. It's easier for her to come and talk to me about something she's done with someone else . . . I think it's good to be like that because you can be a bit more objective. For us, particularly, it's worked quite well.

Another commented:

> I suppose it comes back to the business of losing your privacy sometimes, and it's just the ideal relationship would be to be able to turn her off and turn her on when I was willing to share. That would be the ideal.

When asked about where their own mentoring practices had come from, several of the mentors reported drawing upon their own experiences as student teachers. They would think back to the difficulties they experienced, which some mentors would talk about to the students, and would try to imagine what they would have found most helpful at the time. It is these experiences, more than the training courses at the college, that the mentors reported as a source of ideas on how to carry out the mentoring role and how to help their students. Some of the mentors also spoke of the importance of discussing mentoring with other colleagues in the school. One of the mentors actually viewed mentoring as a whole-school commitment involving all staff, rather than simply the designated mentor.

Most of the mentors also reported some personal benefits to mentoring. They realized that having a student teacher heightened their awareness of their own work. Discussions with their student often made them realize features of their own teaching and helped them to question aspects of their own practice. In some cases, it was also the mentor's keenness to present a good role model that led them to reappraise their own practice:

> I want to give her the best possible role model I can, the best possible guidance. In which case, if she's going to come in and see me do a PE

lesson I immediately think, 'Ah, I've got to get it right because she's watching.' Therefore you become introspective and you make sure you have all the different things you need in a lesson which is done correctly and as you would wish someone else to do it. I've had to rethink quite a few things really.

In considering their own professional development as mentors, they frequently reported that it would be helpful if they had the opportunity to discuss mentoring with teachers in other schools, to exchange ideas and find out how different schools have approached the task. Their view of their own professional development was largely the same as their view of learning to teach: good mentoring was partly a matter of personality and partly a matter of getting ideas and trying them out for oneself.

In developing school-based teacher education, the role of mentor is clearly a crucial one. Consideration needs to be given to how this role is defined, how mentors might influence the professional growth of the student teacher and how this features within the professional training course as a whole. These issues are considered further in Chapter 9.

Facilitating Learning to Teach

This chapter focuses on the tasks facing the teacher educator in designing courses of initial teacher training, and considers the contribution of research to furthering our understanding of professional growth and helping to improve the quality of training courses.

Conceptualizing Teacher Education

As noted in Chapter 1, several writers in the field of teacher education have in the past drawn a distinction between 'teacher education' and 'teacher training' (see Cruickshank and Metcalf, 1990), as if these represent two poles of an ideological dimension concerning the ways in which teachers are most appropriately prepared for their profession. The former is deemed to be concerned with the intellectual development of teachers, whereas the latter is more specifically concerned with the development of particular areas of knowledge and skill that are instrumental to the task of teaching. It has been argued that *teacher education* is involved in the all-round education and development of teachers, emphasizing teaching as a profession involving well-informed judgment; whereas *teacher training* refers to a more mechanistic approach to teacher preparation, more akin to a craft apprenticeship involving the mastery of well-defined routines. Such a distinction, however, may be simplistic and unhelpful. Obviously learning to teach does involve the acquisition of certain knowledge and skills that are essential to adequate classroom performance. It is also the case, however, that learning to teach involves being able to reason about one's own actions, being able to justify particular strategies, understanding the subject matter, children and their ways of learning, and having a conception of the purposes of education and the ways in which schools operate in order to promote education. The continued use of such distinctions may in fact prevent the recognition of the merits of each perspective, hindering the exploration of alternative perspectives and how each refers to different areas of teachers' work and highlights different aspects of learning to teach.

It is the case, however, that over the past decade, 'teacher training' terminology, and a mechanistic ideology associated with it, has become much more prominent in the UK and in several other European and North American countries. It has become fashionable to describe teaching in terms of a knowledge base (Reynolds,

1989), competences (DfE, 1992) or a repertoire of knowledge and skills (HMI, 1988). The assumption has often been that such terminology enables one to be much clearer about what teachers need to know and be able to do, and as a result one can facilitate the professional development of teachers and enable greater precision in the assessment involved in initial certification. Defining teaching in these ways, however, can also present a number of drawbacks.

First of all, it risks being overly prescriptive, placing too tight a definition on 'good' or 'acceptable' or 'competent' practice. If we were to draw up a list of teachers who are commonly regarded as 'good', would the common denominators of their practice really reflect the essence of good teaching? We know that teachers' practice can be quite idiosyncratic and that teachers may be regarded as good exemplars of the profession for quite different reasons. Teachers can be 'good' teachers in many different respects. What counts as 'good' may also be context-dependent: the 'good' teacher in one school with one particular class may not be 'good' in a different type of school teaching different children. By providing a list of competences we may contribute to an illusion that teaching is easy and that once a predetermined knowledge base and set of skills have been learned, the task of teaching has been mastered. We may also be neglecting the creative element of teaching, and failing to acknowledge the individual ways in which teachers develop.

Second, the competency perspective leaves out of account those aspects of teaching that are not easily defined (or are not yet defined) in the language of knowledge and skills. The attitudes student teachers have towards children and towards the task of teaching, the nature of the relationships they establish in the classroom, how they fit into the school as a community and function within it are, for example, areas which appear to be important within the professional development of the new teacher but are areas in which definition in terms of knowledge and skill seems quite elusive.

Third, lists of competences define an end-product in teaching but leave out of account the processes by which teachers achieve competence. Learning, in fact, is frequently viewed as quite unproblematic in teacher education; it seems to be presumed that appropriate course content and experience in schools with relevant feedback on performance will, for most student teachers, result in competent teaching. Yet research repeatedly affirms that learning to teach is a complex process, and, for some students, occasionally a traumatic one. In fact, the use of the term 'learning' itself in describing the professional growth of the student teacher may be misleading since it suggests one generalizable process of development, irrespective of the content to be learned, the context of the learning and the attributes of the learner. Learning in the professional development of teachers, however, is frequently content-, context- and person-specific. The important question becomes not 'How do student teachers learn?' but 'How do particular student teachers learn x in context y?' Learning about the presentation of themselves as teachers is different from learning about planning history lessons. Learning in the mentoring context is different from learning from a textbook or from college-based activities, each with its own range of factors that influence the learning process. Furthermore, different students may learn different things in different ways, or the same experience may have a different significance for different students. In furthering the professional development of student teachers, understanding the complexity of the learning process and how that can be facilitated is as important, if not more so, than agreeing on an ideal end-state.

Fourth, although teaching involves performance, which is perhaps more readily defined in terms of competences, learning to teach also has an existential dimension. As student teachers in this study frequently commented, becoming a teacher is not simply a matter of *doing* what teachers do, it is also a matter of *being* a teacher. The latter involves a personal investment, a feeling of being at ease in the role of teacher, an acceptance of teaching as being part of one's identity, being able to reconcile one's own values with those of the institution and the colleagues with whom one works. This does not mean that the new teacher has to accept those institutional values, but that he or she has to develop a way of working within them. *Being* a teacher is important for student teachers because it is both reassuring and empowering; it signals that they are part of a culture and part of a teaching profession. A personal investment in teaching — being a teacher — is important because, as a teacher, one not only has to act, one invests one's own person in the task. Part of being a teacher is developing relationships with children, establishing a human rapport with others, and contributing through one's own personal qualities to the working environment of the classroom and school.

Fifth, competences neglect the contribution that the school as a community contributes to classroom practice. Although there is a tradition of thinking about teaching as both a lonely and individual profession in which, once the classroom door is shut, the teacher pursues his or her own ways of working, this has not been found to be the case in much recent classroom-based research. Schools accommodate a range of beliefs about children, the role of the teacher, and the nature of good practice. These belief systems help to define the school as a community, and by negotiating their way within this community, the new teachers gain status and acceptance and manages to implement a practice which, for the most part, reconciles their own values with those of the school. What happens in classrooms is not entirely attributable to individual teachers, and any attempts to promote the quality of practice in the classroom need to recognize the professional community that exists in the school, and the effects this has on shaping teachers' practice. The professional community may not always be a positive and supportive one. It is possible for communities to be dysfunctional, destructive and highly constraining, though they are nevertheless influential in the everyday activities of teaching.

In conclusion, it is clear that learning to teach involves more than the mastery of a limited set of competences. It is a complex process. It is also a lengthy process, extending, for most teachers, well after their initial training. The multi-dimensional nature of learning to teach has often not been fully recognized in the design of initial teacher education courses, which are often tightly constrained in terms of both time and human resources. In consequence, teacher educators face the task of attempting to cope with a vast range of competing demands in the process of designing effective initial training courses and find themselves confronting numerous dilemmas.

Dilemmas in Designing a Preservice Teacher Education Course

In many respects, the initial training of teachers, given the current time and re-source constraints in the UK, may be viewed as an almost impossible task. Teacher educators have constantly to juggle external expectations together with their own, sometimes contrary, understanding of how one might most appropriately educate and train teachers. It is a task full of compromises, in which the problems are often only partially understood, and where different interest groups express competing needs. Designing and implementing a teacher education course is therefore more often a matter of managing competing interests than of realizing in practice par-ticular ideas or principles of teacher development. The following are some of the dilemmas that teacher educators, whether school- or college-based, commonly encounter.

Theory versus Practice

This is a long-standing dilemma in teacher education. Ideally, we may wish to have teachers who are not only competent actors in the classroom, but who are also practitioners capable of understanding what they are doing, why they are doing it and how they might have to change their practice to suit changing curricula, con-texts or circumstances. This produces a tension between the need for teachers to *understand* teaching and the need to be able to *perform* teaching. The two may be learned in different ways, and possibly in different places. Furthermore, the tension between these two is enhanced when the culture of the university often supports an emphasis on understanding and theory, and the culture of the school supports an emphasis on action and performance, with the result that student teachers, and those involved in their training, feel they are serving two quite contrary sets of expecta-tions. Designing an initial training course requires decisions to be made about when students are most appropriately based in schools and when they can gain most from being in college or university, as well as decisions on the nature of the tasks that they should pursue in these contexts at different stages of the course.

Some teacher educators (e.g., Smyth, 1992) have argued that it is better for student teachers not to have any early experiences in the classroom at all, and have emphasized the importance of waiting until students have a clearly articulated and critical understanding of classroom processes before they are placed in schools in order to avoid their simply replicating existing practice. Others (e.g., Russell, 1988) have argued that it is only after experience in the classroom that student teachers can acquire an appreciation of what teachers do and are in a position to relate ideas, principles, theories and strategies to practical action. The theory versus practice debate tends to be oversimplified when everything that happens in the college or university is identified as 'theory' and everything in schools as 'practice'. The teacher educator faces real dilemmas, however, in attempting to incorporate the benefits of many different types of study and practice into a coherent and effect-ive course.

Content versus Process

This is often perceived to be a closely related dilemma. It is not difficult to construct a very lengthy and diverse knowledge base that teachers ideally ought to have — knowledge of curriculum, teaching strategies, children, child development, school processes, etc. and it is not unreasonable to expect that teachers should have some understanding of how this knowledge relates to classroom practice. As teacher educators quickly discover, however, much of this knowledge can seem quite irrelevant to student teachers unless it is introduced at a time when they can appreciate the link between the ideas, the practical problems and their own practice as a teacher. The teacher educator is, therefore, faced with the dilemma of focusing on content, providing what is regarded as a vast array of essential knowledge but with the risk that this will be perceived by students as irrelevant and unnecessary because they will be unable to appreciate how it relates to practice; or alternatively focusing on providing the knowledge as it relates to the students' own practical experiences, helping them to appreciate its relevance and usefulness, but with the consequence that the course may fall far short of the comprehensive initial training that one would hope for.

Gatekeeper versus Facilitator

One of the roles generally assigned to teacher educators is that of assessing student teachers, and acting as a gatekeeper to the profession. Teacher educators, however, are also expected to act as facilitators in student teachers' development — acting as counsellors, encouraging students to reflect, to analyse their practice and improve upon it. Inevitably, the two can often create tensions — for example, encouraging student teachers to acknowledge and discuss their weaknesses as a teacher may be difficult when they know they are also going to be assessed by the same person.

Personal Development versus Professional Development

Teaching, perhaps more than many occupations, is one that relies very heavily on personal interactions. Teachers rely on their personality in developing relationships in classrooms. Maturity of outlook is itself sometimes an asset in teaching, which is often highly valued amongst teachers. The personal development that this entails may be as important as the professional development that is aimed at within the formal structured curriculum of teacher education, but is much more difficult to coordinate and manage, and is often more difficult to justify as an essential component of teacher preparation.

Survival versus Ongoing Development

There is a limited amount of time available within initial training programmes, and teacher educators are faced with difficult decisions of what to include and to exclude. Some, for instance, may include a great deal of 'theory' in their courses in the belief that although the students may not appreciate it now, this may be the only opportunity in their professional lives to be introduced to perspectives that might help them to make sense of their practice and make choices in their actions at a later time. Others may be more attentive to the immediate survival needs of students and structure their courses around teaching techniques and the equipment of student teachers with survival tactics.

Support versus Challenge

Learning to teach is a stressful experience for many student teachers, and there is often a need for emotional support and encouragement to help students face up to the demands of the course. If student teachers are to learn and progress, emotional support itself, however, is unlikely to be sufficient. Student teachers need to face new experiences, need to consider alternative practices, and need to analyse their own performance if they are to improve upon it. Mentors and higher education tutors frequently have to judge an appropriate balance of support and challenge, knowing when encouragement or consolation are needed and when challenge is constructive.

Reproduction versus Innovation

New teachers are inevitably thrust into schools which have particular expectations for how they will teach. At the same time, there is often an expectation, within teacher education institutions and also within schools, that new teachers will take new ideas into the school and make some practical and innovative contribution. Within teacher education institutions, where considerable importance is often attached to promoting best practice, the teacher educator has to juggle the competing demands of equipping student teachers with the required knowledge and skills to function in the schools in which they will teach, and, at the same time, preparing them as potential innovators who may improve the quality of existing practice, dealing with the many uncertainties that often accompany the innovation process.

The fact that these many dilemmas are so widespread and so readily recognized by teacher educators raises some interesting questions about the nature of teacher education itself. Why is teacher education so dilemma-ridden? Why do so many competing pressures arise? Several explanations are possible. Perhaps this is attributable to the fact that a number of quite different value positions are held within teaching and teacher education. The ideal roles of teachers are viewed differently even within the same culture and community, leading to various tensions in deciding how teachers are most appropriately prepared and supported for their role. Dilemmas may perhaps also be attributable to the lack of any well-established coherent conceptual systems for understanding the nature of teaching and of professional education. There are no well-worked-out theoretical frameworks for guiding what teacher educators do. As noted earlier, teacher education courses have generally developed far ahead of any understanding about whether and how they actually have their effects. Teacher education courses, whether preservice or inservice, have tended to be shaped by the craft wisdom of teacher educators, within practical, policy and institutional constraints, and, at times, changes have followed so rapidly upon themselves that there has been no opportunity to evaluate innovations in any systematic way.

Yet theorizing about, and researching on, teaching and teacher education — even if there remains a diversity within the research and theorizing, promoting an ongoing debate — are important activities if the quality of what we do in these fields is to be systematically monitored and improved. If we are to better understand how the quality of education in schools can be enhanced, we need to be able to reason about and discuss the nature of the teacher's role and how teachers are prepared for it, and be able to relate our judgments to the evidence. Without the explorations into the nature, contexts and effects of teacher education, the design of teacher education courses will continue to be a high-risk and uncertain affair with highly variable outcomes.

Understanding Mentoring in Initial Teacher Education

With the moves towards school-based teacher training and the greater involvement of practicing teachers in the training process, the role of the mentor has become highly significant, strongly determining the overall quality of training provision. For some student teachers, the mentor can be the main source of information about teaching, the main source of advice and feedback about their own practice, and the main confidant and counsellor when things go wrong. The many ways in which mentors go about their work has only recently come to be studied, and their role and potential effects are still being explored. However, on the basis of the case studies in this project, and drawing upon other recent research (e.g., McIntyre, Hagger and Wilkin, 1993; Furlong and Maynard, 1995), it is possible to infer an analytical framework which accounts for the ways in which mentors might influence student teachers' practice. This is by no means comprehensive, but is proposed as an initial means of conceptualizing professional development interactions between mentor and mentee, highlighting the significant aspects of mentors' work, and providing a basis for identifying the needs of mentors in their own training. Six different processes of mentoring are suggested.

(i) Influencing by Example

In this case, the mentors influence their student teachers by providing a model for the student. It may be a model in the form of their own behaviour — a demonstration lesson or particular teaching strategy — or in the form of suggested lesson plans, ideas for activities or specific recommended actions to take to overcome particular difficulties. The mentor is the source of actions and solutions. The student may use these ideas or demonstrations as examples to copy, or, as was the case with several of the students in this study, they are used as a basis for comparison. Students, on the basis of a range of observed practice, could sift out ideas and strategies with which to experiment, piecing together their own particular practice, following Maggie's analogy of a jigsaw.

(ii) Influencing by Coaching

This involves focused, ongoing support, requiring, for instance, careful observation and follow-up discussion together with repeated practice of particular strategies or skills or types of lesson. Distinguishing features of the coach are observation and discussion, the breaking down of a task into performable parts, and the attention to detail (see Schön, 1987, 1991).

Schön has been one of the main advocates of the importance of coaching in professional practice (see Schön, 1987). Although he has studied a disparate range of professions and mentoring contexts (concerning the training of architects, psychotherapists, musicians and counsellors), he has highlighted a number of features that they all have in common. These different professions, like teaching, involve practitioners relying upon their craft knowledge to solve complex problems. Like teachers, many professionals have developed a body of knowledge which they use in everyday practice, but this knowledge is not articulated. Furthermore, what is important for the novice is not simply the accumulation of the knowledge but an appreciation of how it is used in the framing and reframing of real life problems and the testing out of possible solutions. The development of such knowledge, argues Schön, is dependent upon a mentoring relationship, whereby the experienced teacher initiates the novice into professional practice. The professional knowledge is carried in people's heads and is passed on from practitioner to practitioner by a combination of shared actions and word of mouth. The knowledge isn't easily or meaningfully put into words alone. Architects can write about the principles of design, and about how art and engineering both inform their work, but the processes in which they engage at the drawing board are more mysterious. Schön suggested that mentors communicate their knowledge, understanding and practical skill by relying principally on three strategies which he termed — *joint experimentation*, involving mentor and student working together in solving a problem; *follow me*, in which the mentor talks through their own work; and *the hall of mirrors*, in which the mentor aims to expand the alternative ways in which the student might perceive a particular situation. There were certainly many examples of discussions and collaborative teaching that students and mentors engaged in in this project where Schön's coaching strategies were in evidence.

(iii) Influencing Through Practice-focused Discussion

These might involve abstract discussions about teaching approaches or about theoretical ideas and their implications for practice, or more specific discussions about lessons that students have observed or taught themselves or particular aspects of teaching. Student teachers learn a great deal about practice through talking about it, and often become more aware of aspects of their own practice as a result of such discussion. Talking about practice can also help student teachers clarify their vision of how they would like to teach, setting goals for later attainment.

(iv) Influencing Through Structuring the Context

Student teachers teach in a classroom whose resources and ways of working have already been established by someone else. The children are used to certain activities conducted in particular ways. The classroom itself, its furniture and its resources may be arranged to support this style of working. To some extent the student is having to fit in to someone else's style of teaching. The mentor therefore has a strong *indirect* influence on the practices that the student teacher can feasibly adopt, or which will 'work' in the given context; these structures might be fixed or nego-tiable, and they might or might not be a topic that is discussed within mentoring conversations themselves (see Martin, 1997). Several of the students in this project spoke of the need to 'fit in' to the class teacher's way of working because this was what the children were used to and as a result they would adopt the teacher's routines, mannerisms, and even the distinctive vocabulary which they used in communicat-ing with the children.

(v) Influencing Through Emotional Support

Students often experience a great deal of uncertainty and self-doubt in the process of learning to teach, and the support and encouragement offered by others may be an important factor in maintaining motivation, involvement and the persistence to find solutions to experienced difficulties. Mentors are often viewed as an important source of this encouragement, and mentors themselves have often been found to rate this aspect of their role highly (see Elliott and Calderhead, 1993). Having a supportive class teacher was certainly valued by the students in this study, particularly early in the courses when some of them could easily have been discouraged by their own attempts at teaching. However, teachers who sympathetically recounted anec-dotes of their own problems and difficulties or who advised students 'to go home and have a gin' at the end of a bad day were sometimes regarded as ineffective when the students in fact wanted help in analysing what went wrong and how their teaching could be improved in the future.

(vi) Influencing Through Devised Learning Experiences

Mentors (and college or university tutors) may construct particular school-based tasks to promote student learning. For example, they may require student teachers to work with a small group of children with special needs to sensitize them to children's learning difficulties, or they may require the student teacher to teach in a particular subject area so that they become better acquainted with that content or ways of organizing the class for that subject. In these cases, students are asked to undertake tasks with a particular personal learning outcome in mind. Focused observations, or brief teaching sessions followed by discussions with the class teacher, were particularly valued by students in the project in the early stages of their course.

Skills of the Mentor

Given these different ways in which mentors might influence the professional development of student teachers, it is possible to think about the preparation that mentors may require in order to carry out their work effectively. It was found that the mentors in this study tended to approach mentoring in the same way that they approached teaching. Mentoring often seemed to be regarded as simply another teaching context. However, the above analysis of how mentors influence student teachers would suggest several specific areas where mentors might usefully engage in further professional development.

Developing a Language to Discuss Teaching

Teachers, even though they may well be regarded by their colleagues as expert practitioners, have often developed a great deal of their practice through individual experience, and as a result they have never been placed in the position of having to talk about what they do, and why they do it. Although there were instances in this project when student teachers were in fact confounded by the technical terminology used by their class teachers (particularly when it related to the National Curriculum or Key Stage assessment), it was much more common for conversations about practice to remain at a fairly superficial level. This was attributable, at least in part, to the class teachers' lack of a language to talk about their own practice and their inability to articulate the implicit assumptions and understandings within their practice. In a mentoring context, however, possessing such a language has obvious advantages in helping the student teacher to interpret their observations and reason about teaching and learning.

Being a Competent Practitioner, Able to Demonstrate a Variety of Practices

Coaching and modelling, when this is felt appropriate, require the teacher to be able to demonstrate strategies or lessons, and to be familiar with alternative teaching approaches. This demands a reasonable level of confidence and competence from the mentors themselves, but perhaps as important is a willingness to experiment and develop their own practice.

Willingness to Appraise Their Own Practice

Being able to analyse their own practice in an objective manner, even when it was not exceptional, was highly valued by the students in this project, because it had a reassuring effect (in seeing experienced teachers having some difficulty too) and it also demonstrated how one could turn a particular difficulty into a learning advantage. Teachers who can teach a lesson and then openly evaluate it are making their own knowledge and values accessible to student teachers, and are also encouraging an openness and willingness to engage in self-evaluation, together with the development of reflective, evaluative skills.

Counselling Skills

Learning to teach for many student teachers is anxiety provoking, particularly when students realize that it is far from easy to become the teacher that they would like to be. There are many anxieties, self-doubts and disappointments that accompany that process. A mentor needs to be able to help students to place their experience in perspective, to face their anxieties and to provide any necessary support. That often requires counselling skills that are appropriate for helping adults in stressful situations, which is a new area of expertise for many teachers.

Target Setting

As well as developing a realistic perception of one's own practice, learning to teach involves setting oneself realistic targets for development. When student teachers are unfamiliar with the curriculum, children and the classroom context, and if they perceive learning to teach as relatively unproblematic, they can easily set goals for themselves which are unachievable or inappropriate and which may inevitably lead to feelings of disappointment and failure. Mentors have a valuable role here in drawing upon their own understandings of teaching and teacher development to help student teachers to think about and set appropriate targets that will be motivating, appropriate and achievable.

Understanding Professional Development

Teachers, of course, teach in different ways and there is no one ideal. Student teachers also learn to teach in many ways, coming from diverse backgrounds with differing values and various types of expertise. Helping student teachers to become more accomplished teachers requires some tolerance, or a multiplicity of visions, of what good teaching might be like, but also some perception of how student teachers typically develop, the difficulties they tend to experience and the common stages along the way. One would expect that understanding the nature of teaching, and how student teachers learn to teach, would be of considerable value to mentors.

Relationship Building

Within this study, one of the features of mentors most valued by student teachers, and also valued by several mentors themselves, was the quality of the mentor–mentee relationship. Whilst students acknowledged that it was useful to have a mentor who was a source of ideas about teaching and was someone who could expertly demonstrate a variety of teaching strategies, student teachers found that what influenced their practice most was the quality of the relationship that they established with their mentor. When the relationship was sympathetic, open and understanding, students felt more able to trust their mentor, more able to confide in them with their own perceptions, experiences and difficulties. Where a good relationship existed, discussions about practice were considered to be more honest and students felt more able to accept and respond to criticism. Where students felt that the relationship was not genuine, or that the mentor was maintaining a 'front' and was more concerned with impression management, students reported that they were more cautious and their conversations with mentors more superficial. Similarly, the distant mentor who remained remote from the student and their day-to-day activities, and the arrogant mentor who used the ineptitude of the student as a boost to their own ego, failed to engage student teachers in focused and honest discussions about practice from which the students might learn. Students also reported that when the mentoring relationship was good, even if their mentor taught in a totally contrary style, or even if he/she was not regarded as a particularly effective teacher, the student still learned a great deal from the experience.

One can speculate on what the personal qualities are that enable some teachers to develop supportive and open relationships with their student teachers, and on the kinds of training that might help teachers in this area. It seems likely, for instance, that such relationships will develop more readily where the teacher has a high level of self-awareness, where he/she feels at ease themselves in the teaching role, where he/she is accepting of others and of the difficulties they might experience, and has a positive orientation to the improvement of their own practice. The training experiences that are likely to develop these qualities will probably be different from conventional inservice training courses, and may well be more focused on one's understanding of oneself and others.

Collegiality

A few studies (see Yeomans and Sampson, 1994) have suggested that schools which have a more collegial ethos — where it is common for teachers to jointly plan and teach, and where teachers will join together in evaluating their own and their students' performance — are more supportive environments for student teachers, and many of the students' and mentors' experiences in this study would confirm this claim. In such environments students are exposed to richer and more varied interactions about practice, and are probably in an environment in which it is easier for them to acknowledge what they do not know and what they need to learn. Mentors themselves, by becoming more collegial in their practice, are also developing more potential learning experiences for themselves, their student teachers and their colleagues. The development of collegiality within schools has not been widely studied, however, and much could be gained from further empirical enquiry that would potentially be of use in mentor development as well as school improvement.

Other Implications of Research for Practice in Teacher Education

Much research in the field of teacher education has tended to be small scale, consisting of individual case studies or studies of small groups of student teachers or mentors. Partly, this is a consequence of resourcing. Large-scale studies are beyond the funding capabilities of many sponsors of educational research. Smaller scale qualitative studies, however, have a useful role to play in developing our understanding of the field. While we lack sound conceptualizations of teaching and learning to teach, explorations of the area in order to develop insights and concepts are essential in creating appropriate theoretical frameworks with which research can progress. It is only after reasonable theoretical frameworks have been formulated, once the key concepts and methods for their measurement identified, that larger scale quantitative studies could be meaningful and productive.

In the case of small-scale studies, the interpretation and generalization of findings has to take into account the particular context in which the research was pursued. The findings of this study, for instance, may well have differed in some respects had the study taken place with students in an inner-city college rather than with students in a provincial one. The students' experience in schools would be different, the time afforded for mentoring, the past experience of the mentors, the background of the students themselves, and the constraints upon their learning could also vary, resulting in alternative accounts of student teacher development. Nevertheless, it is through small-scale studies that probe the experiences of student teachers in some depth that we are likely to learn more about the processes of learning to teach. Those processes may vary somewhat in different contexts, though it seems likely that although student teachers' experiences may differ widely, the overall processes of learning may be much less variable.

In addition, small-scale studies of student teachers can also raise questions about conventional conceptions of teaching and teacher education. In this study, several of the findings raise questions about such issues as the recruitment and retention of teachers, where initial teacher training (ITT) is most appropriately based, the time required for ITT and how students' progression is most appropriately catered for, and staff development in teacher training institutions.

The Recruitment and Retention of Teachers

Typically, teacher supply has tended to ebb and flow in regular cycles, where once every ten years or so there is a shortage of teachers, followed a few years later by an over-supply. When the economy is buoyant, often recruitment to initial teacher training courses suffers. Young people who might have entered teaching are attracted to other occupations which are perceived to be better paid, or to offer greater career opportunities, or better working conditions. Conversely, in times of recession, recruitment to teacher training courses is much easier with a large pool of potential entrants on which to draw. Teacher supply is also influenced by other factors, however, including the rate of early retirement, and demographic changes; and certain subject areas in secondary education such as science, technology and modern languages, are much more affected than others by the general shortage of graduates in those fields. On the whole, recruitment and retention of teachers in secondary education has been more affected by fluctuations in the economy than primary education.

Although salaries and working conditions no doubt play a part in attracting potential teachers, it is interesting that with the majority of student teachers studied in this project, the most important factors that drew them into teaching seemed to be personal or intrinsic to the nature of teaching itself. The satisfaction of working with children, of helping them learn, of doing a job that was perceived to be useful and important were all common motivators. It was also the case that most of the students had a commitment to particular ideals that were perceived to be associated with primary education. Most of the students, for example, had a strong commitment to social justice, the equality of opportunity, to the valuing of people as individuals and to children working collaboratively, even before they started their teacher training course. However, these are not just the ideological remnants of 1960s progressivism. They seem to have much more significance than this. They are part of the reasons that many students have for entering primary teacher training in the first place, and are closely tied to the satisfactions that intending teachers, and perhaps experienced teachers as well, expect to obtain from their work. Several student teachers spoke as if these values were an essential and inevitable part of primary education itself.

If we are to attempt to understand the careers of teachers, what motivates them to enter teaching, to gain satisfaction from their work and to commit themselves to improving the quality of their teaching, the role of intrinsic motivation should not be underestimated, and this may need to be more fully recognized by managers and policy-makers who control teachers' working conditions. It would be counter-productive if such policies as the introduction of league tables based on children's test results, and the production of curriculum prescriptions and constraints, for example, change the nature of teaching to such an extent that these aspects of teaching are devalued with the result that teachers no longer experience satisfaction in their work and opt out of the profession altogether.

The Siting of Initial Teacher Training

In recent years, there has been considerable preoccupation amongst policy-makers with where teacher training occurs — whether in schools or in colleges and universities — and with prescribing a required proportion of course time to be spent in schools. However, if we look closely at student teachers' learning experiences, the quality of teacher training seems to depend much more on the quality of interaction between student teachers and their mentors and college tutors, the opportunity to explore different ideas, the opportunity to reflect on practice, and on an environment that supports and encourages experimentation and honest evaluation. Obviously, student teachers need to spend time in schools, observing, practising, experimenting, and talking with experienced teachers about practice, but they also need to spend time away from the site of the action, away from the pressures and the immediacy of the classroom situation, where they can think about their own practice, relate it to ideas and principles within the curriculum, evaluate their work objectively and plan future actions.

Emphasis on the site of teacher training may draw attention away from the importance of the quality of the learning experiences of student teachers and the major factors that influence their development. Given the scarcity of resources in teacher education, using these to maximize the quality of the interactions between student teachers and teacher educators, whether college- or school-based, seems of a higher priority than the actual site of the training. Devoting a large proportion of the available resources to transferring responsibility for teacher education to schools rather than higher education institutions does itself offer no guarantee of improvement.

Time and Progression in Initial Teacher Training

It is clear that the assimilation of the knowledge and practice of teaching is a lengthy process. Student teachers have much to learn and there are different mechanisms by which their knowledge informs or interacts with practice. Students' learning, however, is clearly an active process — the knowledge that is available to them often does not seem relevant until corresponding difficulties with practice have been identified. When faced with having to act in the classroom, student teachers draw upon the strategies that most readily come to mind. Typically, these may originate from memories of past teachers or observed practice within the school. Students are therefore constrained by their own experience, by their own images of teaching. Furthermore, the knowledge they require may not be readily accessible. To break out of this conservatism, students need to be able to relate new knowledge to practice, and to be able to analyse and evaluate the practices they observe and enact.

The processes of learning to teach take considerable time and the common model of professional preparation of one-year postgraduate training, followed by a period of induction, which generally receives little attention, ill fits what we know of this process. The period of induction may well be as important as what typically happens in the preservice preparation. Once teachers have gained some basic competence in teaching, and a level of confidence in their practice, they may need encouragement and support to analyse their practice further. The contribution of an able mentor in the first few years of teaching may be as important as during initial training. Unfortunately, the general trend is to view the qualified teacher as competent, and whatever professional development occurs thereafter is sporadic, short term and left largely to the teacher him/herself to initiate and manage. A more long-term view of professional development is needed. This has implications for the ways in which professional development is viewed in schools and for the development and support they receive from higher education institutions and other professional agencies.

The quality of teaching is a major factor in maintaining and improving education. It is a strange paradox, however, that in the field of education, the importance and funding attributed to induction and inservice training is probably far less than in many other fields. In industry and commerce, for example, it is common for employers to invest upwards of 1 per cent of a company's turnover in staff development, with large multi-national companies committing even more. The culture within our educational system has yet to embrace the importance of staff development, or to appreciate the forms that it could take or the significant contribution it might make to the quality of teaching and learning within schools.

The Staff Development of Teacher Educators

Just as student teachers' practice is constrained by the repertoire of images and strategies that can readily be brought to mind when faced with the need to act, so too are the practices of mentors and university tutors constrained by the images and strategies that they hold for teacher education. Mentors, it was found, would frequently reflect back on their own experience as student teachers to consider what was most useful and helpful to them in similar circumstances when deciding how best to support their student. Mentors indicated little awareness of the range of difficulties that student teachers might face or the various strategies open to them to identify these difficulties and to support students in overcoming them.

Similarly, university tutors are generally appointed to their positions having been judged to be good class teachers who are interested in working with students and who perhaps have some specialist interest in one area of the curriculum or in an aspect of educational research. Upon appointment, they may have had more experience than most teachers in supervising students, and once appointed they would no doubt encounter a wide range of students in diverse school situations. However, there is no training course to prepare teacher educators in higher education in how best to instruct and support student teachers. The expertise that teacher educators have acquired has been developed through their own personal experience, and has often not been shared with colleagues, or subjected to any open and critical scrutiny.

In the interests of improving the quality of initial training, the expertise of teacher educators, in both schools and higher education, needs further exploration. The basis of this expertise needs to be made explicit, and to be open to critical discussion. Further research and development would extend our understanding of this expertise, and may also provide useful material for developing courses and activities for the training of those involved in teacher education.

Research and Initial Teacher Education

As previously noted, national regulations for preservice courses, time constraints, working arrangements with schools, and the craft wisdom of both school and university or college tutors all play a part in shaping the nature and delivery of initial training. In contrast, research in teacher education has tended to play a relatively minor role. Whilst surveys of new teachers in schools have been used to identify general areas of difficulty (HMI, 1987, 1988), occasionally leading to revisions of national frameworks for courses of initial training, research has not been influential to any extent in the design of teacher education courses. This may be due to the low level of research activity in this area up until recently, the inaccessibility of many research reports, or the lack of a research culture within teacher education institutions. Whatever the cause, the potential of research to provide ways of thinking about teacher education, to make our knowledge of teacher education explicit and to test it against empirical evidence, and to explore the relationships amongst key features of teacher education courses has been relatively undeveloped.

The study reported here demonstrates some of the ways in which research might help to inform the everyday practice of teacher educators. This research, however, as with most educational enquiry, also raises many questions about practice which require further clarification. For example, it must be of some concern that students' understanding of subject matter and of children's learning appear to remain at a superficial level throughout initial training. Student teachers, it appears, are learning to manage activities rather than becoming expert in particular subject matter and the pedagogy associated with it. Their ideas about children's learning seem to focus on motivation, engagement and relationships rather than on subject matter. Several possible explanations could be offered for this. First of all, perhaps over the past two or three decades, with the increasing level of sophistication of curriculum resources — mathematics packages, topic resource packs, graded reading schemes — and with the introduction of the National Curriculum, the role of the primary teacher in the classroom has gradually changed. Within the classroom, there is now possibly less pressure upon teachers to be knowledgable about subjects and the teaching and learning of them, and a greater emphasis on managing curriculum resources. The textbook, the National Curriculum, established schemes of work and curriculum packages may have collectively removed the need for teachers to think about subject matter in anything other than layman's terms. Learning how to manage children and resources is what student teachers therefore find to be most important, and this becomes the focus of their attention. They are not learning to be teachers who are custodians and disseminators of subject matter, but to be teachers who are managers of classroom activities. A second interpretation is that learning about subject matter and the teaching and learning strategies associated with it, and being able to implement these in the classroom, is an extremely demanding task, requiring the assimilation of a vast amount of knowledge, and that such a task is only likely to be achieved over a lengthy period of time. Consequently, the understandings of subject matter and its pedagogy that researchers have frequently been looking for in student teachers (see Kruger and Summers, 1988; Bennett and Carré, 1993) is something that one could only reasonably expect much later in a teacher's career.

To explore these interpretations in greater detail requires two types of further study. First, longer term developmental studies of new teachers are required to examine what professional development occurs amongst teachers in their first few years of practice, and to identify the factors that support or impede this development. Second, comparative studies between experienced teachers judged to be good practitioners and novices might help to identify the knowledge, practices and ways of thinking that characterize successful teaching. Such research is not unproblematic, but enquiries in these areas are likely to enhance our understanding of the nature of teachers' expertise and how it develops.

Another area for future research is to explore the particular types of learning in which student teachers engage and how this learning is best fostered. Our understanding of learning to teach remains at quite a superficial level. Student teachers are involved in a variety of different types of task, as they learn about children, the curriculum, teaching strategies and school procedures, as they discover their own strengths and weaknesses, and as they negotiate the transition from student to student teacher to teacher. Acquiring the competences, confidence and self-awareness that this involves are processes that necessitate much deeper investigation if student teachers are to be provided with productive learning experiences and be appropriately supported in their professional development.

Other areas for future research that are highlighted in this project include the nature of personal relationships in primary schools and the development of mentoring skills. The extent to which teachers work collaboratively, jointly plan, teach and evaluate lessons, observe each other's practice and are encouraged to reflect on their own practice, evaluating it objectively, seems to be affected by the quality of relationships amongst teachers in schools, and by whether an ethos exists within the institution to support open relationships and constructively critical dialogue. This raises various questions about how this type of working environment is engineered and managed. What can senior management do, for instance, to encourage a professional development ethos and support the relationships that appear to be associated with teachers' professional improvement? What are the implications for the mentoring role within schools? What other inputs do schools need, in terms of external expertise or institutional support, to be effective in helping staff to analyse and improve the quality of their practice? Research in this area could have a valuable role to play in furthering our understanding of how primary schools support the efforts of teachers and how this in turn might lead to improvements in teaching and learning. Case studies of the dynamics of individual schools would be a useful starting point in exploring these processes.

Teacher education is required to adapt to a constantly changing context. New government guidelines, new expectations, new curricula, and new circumstances in which teachers are expected to work require teacher education courses to change in structure, content and methods of teaching and learning. If teacher education is to maintain a continuous quest for improvement in its preparation of student teachers, not only is there a need for clarification and agreement on purposes, but also a need for the changes and development of teacher education to be based on evidence and tried and tested understandings rather than on speculation and ideology. Research and evaluation should be part of the culture of teacher education institutions, and should be part of the dialogue amongst policy-makers, teacher educators and teachers so that change is evolutionary and based on reasoned argument, evidence and shared, articulated value judgments. Research has indeed a vital role to play in sustaining the quality of teacher education and providing the basis for the professional development of teachers on whom the education of children in our schools ultimately depends.

References

ASHTON, P.M.E. (1983) *Teacher Education in the Classroom: Initial and Inservice*, London, Croom Helm.

BENNETT, N. and CARRÉ, C. (eds) (1993) *Learning to Teach*, London, Routledge.

BENTON, P. (ed.) (1990) *The Oxford Internship Scheme*, London, Calouste Gulbenkian Foundation.

BERLINER, D.C. (1987) 'Ways of thinking about students and classrooms by more and less experienced teachers', in CALDERHEAD, J. (ed.) *Exploring Teachers Thinking*, London, Cassell, pp. 60–83.

BERLINER, D.C. (1988) 'The development of expertise in pedagogy.' Paper presented at the meeting of the American Association of Colleges for Teacher Education, February, 1988, New Orleans, LA.

BROADFOOT, P., OSBORN, M., GILLY, M. and BRÛCHER, A. (1994) *Perceptions of Teaching: Primary School Teachers in England and France*, London, Cassell.

BUCHBERGER, F. (1992) *ATEE Guide to Institutions of Teacher Education in Europe*, Brussels, Association for Teacher Education in Europe.

BULLOUGH, R.V., KNOWLES, J.G. and CROW, N.A. (1991) *Emerging as a Teacher*, London, Routledge.

CALDERHEAD, J. (1987) 'The quality of reflection in student teachers' professional learning', *European Journal of Teacher Education*, **10**, 3, pp. 269–78.

CALDERHEAD, J. (1991) 'The nature and growth of knowledge in student teaching', *Teaching and Teacher Education*, **7**, 5/6, pp. 531–5.

CALDERHEAD, J. and GATES, P. (eds) (1993) *Conceptualizing Reflection in Teacher Development*, London, Falmer Press.

CALDERHEAD, J. and ROBSON, M. (1990) 'Images of teaching: Student teachers' early conceptions of classroom practice', *Teaching and Teacher Education*, **7**, 1, pp. 1–8.

CARR, W. and KEMMIS, S. (1986) *Becoming Critical: Education, Knowledge and Action Research*, London, Falmer Press.

CLANDININ, D.J. (1986) *Classroom Practice: Teacher Images in Action*, London, Falmer Press.

CLARK, C.M. (1988) 'Asking the right questions about teacher preparation: Contributions of research on teacher thinking', *Educational Researcher*, **17**, 2, pp. 5–12.

CLARKE, A. (1995) 'Professional development in practicum settings: Reflective practice under scrutiny', *Teaching and Teacher Education*, **11**, 3, pp. 243–61.

CLIFT, R.T., HOUSTON, W.R. and PUGACH, M.C. (eds) (1990) *Encouraging Reflective Practice in Education*, New York, Teachers College Press.

COURT, D. (1988) 'Reflection-in-action: Some definitional problems', in GRIMMETT, P. and ERICKSON, G. (eds) *Reflection in Teacher Education*, New York, Teachers College Press, pp. 143–6.

CRUICKSHANK, D.R. and METCALF, K.K. (1990) 'Training within teacher preparation', in HOUSTON, W.R. (ed.) *Handbook of Research on Teacher Education*, New York, Macmillan, pp. 469–97.

DfE (1992) *Initial Teacher Training (Secondary Phase)*, Circular 9/92, London, Department for Education.

DfE (1993) *The Initial Training of Primary School Teachers: New Criteria for Courses*, Circular 14/93, London, Department for Education.

DfEE (1996) 'Shake up of teacher training', *DfEE News*, Number 302/96.

ELBAZ, F. (1983) *Teacher Thinking: A Study of Practical Knowledge*, London, Croom Helm.

ELLIOTT, B. and CALDERHEAD, J. (1993) 'Mentoring for teacher development', in McINTYRE, D., HAGGER, H. and WILKIN, M. (eds) *Mentoring: Perspectives on School-based Teacher Education*, London, Kogan Page, pp. 166–89.

EURYDICE (1995) *Key Data on Education in the European Union*, Brussels, EC.

FEIMAN-NEMSER, S. (1990) 'Teacher preparation: Structural and conceptual alternatives', in HOUSTON, W.R. (ed.) *Handbook of Research on Teacher Education*, New York, Macmillan, pp. 212–33.

FULLER, F. and BOWN, O. (1975) 'Becoming a teacher', in RYAN, K. (ed.) *Teacher Education, 74th Yearbook of the National Society for the Study of Education*, Chicago, IL, University of Chicago Press.

FURLONG, J. and MAYNARD, T. (1995) *Mentoring Student Teachers: The Growth of Professional Knowledge*, London, Routledge.

FURLONG, J., WHITTY, G., BARRETT, E., BARTON, L. and MILES, S. (1994) 'Integration and partnership in initial teacher education — dilemmas and possibilities', *Research Papers in Education*, **9**, 3, pp. 281–301.

GRIMMETT, P. and ERICKSON, G. (1988) *Reflection in Teacher Education*, New York, Teachers College Press.

GROSSMAN, P.L. (1992) *The Making of a Teacher: Teacher Knowledge and Teacher Education*, New York, Teachers College Press.

GUYTON, E. and McINTYRE, D.J. (1990) 'Student teaching and school experiences', in HOUSTON, W.R. (ed.) *Handbook of Research on Teacher Education*, New York, Macmillan, pp. 514–34.

HAWKEY, K. (1995) 'Learning from peers: The experience of student teachers in school-based teacher education', *Journal of Teacher Education*, May–June, **46**, 3, pp. 175–83.

HMI (1982) *New Teacher in School*, London, HMSO.

HMI (1987) *Quality in Schools: The Initial Training of Teachers*, London, HMSO.

HMI (1988) *The New Teacher in School*, London, HMSO.

HMI (1991) *School Based Initial Training in England and Wales*, London, HMSO.

HMI (1992) *The New Teacher in School*, London, HMSO.

JOHNSTON, S. (1992) 'Images: A way of understanding the practical knowledge of student teachers', *Teaching and Teacher Education*, **8**, 2, pp. 123–36.

KNOWLES, G. and COLE, A.L. (1994) *Through Preservice Teachers' Eyes: Exploring Field Experiences through Narrative and Inquiry*, New York, Merrill.

KRUGER, C. and SUMMERS, M. (1988) 'Primary school teachers' understanding of science concepts', *Journal of Education for Teaching*, **14**, 3, pp. 259–65.

LACEY, C. (1977) *The Socialisation of Teachers*, London, Methuen.

LAFFITTE, R. (1993) 'Teachers' professional responsibility and development', in DAY, C., CALDERHEAD, J. and DENICOLO, P. (eds) *Research on Teacher Thinking: Understanding Professional Development*, London, Falmer Press, pp. 75–86.

LANIER, J.E. and LITTLE, J.W. (1986) 'Research on teacher education', in WITTROCK, M.C. (ed.) *Handbook of Research on Teaching*, New York, Macmillan, pp. 527–69.

LAWLOR, S. (1990) *Teachers Mistaught*, London, Centre for Policy Studies.

LYONS, N. (1990) 'Dilemmas of knowing: Ethical and epistemological dimensions of teachers' work and development', *Harvard Educational Review*, **60**, 2, pp. 159–80.

MARTIN, D. (1997) 'Mentoring in one's own classroom: An exploratory study of contexts', *Teaching and Teacher Education*, **13**, 2, pp. 183–97.

MILES, M.B. and HUBERMAN, A.M. (1984) *Qualitative Data Analysis: A Sourcebook of New Methods*, Newbury Park, California, Sage.

MCINTYRE, D., HAGGER, H. and WILKIN, M. (1993) (eds) *Mentoring: Perspectives on School-based Teacher Education*, London, Kogan Page.

MCNALLY, J., COPE, P., INGLIS, B. and STRONACH, I. (1994) 'Current realities in the student teaching experience: A preliminary enquiry', *Teaching and Teacher Education*, **10**, 2, pp. 219–30.

NODDINGS, N. (1986) 'Fidelity in teaching, teacher education and research on teaching', *Harvard Educational Review*, **56**, 4, pp. 496–510.

O'HEAR, A. (1988) *Who Teaches the Teachers?* London, Social Affairs Unit.

OLSON, J.K. (1992) *Understanding Teaching: Beyond Expertise*, Milton Keynes, Open University Press.

PLANEL, C. (1995) 'Children's experience of the learning process and the role of the teacher: A comparative study of English and Franch primary school classrooms', *EERA Bulletin*, **2**, 1, pp. 13–20.

REYNOLDS, M.C. (1989) *Knowledge Base for the Beginning Teacher*, Oxford, Pergamon.

RUSSELL, T. (1988) 'From pre-service teacher education to first year of teaching: A study of theory and practice', in CALDERHEAD, J. (ed.) *Teachers' Professional Learning*, London, Falmer Press, pp. 13–34.

RUSSELL, T., MUNBY, H., SPAFFORD, C. and JOHNSTON, P. (1988) 'Learning the professional knowledge of teaching: Metaphors, puzzles and the theory–practice relationship', in GRIMMETT, P. and ERICKSON, G.L. (eds) *Reflection in Teacher Education*, New York, Teachers College Press, pp. 67–89.

RUST, F.O. (1994) 'The first year of teaching: It's not what they expected', *Teaching and Teacher Education*, **10**, 2, pp. 205–18.

RYLE, G. (1949) *The Concept of Mind*, London, Hutchinson.

SCHÖN, D.A. (1983) *The Reflective Practitioner*, New York, Basic Books.

SCHÖN, D.A. (1987) *Educating the Reflective Practitioner*, San Francisco, CA, Jossey-Bass.

SCHÖN, D.A. (ed.) (1991) *The Reflective Turn: Case Studies In and On Educational Practice*, New York, Teachers College Press.

SHULMAN, L.S. (1986) 'Those who understand: Knowledge growth in teaching', *Educational Researcher*, **15**, 2, pp. 4–14.

SHULMAN, L.S. (1987) 'Knowledge and teaching: Foundations of the new reform', *Harvard Educational Review*, **57**, 1, pp. 1–21.

SMYTH, J. (1992) 'Teachers' work and the politics of reflection', *American Educational Research Journal*, **29**, 2, pp. 267–300.

STALLINGS, J.A. and KOWALSKI, T. (1990) 'Research on professional development schools', in HOUSTON, W.R. (ed.) *Handbook of Research on Teacher Education*, New York, Macmillan, pp. 251–66.

VALLI, L. (1990) 'Moral approaches to reflective practice', in CLIFT, R.T., HOUSTON, W.R. and PUGACH, M.C. (eds) *Encouraging Reflective Practice in Education*, New York, Teachers College Press, pp. 39–56.

VALLI, L. (ed.) (1992) *Reflective Teacher Education: Cases and Critiques*, Albany, New York, State University of New York Press.

VEENMAN, S. (1984) 'Perceived problems of beginning teachers', *Review of Educational Research*, **54**, 2, pp. 143–78.

WILSON, S.M., SHULMAN, L.S., and RICHERT, A. (1987) '"150 different ways" of knowing: Representations of knowledge in teaching', in CALDERHEAD, J. (ed.) *Exploring Teachers' Thinking*, London, Cassell, pp. 104–24.

WUBBELS, T. (1992) 'Teacher education and the universities in the Netherlands', *European Journal of Teacher Education*, **15**, 3, pp. 157–72.

YEOMANS, R. and SAMPSON, J. (1994) *Mentorship in the Primary School*, London, Falmer Press.

ZEICHNER, K.M. (1983) 'Alternative paradigms of teacher education', *Journal of Teacher Education*, **34**, 3, pp. 3–9.

ZEICHNER, K.M. and GORE, J.M. (1990) 'Teacher socialization', in HOUSTON, W.R. (ed.) *Handbook of Research on Teacher Education*, New York, Macmillan, pp. 329–48.

ZEICHNER, K.M. and TABACHNICK, B.R. (1981) 'Are the effects of university teacher education "washed out" by school experience', *Journal of Teacher Education*, **32**, 3, May–June, pp. 7–11.

ZEICHNER, K.M., TABACHNICK, B.R. and DENSMORE, K. (1987) 'Individual, institutional and cultural influences on the development of teachers' craft knowledge', in CALDERHEAD, J. (ed.) *Exploring Teachers' Thinking*, London, Cassell, pp. 21–59.

Author Index

Subject Index